Uncertain Friendship

AMERICA AND THE WORLD

EDITOR: Robert A. Divine

Uncertain Friendship:

American-French Diplomatic Relations Through the Cold War

MARVIN R. ZAHNISER

The Ohio State University

John Wiley & Sons, Inc.
New York · London · Sydney · Toronto

Copyright © 1975 by John Wiley & Sons, Inc.

All rights reserved. Published simultaneously in Canada.

Library of Congress Cataloging in Publication Data:

Zahniser, Marvin R
    Uncertain friendship.

    (America and the world)
    Bibliography: p.
    1. United States—Foreign relations—France.
2. France—Foreign relations—United States.
3. World politics. I. Title.
E183.8.F8Z33   327.73′044   75-23047
ISBN 0-471-98106-0
ISBN 0-471-98107-9 pbk.

Printed in the United States of America

10 9 8 7 6 5 4 3 2 1

To Adrienne

Foreword

"Lafayette, we are here!" an American officer proclaimed at the tomb of the revolutionary hero when the advance units of the AEF arrived in France to help reverse the course of the First World War. By the time American forces had liberated Paris in 1944, one might claim that the revolutionary debt had been amply repaid. Yet despite these twentieth century repayments for the vital role France played in the winning of American independence, the course of Franco-American relations has seldom been as smooth as the Lafayette legend would indicate. The original alliance, based on expediency, became a casualty of the French Revolution and ended after mutual recrimination in 1801; Napoleon's Continental System irritated Americans and nearly led to war in the first decade of the nineteenth century—only Britain's more injurious acts avoided a showdown with France; Andrew Jackson's belligerent handling of the claims issue brought Franco-American relations close to the breaking point in the 1830s; and Louis Napoleon's grandiose Mexican adventure led to yet another period of grave tension in the 1860s. In the twentieth century, though France and America twice fought together as allies, the conflict of interests symbolized by the antagonism between Georges Clemenceau and Woodrow Wilson, and later between FDR and de Gaulle, continued to make the relationship a difficult and often tempestuous one.

Marvin Zahniser succeeds in revealing the uneven course of Franco-American relations by stressing the continuing conflict between the vital interests of these two nation-states. Using a realistic appraisal that cuts through the rhetoric that both governments were so fond of invoking, he points to the common emnity toward Britain that led to alliance in 1778, and the shared opposition to Germany that brought the two countries together in 1917 and 1941. At other times, Professor Zahniser argues, it was divergent interest—commercial, territorial, and strategic—that created currents of hostility that made for, at best, an uncertain friendship. His analysis reveals that Charles de Gaulle, far from personifying an aberration in Franco-American relations, embodied the very contradictions that reappear throughout nearly two centuries of diplomatic interaction between Paris and Washington. France and America have often needed each other; they have embraced on occasion, but they have never developed the trust and confidence of full-fledged allies.

This book is one in a series of volumes tracing the history of American foreign policy toward those nations with which the United States has had significant relations over a long period of time. By stressing the continuity of diplomatic themes through the decades, each author seeks to identify the distinctive character of America's international relationships. It is hoped that this country-by-country approach will not only enable readers to understand more deeply the diplomatic history of their nation but make them aware that past events and patterns of behavior exert a continuous influence on American foreign policy.

ROBERT A. DIVINE

Acknowledgments

MANY STUDENTS in my seminars at The Ohio State University have written papers on French-American relations that have been helpful in preparing this study. In particular I would like to thank Ronald J. Boggs, Steven E. Breyfogle, John A. Cooley, Thomas H. Hartig, Melvyn P. Leffler, Lois Livesay, Stephen M. Millett, Charles Robinson, and William O. Walker, III.

My thanks also goes to my colleagues John M. Rule and John A. M. Rothney, who saved me from several grievous errors; to The Ohio State University which made released time available to further this manuscript; to Greenville College and its library director, Cornelia May, who helped forward a summer's work on this book; to Margaret Kalatta, who typed—and retyped —the manuscript with great patience and efficiency, and to Rocky Coss, my research assistant. Professor Robert A. Divine made many valuable suggestions that improved the manuscript, as did Professor Armin Rappaport.

My enormous debt to my wife is indicated by the dedication of this book to her.

At this point I must add that all errors of fact and interpretation are solely my responsibility.

Marvin R. Zahniser
The Ohio State University
Columbus

Contents

Uncertain Friendship

CHAPTER I

Colonial Backgrounds

I know not which are most rapacious, the English or the French, but the latter have, with their knavery, the most politeness.

Benjamin Franklin, 1767

. . . the *French*, who all the world acknowledge to be an enterprizing, great and politick *Nation*, are so sensible of the *Advantages* of *Foreign Colonies*, both in reference to *Empire* and *Trade*, that they use all manner of *Artifices* to lull their *Neighbours* A Sleep, with fine *Speeches* and plausible *Pretences*, whilst they cunningly endeavor to compass their *Designs* by degrees, tho' at the hazard of encroaching on their *Friends* and Allies, and depriving them of their *Territories* and *Dominions* in time of *Profound Peace*, and contrary to the most *Solemn Treaties*.

Daniel Coxe, 1727[1]

AMERICAN REVOLUTIONARIES WERE OVERJOYED in April 1778 when news arrived that France and America had joined hands formally through treaties of alliance and commerce. Despotic and tyrannical England would soon be hammered by paralyzing blows directed from both Old and New World bases. Independence and the end of the war, if not in sight, could now at least be contemplated. Parades were held, guns fired in salute to France, and toasts proposed to good King Louis.

George Washington expressed the general sentiment that France had acted wisely in granting America exceedingly generous treaty terms. Bonds of common interest, he believed, would now be strengthened by the gratitude of an appreciative American people. Richard Henry Lee wrote to his Virginia compatriot

---

[1] Franklin's comment is found in Carl Van Doren, *Benjamin Franklin* (New York, 1956), pp. 367–368. The Coxe statement is cited in Max Savelle, *The Origins of American Diplomacy: The International History of Angloamerica, 1492–1763* (New York, 1967), p. 517.

Patrick Henry: "I look at the past condition of America as at a dreadful precipice, from which we have escaped by means of the generous French, to whom I will be everlastingly bound by most heartfelt gratitude. . . . Surely Congress will never recede from our French friends. Salvation to America depends upon our holding fast to our attachment to them. . . ."[2] In the general jubilation over the acquisition of a powerful ally in time of need, muted cautionary warnings could still be heard. Great powers were seldom known to act from disinterested motives. The Founding Fathers were certain that France had neither acted precipitately nor taken this fateful action of allying itself with struggling America without due regard to French advantage. And experience itself argued against too warm an embrace of France. Some of the colonists' most bitter memories were associated with struggles against French trade monopolies, French attacks and French incitement of their pitiless Indian allies against American frontier settlements. A recollection of France's history and role in the founding and settling of the North American continent, and its latent but continuing American ambitions, was certain to check the enthusiasm of many American leaders for the treaties of 1778.

* * * * *

Colonial American perceptions of France were partly products of that larger struggle for empire, glory and gold waged by the powers of Europe since the sixteenth century. Although separated by an ocean from their English homeland, the American colonists nevertheless tended to identify their international interests with those of England, and to view French actions and policies from a London perspective. Moreover, British eyes increasingly came to see France as the *bête noire*, the most logical challenger to Britain's growing commercial and territorial empire.

On the North American continent the struggle for position and empire was very old by 1763. In that contest Americans

---

[2] Quoted in Bernard Faÿ, *The Revolutionary Spirit in France and America* (New York, 1927), p. 104.

had participated as combatants, as advisers to the Crown, and as commercial competitors of French interests both in the New-foundland fisheries and on the fur and farming frontiers of the continental interior. Americans did not, therefore, see France exclusively through British eyes but by their own lamp of experience as well.

Colonial Americans were likely to take an exceedingly harsh view of Frenchmen in America. It was the French who skillfully allied with the western Indians and used them to massacre the advancing pioneers of English settlements. Frenchmen built forts along the western rivers that threatened to stem American western advance and thus deny land speculators and fur traders profits they considered part of their birthright. Fervent Protestants also deplored the influence of the Roman Catholic Church within the French régime and the persistent clerical drive to win Indians to Mother Church.[3] The very mention of French *habitants* early evoked in American minds the image of a polished savage, an inciter of Indian attacks who was devoted to the Catholic Church, determined to advance the cause of France in the New World, and an active, often unscrupulous competitor for the riches of the fishing banks and the fur frontiers.

English and colonial interests rather than judicious analysis led Americans toward making such unflattering generalizations about the French. In fact, many Frenchmen sailed to their New World destinies with motives and goals strikingly similar to those of contemporary English adventurers. Reuben Gold Thwaites concluded many years ago that French motives in the exploration and founding of New France were essentially four in number: the hope for profits in the fur trade and possibly in mining precious metals that would enable France to match the wealth of Spain; the desire to bring Christ's message to the Indian; the wish for martial experience, for "Gallant Exploits" by the army and navy personnel; and the desire to discover some short cut to the spice-producing regions of East Asia.

---

[3] Howard M. Jones, *America and French Culture, 1750–1848* (Chapel Hill, 1927), p. 352. See also William Livingston's lament, made in 1754, that the French sponsored "an *impious*, an *absurd*, a *persecuting*, Blood *shedding* Religion . . ." Quoted in Savelle, *Origins of American Diplomacy*, p. 547.

These motives Thwaites has called "the controlling and often warring interests of New France" for a hundred and fifty years.[4]

Although French sea captains participated in the early exploration of the North American continent, French settlers did not follow quickly enough to preempt a significant portion of the seaboard areas. Why this was so is itself a complex story. France explored the New World probably as early as 1497 when French fishermen visited and exploited the Grand Banks of Newfoundland for cod. Some twenty-five years later, Francis I (1515–1547) summoned to his court a Florentine mariner, Giovanni Verrazano, who was commissioned to explore the New World and to find, if possible, a route to China so that France could gain the promising profits of an Oriental trade.

Verrazano embarked in early summer of 1523, crossed the Atlantic, and explored the coast of North America as far as Newfoundland. It was his explorations that established France's original claim to North America. The succeeding voyages to the Gulf of St. Lawrence were made by Jacques Cartier and were financed or supported by Francis I. Later French settlements in North America were pretty well marked out by Cartier's explorations up the St. Lawrence, but her insecure position in Europe made it difficult for France to cultivate these initial impulses until after 1600.

That France should have made no very great commitment to exploration and settlement in the sixteenth century is not surprising. Nations not yet well established or in fear for their existence are unlikely to see much advantage in promoting expensive overseas settlements. Although the French had largely gained control of their claimed territory by the expulsion of English armies in 1453, France was still threatened by the ambitions of a powerful enemy. Charles V, the Hapsburg Emperor whose imperial dominions included Spain and the Spanish colonies, the Netherlands, Austria, Germany, and northern Italy, wished to annex the duchy of Burgundy, an area of France taken from his grandmother by Louis XI. Other issues arose to plague France involving Naples, Milan, and the Netherlands.

---

[4] *France in America: Fourteen Ninety-Seven to Seventeen Sixty-Three* (New York, 1905), p. 17.

The result was a series of wars fought between 1521 and 1559, wars that threatened to wreck the strong diplomatic and economic position of France within Europe.

When Henry of Navarre assumed power in 1589, France moved toward a state of internal tranquillity and adequate international security. Henry IV's vision of national grandeur included colonial projects for the Americas. Accordingly, Henry granted monopolies to private investors for the North American fur trade, an area attractive because of its ready profitability. Success only came through the efforts of a Huguenot, Pierre de Gaust, Sieur de Monts, leader of a company of merchants who obtained a grant to the region between the fortieth and forty-sixth parallels. Here, on the Bay of Fundy in the country called Acadia, de Monts established a colony at Port Royal Harbor in 1605.

De Monts' efforts to encourage a prospering fur trade from a coastal base was questioned by a French navigator and cartographer, Samuel de Champlain. After taking part in exploratory expeditions under de Monts in 1604–1607, Champlain argued that de Monts must move his base to the St. Lawrence. It was Champlain who subsequently led the expedition that founded Quebec in 1608, who inaugurated a program of systematic interior exploration, and who initiated the policy of French interests allying themselves with those Indians willing to serve the common economic good.

Champlain's vision of a settled and economically exploited St. Lawrence Valley brought him into conflict with private companies controlling the fur trade. Furs, not founding settlements, was the primary concern of the companies. It was not until the advent of Cardinal Richelieu, Louis XIII's first minister and grand master of navigation, that Champlain's desires were given substance. Richelieu was impressed by the brilliant economic achievements of the Netherlands and decided that comparable power for France could be obtained by cornering a major share of the colonial maritime trade. Constructing a large navy and chartering powerful companies to develop the colonies therefore became a significant aspect of his policies to promote French power. Richelieu had all earlier concessions revoked and his chosen company of one hundred associates received a royal charter in 1627. This company was given title to the land from Florida to the Arctic Circle and from the Great Lakes to the Atlantic Ocean. In return, the Company was expected to bring out some 4000 settlers during the succeeding fifteen years.

During the Company's thirty-six year tenure, all efforts failed to increase significantly the number of habitants. War, misfortune, inadequate planning, and miscalculation of what settlers would do when brought to New France frustrated Richelieu's great plan. Neither the Company's economic incentives nor the Jesuits' appeals to religious motivations attracted settlers. Even a group of wealthy *seigneurs* who formed the Company of Habitants in 1645 found recruitment of settlers a difficult challenge. By 1653 Canada was still a weak, vulnerable colony with a population of only 2000. The very existence of the colony was questioned after 1641 when the Iroquois went on the warpath against the French and their Indian allies, the Hurons. The Iroquois, who dominated the country that joins the Hudson River and the Great Lakes, were angry because French fur trappers and their Indian allies were hunting and trapping in territory the Iroquois regarded as their own. English buyers in Albany gave active encouragement to their Iroquois allies. The resulting wars, which had such crippling effects on New France's economic and demographic growth, continued intermittently until 1701.[5]

In order to cope with the great crisis brought on by the wars of the Iroquois and to clear the path to a new program of colonial defense reform, the government of Louis XIV revoked the charter of the One Hundred Associates in 1663. New France (Canada) was now placed under direct state control. Private enterprise, so generally successful in establishing English colonies on the North American continent, was for the time dropped by France as the most efficient path to mature colonization.[6] It was Jean-Bap-

---

[5] There was a respite from 1667 to 1682. See G. T. Hunt, *The Wars of the Iroquois: A Study in Intertribal Trade Relations*, 2nd. ed. (Madison, 1960).

[6] See W. J. Eccles, *Canada Under Louis XIV, 1663–1701* (Toronto, 1964) for a perceptive discussion of why French governmental aid was necessary if New France was to prosper.

tiste Colbert, Louis XIV's great controller general of the finances (1662–1683), who argued so persuasively that only the state could energize those diversified economic enterprises which could make it rich and therefore powerful. Colbert wished to see Canada develop thriving manufacturing, lumbering, and fisheries and become self-supporting in the necessities of life. The fur trade, he believed, must yield to central economic control. Concentrate population and encourage wealth-producing industries by subsidies and private diversification; this policy would place Canada on the road to salvation, strengthen her militarily, and increase her value to France's commercial empire.

Colbert's vision, like that of Richelieu, was broken by events beyond his control. Outbreak of war with the Dutch in 1672 meant that Canada-bound subsidies must be stopped and those monies directed into the war treasury. Under the best circumstances, Colbert's plan was problematical. Projected funding and subsidy costs were high and expectations of profitable fur returns were many years away. Temptations of the fur trade also made it difficult to implement a "compact colony" policy. Colbert himself unwittingly contributed to diffusing the meager French population when he encouraged exploration to discover an ice-free port for the colony. As René Robert Cavelier, Sieur de la Salle, explored the Mississippi river basin in the later 1670s, he established forts that initiated new and wider patterns with the Indians.

Hitherto French merchants had largely been content to wait for the Indians to bring their pelts to the colony. But the easy access of the new posts stimulated merchants to meet the competition by establishing bases closer to the Indian sources of supply. The rush into the interior was to have momentous consequences for the development of New France. In 1670 the colony was still compact, concentrated in the area of the St. Lawrence Valley. Fifteen years later, despite persistent government opposition, New France and Louisiana encompassed a vast hinterland embracing the entire Great Lakes and Mississippi Valley regions. Viewed from Paris it was plain that French resources were vastly overcommitted, that the population dispersion had weakened New France in its competition with the

English colonies. But through an ingenious use of agents, traders, missionaries, and soldiers stationed at strategic posts, and with the help of its Indian allies, the government hoped to maintain its authority and economic position in this vast arc of empire. With the English colonies thrusting ever westward, ambitious, well-populated, and resourceful, it became evident to French and British statesmen, and to their colonial subjects as well, that a great crisis involving clashing empires could not be postponed indefinitely.

This awareness of conflicting interests perhaps dawned in the 1680s and 1690s. English support of the Iroquois in the struggle to corner the western fur trade, and the English drive to establish their position in the Hudson Bay were direct challenges to France. France responded by launching savage raids against the western border settlements of New York and New England and by encouraging La Compagnie du Nord, an association of Canadian merchants, to destroy installations of the Hudson's Bay Company. These raids caused great anxiety in the English settlements and provoked a series of military responses. The struggle for the continent was now to involve the colonists directly in the roles of soldiers, propagandists, strategists, and as pressure groups urging home governments to take appropriate countering actions.

French strategy to preserve and enhance their position evolved from the recognition that the overflow of population from the English settlements into the Mississippi Valley could eventually reach flood proportions. In that event, the possessions of both France and Spain in America would be placed in mortal peril. Confronting the British plantations by erecting strategic fortifications from the Great Lakes to the Gulf of Mexico was advanced as a sound defensive strategy in 1701, the first year of the War of the Spanish Succession. Little was done during the war to implement that strategy, but the Peace of Utrecht (1713) underlined for France this fact that only vigorous action could save her North American colony. Hudson Bay, Newfoundland, and Acadia were all ceded to Great Britain at Utrecht, though New France of the Laurentian Valley, Cape Breton Island, and Louisiana were retained by France. England also gained superiority over the weakened Iroquois' confederacy and the right to barter with the western tribes. France's fur trade and fisheries were now directly threatened by British encroachment.[7]

How to annul the potentially disastrous effects of Utrecht became one pressing question for French statesmen. Measures were immediately implemented that were partially successful, but these alarmed the English colonists further and made another clash with Great Britain inevitable. In the North Atlantic, on Cape Breton Island, the French constructed the formidable fortress of Louisbourg, designed as a naval base to protect approaches to the St. Lawrence and as a fishing station to replace those lost in the cession of Acadia and Newfoundland. To undermine the Hudson's Bay Company fur trade, a series of trading posts were established from Lake Superior almost to the Stony Mountains. To prevent Britain from gaining influence over the Trans-appalachian Indians, France also extended its system of fortified trading posts from Nova Scotia to the Carolinas.[8]

As France implemented these blocking measures the English colonists grew increasingly alarmed, a feeling that was shared by the British government. It was obvious that New France was prospering as it never had before 1713, that France had largely annulled the Peace of Utrecht as it related to the North American settlement. To many it seemed possible that an ambitious French government might soon consolidate its hold on the Mississippi Valley and pin the English settlements in areas east of the Appalachians through well-placed forts and alliances with the Indians. "Encirclement" is never a pleasant state for any people to contemplate. For colonial America, the competing enemy was particularly dangerous. Frenchmen were clever, ambitious, known to encourage Indians to scalp and rape among white settlers, and devotees, in about equal portions, of the slippery Jesuits and an absolutist Monarchy! If London's view

---

[7] Max Savelle, "The American Balance of Power and European Diplomacy, 1713–78," in *The Era of the American Revolution. Studies inscribed to E. B. Greene*, Richard B. Morris, Ed. (New York, 1939), p. 141.

[8] The broad lines of French strategy to 1763 were recommended in 1716 by the Marquis de Vaudreuil, Governor of New France. Savelle, *Origins of American Diplomacy*, pp. 234–235. An excellent study is Guy Frégault, *Le Grand Marquis: Pierre de Rigaud de Vaudreuil, et la Louisiane* (Montreal and Paris, 1952).

of New France's citizenry was somewhat less diabolical, there was, nonetheless, an appreciation of the French continental threats to expanding English interests.

Great Britain and France finally came to blows in 1744 when Great Britain entered the War of the Austrian Succession, a war in which France was already engaged. With but six years respite (1748–1754), France and Britain grappled until 1763 in a war with world-wide repercussions, a war in which the North American continent increasingly became a central concern. France felt particularly pressed to protect its American interests. She feared that if Britain were to add the resources of New France to her already vast colonial empire, the balance of power in Europe would be decisively altered.[9] On the Anglo-American side, the argument that the thirteen colonies would never be secure without a total overthrow of New France gradually gained acceptance. The stage was thus set for a desperate contest, a contest that ended in 1763 with the collapse of France's American Empire.

British strategy in America for the Great War for the Empire (1756–1763)[10] centered around gaining or maintaining control of the Ohio Valley and Canada. Forts and posts guarding the approaches to Canada early became focal points of struggle. Early French success in defending their forts and in carrying the attack to English outposts and frontier settlements precipitated a crisis in the British government that thrust the brilliant and resolute William Pitt into power. Pitt was both energetic and lucky, for in 1758 Forts Louisbourg, Duquesne, and Frontenac fell, opening the way to Canada. In 1759 the French fleet was shattered, making it impossible to supply forces in Canada with the necessities for continuing the struggle. With the fall of Quebec in September 1759 and the surrender of Montreal one year later, British aims in Canada were completely successful.

America rejoiced that the deadly foe had been so decisively

---

[9] John C. Rule argues that France was really on the defensive, 1750–1755, before what it regarded as an aggressive British imperialism. "The Old Regime in America: A Review of Recent Interpretations of France in America," *William and Mary Quarterly*, 3rd. Ser., XIX, No. 4 (October 1962), pp. 585–586.

[10] Sometimes misleadingly called the French and Indian, or the Seven Years' War.

defeated. In the Treaty of Paris (1763) France transferred Canada, and all French territory east of the Mississippi River with the exception of New Orleans, to Great Britain. Two small islands south of Newfoundland, St. Pierre and Miquelon, were also exceptions and were to be used by France as bases to exploit the Newfoundland fisheries. Besides losing several islands in the West Indies, France also was forced to yield her fortifications in India. Britain likewise received Florida from Spain and all Spanish possessions east of the Mississippi. As for the Mississippi River south of New Orleans, still French territory, it was made free and open to the subjects of both England and France. Immediately after the peace was signed, France ceded to Spain all of Louisiana west of the Mississippi and New Orleans. By the transfer France concluded her role as a territorial power on the continent of North America.

For Americans it was a most satisfactory peace. No longer would they live in continual fear of French or Spanish attacks. Americans were now free to expand westward, to fulfill their presumed territorial destiny.

* * * * *

There is a maxim that statesmen often abuse in international relations: never be too harsh on your enemy of today for tomorrow he may be your ally. Contemporary Americans have observed their own government apply this principle in its relations with Germany and Japan following World War II. As the Cold War took shape it quickly became obvious that these determined enemies of the war years might soon have value as friends, or even allies. They were, therefore, wooed with generous treatment and those mating gestures peculiar to nation-states. This flexible approach in determining one's national friends is not peculiar to Americans of the post-1945 era. Colonial Americans were just as flexible, just as willing to reassess their true interests to determine who ought to be considered a friend and who an enemy.

It is generally accepted by historians that removal of the

French and Spanish threats to American security cast a shadow over British-American relations. Americans became rather less willing to subordinate their views to London's economic and political policies once American fisheries and territory were relatively secure. As the years sped by, observant men even began to whisper that perhaps Britain was America's real problem, that it was Britain who was levying unjust taxes, penning up Americans east of the Appalachians, and bullying colonial merchants. Likewise, in French-American relations after 1763, new themes were explored. The image of France as an ancient and savage enemy, the citadel of decadent Catholicism and governmental tyranny, slowly receded and a refurbished image of France came into focus. This new France, remarkably enough, possessed an enviable culture, was the base of advanced political and economic thought, and in certain areas of science was instructor to the world.

Old thought patterns fade slowly, of course, and these new concepts about France evolved by degrees. If the New England clergy remained reluctant to relinquish their sermons denouncing Frenchmen as papal tools, many Americans found their religious prejudices softening as more tolerant attitudes became fashionable. The very heterogeneity of American society and the diversity of religious traditions argued powerfully for toleration of other religious viewpoints if social tranquillity was to be fostered.[11] Internal politics thus worked to mellow Protestant Americans' fear of Catholic France. The growth of deism in America also helped to blunt the edges of American religious prejudice. Heated Protestant-Catholic debates over points of policy or theology seemed largely irrelevant to men who liked their religion punctuated by rationality, skepticism, and philosophical detachment. In this orientation Benjamin Franklin, Thomas Jefferson, and John Adams could join hands with Voltaire, Condorcet and Diderot. So the old religious barriers to common understanding were lowered through gradual

---

[11] See Daniel Boorstin, *The Americans: The Colonial Experience* (New York, 1958) pp. 132–139. Also Carl Bridenbaugh, *Mitre and Sceptre* (New York, 1962), and Charles H. Metzger, *Catholics and the American Revolution* (Chicago, 1962).

diminuation of the Protestant-Catholic conflict and through the growth of a larger religious toleration.[12]

Once the military threat of France was removed, many colonials freely recognized that culture-starved America had much to gain by emulating France. One sign of this new acceptance of things French was the increased study in the colonies of French language and literature. Ever larger numbers of French dictionaries, novels, and scientific treatises were ordered by Americans, reflecting this growing interest in French thought and culture. French dancing masters, hairdressers, and tutors emigrated to America after 1763 to fill the growing demands of America's polite society.

Even as Americans reoriented their deepest feelings about France and the French, social and political developments within France favorably predisposed French intellectuals and statesmen toward America. In the 1760s heightened interest in America was generated by the *Economistes* (physiocrats) who argued that a nation's true wealth consisted solely of the products of the soil. To these rationalists of medieval economic ideals, agricultural America held a magnetic appeal. This was especially true after Benjamin Franklin's visit to France in 1769, during which he publicly embraced the doctrines of the *Economistes* and supported America's political and economic differences with England by citing physiocratic theory.[13]

Franklin also introduced American viewpoints to a wider French audience through his contributions to a physiocratic monthly journal, *Ephémérides du citoyen.* In this journal Franklin published articles on the American Indians, rural customs of America, a proposed philanthropic voyage to New Zealand, twelve economic principles, and his rigorous and humiliating examination before the House of Commons. After examining the writings of Franklin, John Dickinson's *Letters From a Farmer in Pennsylvania,* and Benjamin Rush's scientific treatises, editors of the *Ephémérides* soon concluded that mankind must

---

[12] Jones, *America and French Culture,* p. 365; Faÿ, *The Revolutionary Spirit in France and America,* pp. 41–43.

[13] Durand Echeverria, *Mirage in the West: A History of the French Image of American Society to 1815* (Princeton, 1957), p. 20.

see in the American character "une idée de la dignité dont l'espèce humain est susceptible."[14]

Such flattering sentiments were certainly not accepted by the entire intelligentsia of France. In the mid 1760s, for example, there was a vigorous debate over the nature of these new people, the Americans. Were Americans exalted Europeans, liberated and strengthened by the New World environment, or were they Europeans who had been debased by transplantation? Scientific evidence of the highest authority appeared for a time to be quite contradictory. Every man could thus support his own prejudice, and not a few were hostile to Americans.[15]

But as France lurched through the last years of the *ancien regime*, its government increasingly under fire for corruption, bureaucratic inertia, and unresponsiveness to social distress, America appeared ever more attractive to social philosophers. It became, in the words of Durand Echeverria, the Mirage in the West. It was possible after all, many argued, for man to escape from poverty, corruption, and injustice; men could live in equality and with full enjoyment of liberty. America was living proof of that. America was the *avant garde*, the new order, and it was to America that reformers and lovers of humanity could turn for guidance as they restructured their own institutions.

This more generous view of America, arising largely in response to France's internal needs, was strengthened by government policy. Because France had been eliminated as a North American power by the Treaty of Paris of 1763 did not mean that she had lost interest in the Americas. In fact, the opposite was true. The very extent of France's debasement in the Great War for the Empire, a war in which she had lost territory or prestige in India, in America, on the high seas, and on the Continent, was reason enough for France to plot a comeback. Her lowered status at the courts of Europe and the humiliations inflicted upon her by the rigors of court protocol added incentive

---

[14] Quoted in Alfred Owen Aldridge, "The Debut of American Letters in France," *The French-American Review*, III, No. 1 (January–March, 1950), p. 2.

[15] The debate is discussed in Durand Echeverria, "Roubaud and the Theory of American Degeneration," *Ibid.*, pp. 24–33.

to the plans for revenge. The partition of the vast territories of Poland in 1772 without France being consulted, though her supposed friend Austria was one of the participants, illustrated the low status of France among the Constellation of Powers. France's conception of her proper role in Europe absolutely forbade acceptance of her diplomatic position after 1763. Within the context of French plans for revenge on Great Britain, the American colonies became increasingly important.

It was not the thinking of French Foreign Minister Étienne-François Duc de Choiseul that France might snatch the American colonies from Britain and add them to her own dominion. Nor did Choiseul see much advantage in jockeying to recover the lost Louisiana territory as a counterforce to British power in America. Britain's American colonies were rather seen by Choiseul (and after 1774 by Foreign Minister Charles Granier, Comte de Vergennes) as a major factor in the balance of power. If America's trade, resources, and population were subtracted from the British equation, and in such a way that America would throw its economic favors to France, Britain would receive a stinging blow. Although in itself the defection of the American colonies would not decisively alter the balance of power in France's favor, it would be a handsome start toward that goal.

Choiseul thus started France on a course of observation and report concerning the temper of the American colonies. Agents were sent to the colonies as early as 1764 and their reports were duly read and analyzed. Each sign of America's disaffection from England—the Stamp Act Crisis of 1765-1766, the enactment of nonimportation measures in 1767, the Battle of Golden Hill and the Boston Massacre in 1770, the burning of the *Gaspée* in 1772, and the creation of committees of correspondence in 1773 —caused palpitations in the French Foreign Ministry. Each crisis raised the possibility that Americans might now strike for independence; every disturbance meant that France must reassess the diplomatic scene to determine what support it might be able to give the Americans.[16]

When sustained violence erupted in America following Lexing-

---

[16] Richard W. Van Alstyne, *Empire and Independence: The International History of the American Revolution* (New York, 1965), pp. 49–52.

ton and Concord in April 1775, events and circumstances of the past twelve years made it possible for France and America to embrace, however discreetly. Long-standing hatreds and misconceptions between peoples generally subside when common fears or needs make cooperation appear to their mutual advantage. America, uncertain as to her future course, but heading toward conflict with the world's greatest maritime power, prepared to grasp the hand of France. A wary and ambitious France was willing to offer that hand if only she could reassure herself that such a move would not bring disaster upon France.

*   *   *   *   *

By 1775 Americans had had over 150 years of experience with France and Frenchmen. Patterns of exploration and settlement in the New World and different allegiances had precipitated French-American conflicts throughout America's colonial era. Out of those experiences flowed hatred and misunderstanding. As the Great War for the Empire drew to a close, Americans rejoiced at the final humiliation of their ancient enemy. Long historical experience, idealogical commitments, economic rivalry, and spilled blood all argued in support of American jubilation. But expulsion of France from America, French desire to regain her former international status, and colonial America's growing unhappiness with British rule made it possible, in fact mandatory, that Americans and Frenchmen reexamine their feelings. In these moments of shared desperation and ambition France and America found it possible to overlook a turbulent past and to consider joining arms as partners against the common enemy.

CHAPTER II

Establishing American Independence

What a miraculous change in the political world! The ministry of England advocates for despotism, and [is] endeavouring to enslave those who might have remained loyal subjects of the King. The government of France an advocate of liberty, espousing the cause of protestants and risking a war to secure their independence. The king of England considered by every whig in the nation as a tyrant, and the king of France applauded by every whig in America as the protector of the rights of man! . . . Britain at war with America, France in alliance with her! These, my friend, are astonishing changes. Perhaps one principle, self interest, may account for all.

Elbridge Gerry, 1778[1]

How a divided colonial people could overthrow their powerful political masters in a seven-year struggle, obtain the open or covert support of Europe's second power, emerge with their political institutions intact, and with an enormous land base as a stake for the future is truly a remarkable story. Nationalists with a religious bent have often pointed to the Revolutionary years as evidence that America has been specially favored by some divine providence.

Students of foreign policy take particular interest in the years of the American Revolution for different but, nevertheless, compelling reasons. So many principles of interstate relations are illustrated in these years that the era is considered a fascinating case study in international behavior. Certainly the Founding Fathers received a liberal education in the opportunities and dangers awaiting a small power maneuvering in the rolling and uncertain waters of great power diplomacy. If they showed little system in their thought about international relations before

---

[1] Gerry to ———, May 26, 1778, in James T. Austin, *Life of Elbridge Gerry*, 2 vols. (Boston, 1828), I, p. 276.

1776, the same could not be said by 1783. For as the war ended, certain common great-state practices of a cynical and opportunistic century were not only understood as practices by American diplomatists, but had been applied as principles needed to achieve American independence.

In this educative process France was to play a central role. As America's covert friend to 1778, as her formal ally from 1778, in her efforts to make America her diplomatic satellite in the peace negotiations, and in her willingness to deny America certain basic objectives of the war, France became America's tutor in international diplomacy and ethics. France was eventually astonished at the adeptness of her pupil who not only managed to gain independence on exceedingly magnanimous terms, but who also was willing to violate the spirit of its alliance with France to realize American ambitions.

French-American relations during the war years can be viewed as having two stages: to the alliance treaty of 1778 and from alliance to the signing of the various treaties ending the war. In the first period, when America was actually seeking for aid and allies, France pursued a variety of policies which alternately encouraged and discouraged the American government. France would not conclude an alliance with America; she would not join battle for America; but she did encourage America by an extensive aid and trade program. While France did her part to keep the coals of rebellion glowing, she laid the groundwork to enter the contest as opportunities warranted. Her navy was strengthened, new financial resources were sought, potential enemies were pacified, and a continuing effort was made to assure France of Spanish assistance when the struggle commenced.

From the American vantage point, the second period of its relationship with France had far greater advantages. The alliance treaties, naval aid and ground armies, and a more extensive fiscal support program all made a vital contribution to the success of American arms. What most Americans did not properly appreciate was that the "American Question" became internationalized once France and Spain linked arms to subdue England. The years of maximum aid to America were exactly the years of greatest danger that American interests would be traded to achieve higher goals: peace for Europe, a new balance of power, or enhanced prestige for some mediation-prone monarch. But as the world-wide military struggle seesawed and the Powers reached the point of financial or psychological exhaustion, the diplomatic mouse, America, seized its chance and scurried to safety. Internationalization of the war, a phrase pregnant with potential disaster for America, actually worked to complete the American puzzle. And a beautiful puzzle it was when complete: independence, vast unsettled territory to the Mississippi, a foothold in the Grand Banks fisheries, and the great powers reasonably well-disposed toward the fledgling nation.

From a modern perspective it is instructive to follow French rationale for intervention, the gradual way France became involved in the war (until the aid program assumed a logic of its own), the means by which the French government worked to control the American peace program while appearing not to do so, the difficulty of getting the war stopped on an honorable basis, and the disappointment France experienced despite her prolonged struggle. France carefully gauged her program according to many sound diplomatic maxims. She entered the war strictly for her own advantage, at an opportune moment, and when her military preparations were in reasonably good order. She secured a powerful ally in Spain. She largely neutralized potential opposition to her course among the powers of Europe. She allied herself to a small power, it is true, but a determined and resourceful one, not a quitter by any standard. Yet the laurels of victory hung limply in her hand as peace was concluded. Her debt was crushing, her ally of 1778 was acting exceedingly independent, her family ally Spain was angry that her goals had not been achieved, and French standing in the diplomatic community was not noticeably higher than before she entered the lists.

*   *   *   *   *

In October and November, 1775, the reassembled Second Continental Congress took steps to appoint committees and secret agents to approach the powers of Europe for assistance.

Much had transpired, however, before Connecticut businessman Silas Deane arrived in Paris in July 1776 to solicit aid on behalf of Congress. In late 1775, as Americans debated fiercely whether to strike for independence, various Frenchmen appeared in Philadelphia inquiring solicitously about American plans and needs. French foreign minister Vergennes, for example, sent naval officer Achard de Bonvouloir in September to assure American leaders that France had no desire, nor would she take advantage of this crisis, to repossess Canada. Further, it was communicated, France was by no means unfriendly to the cause of American independence and "would be pleased to see fortunate circumstances enable them [Americans] to frequent our ports. . . ."[2] Bonvouloir carried the message to the Secret Committee of Correspondence of the Congress which received it gratefully, and in turn gave him assurances that Congress was moving toward a proclamation of American independence. In December 1775 the same Committee was contacted by two private French commercial agents, Messrs. Penet and Pliarne, who contracted with Congress to supply powder and munitions in return for American produce.

French merchants were not alone in wanting to supply America's military needs. An enormous clandestine trade sprang up with Dutch merchants operating through St. Eustatius in the West Indies. Spanish merchants as well leaped to the opportunity to supply the rebellious Americans. But the trade had to be surreptitious in nature until America made the very basic decision of whether or not to seek independence. When George III declared the American colonies in rebellion late in August 1775, and when Parliament cut off all trade with them in December, American debate concerning what course to take became ever more vigorous. To lift its self-imposed embargo and to proclaim America's ports open to all would be the act of a sovereign power—tantamount to a proclamation of independence. Throughout 1775, therefore, because Congress was unwill-

---

[2] Vergennes to Comte de Guines, Versailles, August 7, 1775, in Henri Doniol, *Histoire de la participation de la France à l' etabilissement des Etats-Unis d' Amérique.* 5 vols. (Paris, 1884–1892), I, p. 156. Guines gave the instructions verbally to Bonvouloir.

ing to take so drastic a step, America resorted to encouraging the clandestine trade with foreign merchants.[3] But as time and events slipped by, both logic and emotion argued that independence be proclaimed. In 1775 alone, events pointed toward a hardened American attitude. Lexington and Concord in April, capture of Forts Ticonderoga and Crown Point in May, augmentation of the Continental forces, the battle of Breeds-Hill in June, and the expedition commenced against Canada in August all pled for a formal breach with Britain. The appearance of Thomas Paine's eloquent call to independence in "Common Sense" in January 1776, together with a widened British offensive, pushed the Congress toward radical steps. If the cause was to be saved, it must first be defined. If independence was indeed the objective, then a program must be implemented to achieve that goal.

Since relatively few Americans were ready to turn back the clock and assume the usual role of England's star of Empire, and since the ministry of Lord North was not ready to grant the substance of America's evolving demands, a declaration of independence became a matter of necessity. Without such a declaration, Richard Henry Lee pointed out, "no State in Europe will either Treat or Trade with us so long as we consider ourselves Subjects of Great Britain. . . . It is not choice . . . but necessity that calls for Independence, as the only means by which foreign Alliances can be attained and a proper confederation by which internal peace and union may be secured. . . ." Probable failure of the American attempt to conquer Canada underlined for Congress the need to obtain an enlarged commerce and a wealthy ally willing to augment American military efforts with a powerful protective navy.

Congress tipped its hand on April 6, 1776 when it opened American ports to all trade except that of British vessels. Simultaneously it debated and hammered out three great measures: a declaration of independence, a treaty plan to be offered to

---

[3] See Richard W. Van Alstyne, *Empire and Independence: The International History of the American Revolution* (New York, 1965), Chapter IV for an excellent account of the trade's growth.

[4] Van Alstyne, *Empire and Independence*, p. 106.

France, and a political structure to unite the colonies in some form of confederation. When independence was proclaimed on July 4, 1776 the hands of Congress were freed to organize a new government and to conduct foreign affairs as did other sovereign nation-states. Establishment of diplomatic relations with other nations could now be sought and trade treaties and alliances made.

Exactly how a new nation-state should proceed to establish diplomatic relations with the Powers of Europe became a matter of lively debate. British frowns and probable retaliation against nations exchanging diplomatic formalities with America were the major complications. Some Congressmen argued that the shotgun approach should be used, scattering agents to the courts of Europe in indiscriminate fashion. In this way America's cause could be explained, American trade favors dangled as bait for diplomatic relations, and potential friends or enemies could be quickly ascertained. If America's overtures were rejected, the method of approach could not be blamed; nations, after all, decided questions of state on the basis of self-interest. Others, such as Benjamin Franklin, were aghast at such tactics. They would smack of desperation, he argued, and would therefore encourage potential friends to sit on the sidelines awaiting some decisive events. And they would violate the European sense of punctilio and proportion, a matter of pronounced importance to the ancient courts of Europe.[5]

There was, at least in Congress, some realization that relations with France would largely determine the extent of America's diplomatic success in Europe. If France remained neutral, then no other power would dare to defy the might of Britain's navy. If France chose to aid America through secret grants and clandestine trade, this would likely become the pattern for other well-disposed powers. An open alliance with America would sound the trumpet of warfare with Britain; powers resentful of English wealth and power might then rush in to stab Britain as she

---

[5] Felix Gilbert, *To the Farewell Address: Ideas of Early American Foreign Policy* (Princeton, 1961), pp. 79–81; Verner W. Crane, *Benjamin Franklin and a Rising People* (Boston, 1954), p. 17.

staggered from New and Old World blows. This situation, of course, promised America most by way of aid and military assistance. It then became essential to determine how best to entice France into the war. This raised other crucial questions that have not been settled to the present day: should America become embroiled in Old World politics through treaties of alliance or should America define the relationship as one based primarily on trade. The discussion was influenced by the somber realization that precedent for future policy was being made. As in most discussions where statesmen hope to shape ideal policies, necessity ultimately decided the issue.

After lengthy debate, Congress composed instructions in September 1776 that were to guide American diplomats if they concluded a treaty with France. Friendship and commerce in perpetuity were to be offered to France. In turn France would be asked to pledge herself to follow principles on the high seas that were advantageous chiefly to small navy powers: that goods on board neutral ships be regarded as neutral, that neutrals be free to trade between ports of a belligerent, and that contraband lists in wartime be narrowly defined so as not to include naval stores or foodstuffs. France was also to be asked to protect American citizens and vessels from the Barbary corsairs and to agree that French and American naval vessels be allowed to travel in the others' convoys. And if war with England resulted from French recognition of American independence, would America be willing to conclude a military alliance with France? The answer was negative, partly because such an alliance seemed unnecessary and partly because the Americans were reluctant to associate themselves with the tainted methods of European diplomacy. America would, however, pledge not to assist France's enemies with trade, ships, contraband, money, or men. For this pledge France should be asked to promise not to take and hold any British territory on the North American continent or any adjacent islands. If France was not satisfied with these commitments, several other clauses could be written into the treaty: one to specify that America would never resume its allegiance to Britain; another that France should enjoy all trade privileges granted to Britain; and finally that neither power should make a separate peace with their common enemy until six months after notification that negotiations had started.[6]

To a disinterested observer, America's proposed terms might seem highly presumptuous. For an upstart country, uncertain of its very survival, to propose such self-indulgent terms might be misunderstood by France. Congress was not intentionally brash, however, just ill-informed about the attracting power of American trade. If trade and friendship proved unequal to the task of wooing France to America's side, then the high card must be played: France should be threatened with America's return to its British allegiance. As the instructions phrased it, ". . . it will be proper for you to press for the immediate and explicit declaration of France in our Favour, upon a Suggestion that a Re-union with Great Britain may be the Consequence of a delay."[7]

Congress commissioned Silas Deane to proceed to Paris, posing as a merchant, to sound the possibilities for trade and treaty. When Deane was appointed, none could have envisioned the remarkable impact he would exert in shaping American wartime politics. Deane eventually became the center of bitter Congressional fighting over the terms of peace, the appointment of diplomatic personnel, Congressional purchase policy of wartime supplies, and the ethical standards by which America's public servants were to be guided. No one was more surprised by these developments than Deane. He erred in failing to realize the danger of crossing a self-righteous paranoid, or to recognize the rising standards for the conduct of government officials. The paranoid he challenged was Arthur Lee, one of the Lee dynasty of Virginia. And the propriety he violated was not yet commonly accepted. Deane saw no reason why private profit and public office should be mutually exclusive. What was good for Silas Deane and his financial associates he perceived as being beneficial for America. Because some people questioned this premise, and the actions that flowed from it, Deane was eventually

---

[6] William C. Stinchcombe, *The American Revolution and the French Alliance* (Syracuse, 1969), pp. 8–9.

[7] Quoted in Samuel Flagg Bemis, *The Diplomacy of the American Revolution* (Bloomington, 1957), p. 47.

called home for consultation and review of his activities.

Deane's problems with Arthur Lee highlight the extent of early French involvement in supplying America with essential materials. After earnest debate within the French government in late spring 1776, several decisions were reached relating to the American rebellion. First, France would funnel secret aid to America in the form of outdated French arms, monetary subventions, and encouragement of private trading. This policy was risky, but Vergennes was convinced that Britain wanted no new open enemies until the American question was settled. Juxtaposed to the secret aid discussions of May 1776 were those relating to American vessels entering French ports and the defense of France's neutral rights. Despite vigorous and continuing British protests, the French government decided to welcome rebel American merchantmen into French ports. Even more damaging to Great Britain, however, was the French announcement that French merchantmen engaged in trade between France and her colonies would not permit British vessels of war to search their cargoes. Clandestine contraband trade to Cap Français in Haiti, destined for transfer to the American flag, was therefore protected from prying British eyes.[8]

The mechanics of transferring contraband aid to America involved the French government with Caron de Beaumarchais, an ardent pro-American who had some standing with the government. Already known to theatre audiences as the author of "The Marriage of Figaro" and "The Barber of Seville," Beaumarchais made the acquaintance of Arthur Lee while in London on a secret mission for the French government. Lee, a confidential correspondent of the Committee of Secret Correspondence, discovered a fellow-soul in Beaumarchais; at least Beaumarchais shared Lee's enthusiasm for the American cause and his desire to see the French government step forward as America's protector. Beaumarchais took it upon himself in the summer of 1775 to forward his assessments of the American situation to Vergennes. In February of 1776 he warned the French Foreign Office that if Americans were not soon aided with ample powder and muni-

---

[8] Lawrence S. Kaplan, *Colonies Into Nation: American Diplomacy, 1763–1801* (New York, 1972), pp. 91–92.

tions, they might in revenge join hands with England to conquer the French sugar islands. Secret aid, Beaumarchais urged, could preclude this imminent disaster but speed was essential. Vergennes found this communication useful since it agreed with his own thinking. It was therefore sent to the King for his personal comment.

For reasons not entirely clear, Vergennes decided to channel French aid through a dummy company organized by Beaumarchais. Arthur Lee, one of Beaumarchais' principal American friends, thus assumed some importance as an adviser to Beaumarchais on American needs and priorities. Lee apparently understood that French aid was to be a gift, even if contracts were signed and bills submitted for the sake of appearance.

With the arrival in July 1776 of Silas Deane, a merchant with connections even into the French Foreign Office, Lee's value to the French government largely vanished. Although a patriot, Lee was petty, revengeful, suspicious and defensive beyond reasonable bounds. This blow to his ego provoked Lee to regard Silas Deane as his personal foe. Deane was careless, Deane was corrupt, Deane was not a patriot—on and on the charges flew until Deane was eventually brought home by a Congress whose confidence in his ability and honesty had been shaken. One particular charge of Lee's was especially damaging: that the French had promised their arms and ammunition *gratis*, whereas Deane proceeded to contract for it and to arrange methods of payment. Why did Deane pay for what ought to have been free? Lee assumed that Deane and his cohorts were craftily milking the American government through the contracts and that all who cooperated in this scheme were tainted with the stench of corruption. Congress was not free to review Lee's charges when French aid was tenuous, but once secure in the French Commitment, politics was given its due, and with a vengeance. Family standing, leadership in the revolutionary cause, personal reputations, factional and state politics, patronage, and peace policy all eventually became interwoven in the Lee-Deane quarrel.

Even Deane's enemies conceded that he was energetic in pursuing his duties. He exploited his Paris and Bordeaux contacts to speed supplies to America. He worked with Beaumarchais to channel the desperately needed arms and ammunition. Deane even approached the French Foreign Office in September 1776 to urge that France take the decisive step to ally itself with America. Now was the golden moment Deane urged. As the crisis mounted in Britain, surely a "Great Genius, a Man of Liberal and extensive views" would come forward to manage British fears. Deane followed this allusion to William Pitt, Earl of Chatham, who had despoiled France in the Great War for the Empire, with a warning. Whose New World Empires would be safe, he asked, once Britain had amassed superior naval and land forces in America? Upon receipt of news that America had declared its independence, Deane followed up his earlier queries by proposing an alliance with France. Entirely unauthorized, Deane proposed that France, Spain, and America join hands to deprive Britain of her West Indies possessions, to pledge free trade among themselves, and to exclude British merchantmen from the coasts of North and South America; and that France and Spain immediately dispatch a fleet to protect the interests of the United States.[9]

Prudent governments rarely respond formally to such desperate invitations. A cautious man, Vergennes certainly was not intrigued by such an offer. Objective factors must determine French policy in this crisis. Would Spain join in a common attack on Britain? When, and upon what conditions would she do so? How long would Britain allow France to supply America without directly challenging France? Would the state of French finances permit an extended and severe trial by arms? Was it absolutely certain that Americans had resolved to bulldog their way to independence or would America opt out when the going got tough? These were some of the questions that the French government constantly reviewed. The answers formulated throughout 1776 were not reassuring.

Although Spain agreed to subsidize America secretly, her distaste for an open conflict with England was not hidden. Moreover, it never struck the Spanish as particularly advantageous to

---

[9] See Deane's "Proposed Articles of a Treaty between France and Spain and the United States, presented to M. Gerard, Nov. 23, 1776," in Vol. 19, *Collections of the New York Historical Society* (New York, 1887), pp. 361–364.

encourage a potentially rapacious American neighbor, already talking about its need for free access to the Mississippi. Despite what the Americans said, Spain and America had directly clashing interests in the New World and it was not wise for Spain to strengthen a notoriously land-hungry people. But Spain had its price for entering the war, and it was Vergenne's unpleasant task to ascertain the price. Once determined, the French court must then decide if the price was payable. All was in limbo, however, as 1776 drew to a close.

And on the American front? The picture there was clearly mixed. England had not met with unbroken military successes. On the other hand, neither had the Americans. Particularly frightening was the narrow escape of General Washington's army as it evacuated New York City in September. A little British luck, some said, and the American war effort would have ended in disaster on Manhattan Island. It was encouraging to the French government that Americans had declared their independence, but American pretensions had to be supported by more than noble verbiage. Everything considered, France would do well to continue its aid, gain the needed pledges from Spain, maintain a friendly facade with England, and determine if America and Britain had reached the point where reconciliation was impossible. Any bolder course would risk catastrophe for France. Any lesser measure might push America toward reconciliation and France's unique opportunity to wound Great Britain would vanish.

*   *   *   *   *

Congress was quite aware that French aid and goodwill were central to America's hopes. It then became a matter of urgency to have astute representation at the Court of Louis XVI. Silas Deane had his good points, to be sure, but others were probably more suitable for a diplomatic role. At least Deane should have supporting personnel in his entreaties to the French court. Multiple representation would have the further advantage that each faction in Congress would have its man on the scene to frustrate possible skulduggery, check the pulse of Europe, and make honest reports to home contacts. Accordingly, Arthur Lee, Benjamin Franklin, and Thomas Jefferson (who declined the appointment) were ordered to Paris to join Deane.

When Congress selected Franklin, it was giving France America's most accomplished and renowned personality. As events were to prove, he was superbly endowed with those qualities of heart and mind that distinguish the superior diplomat. Franklin was such a marked personal success in France and was so well liked by the French court that it is difficult to keep his mission in perspective. Many historians have pronounced him America's first and greatest diplomat. His rallying of French opinion to the American cause, his astute, even cynical use of the press to present American perspectives on war and peace, his cultivation of the intelligentsia through lodge and social activities, and his skillful role in winning aid and concluding peace certainly lend support to the Franklin legend.

It is difficult, however, to take some of the plaudits given to Franklin at face value. He did not alter French policy by heroic efforts at crucial moments. He did not ferret out French military talent, without which the good cause would have been lost. Nor did Franklin singlehandedly play a crucial role in arranging the favorable peace with Great Britain.

He did offer wise counsel to America in dealing with the European courts; he possessed a keen sense of timing in presenting petitions for aid; he realized the importance of wooing French public opinion; and he confirmed for Frenchmen an image of America that they so desperately wished to hold. His most crucial contribution, one that perhaps no other American could have made so well, was helping to establish a climate of opinion that made it easier for the French government to adopt pro-American positions.

There is little doubt that Franklin was a marked success in this endeavor. Since many Frenchmen preferred to believe Americans epitomized the exalted virtures of the Quakers, Franklin adopted an extremely plain demeanor: no wigs, plain clothing, and a little fur cap thrown in to symbolize frontier virtues as well. As a people fascinated by science, it was natural for the French to admire Franklin, one of the most famous natural philosophers of his era. In the literary salons of Paris, Franklin was instantly accepted as a wit and author of wide renown. Franklin even played the role of rogue with the ladies, not a difficult one for him, and a role that delighted his French friends but scandalized John Adams. Franklin was not only the complete and enlightened man in French eyes, but he also came to represent the kind of man produced by the invigorating American environment and by a government not burdened by anachronisms. In his exalted simplicity he represented what mankind could become if given a new chance. Franklin had obvious utility for those dissatisfied with the French government and certain values supporting the French social system. Many flowery plaudits for Franklin were, therefore, most meaningful when viewed as barbs intended for some French institution. Although there is little doubt that Franklin was enormously popular, it would be misleading to assume that esteem for him translated directly into actions favorable to his government or to believe that compliments thrown his way did not often convey other meanings.[10]

The team of Franklin, Lee, and Deane, although not a personally cordial one, was energetic in soliciting French assistance. Blankets and clothing, as well as arms and ammunition, were absolutely necessary to keep the American army in the field. Monetary aids were equally mandatory to maintain American credit in Europe. At times the commission, and later Franklin alone, had to beg for their country. Although France was often swayed by these entreaties, the Americans nevertheless felt humiliated to be this dependent upon a foreign power. But French assistance was so essential that the Americans swallowed their pride and repeated the beggar's ritual with regularity at the French Foreign Office. Franklin had to ask for a French loan even after the peace treaty had been signed with England; although he presented the case with his usual finesse, eating humble pie for his country's sake was no pleasant task for him.

---

[10] An engaging account of Franklin's activities as a diplomat is found in Carl Van Doren, *Benjamin Franklin* (New York, 1938). The foundations of Franklin's thinking about foreign affairs is thoroughly explored in Gerald Stourzh, *Benjamin Franklin and American Foreign Policy* (Chicago, 1954).

Congress was anxious that its diplomatic team make the strongest possible case for French and Spanish intervention. A general European war, so the Congress reasoned, seemed the most expeditious way to relieve British pressure on America; if ever America had a vested interest in starting the engines of war, this was the moment. And it was within French power to push the button. In March of 1777, therefore, Franklin and Deane broached the subject of an alliance to the French Foreign Office. Not only could France have access to American commerce, they said, but also to half the fishery, and all the British sugar islands that America would help her to conquer. If Spain entered the contest America would be happy to declare war on Portugal and "will continue the said war for the total Conquest of that Kingdom, to be added to the Dominion of Spain." As for itself, the United States modestly asked only that it be allowed to keep Canada, Newfoundland, Nova Scotia, St. Johns, Bermuda, the Floridas, and the Bahamas![11]

French silence on this alliance offer was eloquent comment on its rather one-sided terms. But the silence also bespoke the tensions building within the French government concerning war policy and the growing antagonism between France and England. As France rushed frantically to put her fighting navy into combat readiness, and as it became clear how extensively France was supplying the American rebels, British anxiety and anger naturally increased. As long as the government of Lord North hoped to end the American War by an early decisive stroke, or by negotiation, French supplies to America were discounted. But as the war dragged on with no immediate end in sight, it became easier for all factions in England to point the finger of responsibility at France. Cries for revenge arose from all sides, whether or not it plunged England into a general European war.

In 1777 the extent of French involvement with America, together with French hopes and fears, began to exert their own pull upon state policy. Subventions to America, a less reluctant Spain, an appetite for spoils, a continuing and successful resistance in America, a better prepared navy, and rising blood all combined to change the "if" of French intervention to "when."

---

[11] Van Alstyne, *Empire and Independence*, p. 123.

France's decision in August to send four thousand troops and at least five ships-of-the-line to West Indian waters was a major one. To Britain, it was the fire bell in the night, the sign that the conflagration was all but upon her. Britain reacted by commissioning six additional ships-of-the-line.

Exactly when the French government decided that the pressures for war were irresistible is uncertain. Perhaps the decision to send naval reinforcements to the West Indies was really the crucial one since military considerations then became a central concern. When news arrived from America that the British army of General John Burgoyne had been captured at Saratoga in mid-October 1777, Franklin mounted a new campaign to bring France openly into the war. Franklin warned Vergennes that however cheerful the American situation appeared from Paris, he should remember how desperate it seemed in America. Don't be too certain, Franklin emphasized, that in discouragement and desperation America would not finally return to its British allegiance.

This bugaboo of the French Foreign Office assumed greater proportion when William Eden, a friend of Lord North and undersecretary of state for the Northern Department, decided to approach Franklin and sound him out on possible peace terms. Eden thought it best to pose questions to Franklin through his secretary, Dr. Edward Bancroft, a man with double loyalties and salaries. Bancroft submitted Eden's letter to Franklin for his personal response. Franklin shrewdly turned it over to the French Foreign Office. In one stroke he revealed America's opportunity to slip out of the war but her present determination to fight on.

Saratoga had an even greater immediate impact in London than it did in Paris. American demands that had outraged George III in 1775 began to have a plausible ring after Saratoga. After a flurry of consultations within the Ministry and with George III, bills were introduced into Parliament to repeal legislation that had estranged America after 1763. Even the possibility of some autonomous status within the Empire was envisioned. Before dispatching a peace commission to America, the North government decided to approach Franklin and Deane. A good word from these gentlemen might be decisive in assuring the peace proposal a friendly reception in America. Accordingly,

William Eden sent Paul Wentworth to Paris to sound out Franklin and Deane on the peace proposals. Franklin was privately overjoyed to see Wentworth. Eden's private agent was living proof of Britain's desperation and America's opportunities. Vergennes, one may be certain, was kept fully informed of Wentworth's efforts to seduce the wily Americans.

It was now time for France to make a decision. America was apparently up for the highest bidder. Fifteen years of diplomatic humiliation, dreams of revenge on England, previous commitments to America, and stark opportunism all cried out for France to act. If only Spain would join her in this endeavor, Court and Crown would approach the contest with buoyant attitudes. Vergennes made desperate last minute efforts to gain a Spanish commitment, but to no avail. Without handsome French promises concerning the division of spoils, Spain saw little advantage in fighting a war partly to free an aggressive colonial possession of England. Spain was absolutely right in her assessment of late 1777; an independent America, as the next four decades were to prove, inflicted repeated humiliations on Spain and Spain was helpless to retaliate.

Vergennes believed the Spanish disgustingly obtuse and decided that France must act. Not to grasp at such a promising opportunity would expose France to well-deserved contempt and the Crown to further humiliations. Spain or no Spain, France must move ahead. On December 17, 1777 Vergennes hastily promised American diplomats recognition and a mutually agreeable treaty. And why a treaty? It was expedient not only to please the Americans and to regularize the partnership, but also to place some French lead strings on their distant ally. With a treaty France would have some guarantee that America would remain in the war, giving France hope that the spoils gained would be roughly commensurate with French effort.

Perhaps there is no better evidence of French determination to wreck the British Empire than the liberal treaties it signed with America. As Samuel Flagg Bemis has underscored, France had other pressing questions that explained her apparent generosity. If war with England did come as a result of the alliance, Vergennes wished no enlargement of the war beyond the addition of Spain. Vergennes especially wanted no European jealousies of France aroused, jealousies that would certainly flower if it appeared France intended to add America to its empire. And in a war with England, well disposed neutrals could help significantly in supplying France and America with foodstuffs, naval stores and non-contraband products. France's military and diplomatic situation thus argued eloquently for generous treaties with America.[12]

After relatively brief negotiations, two treaties were signed on February 6, 1778. In the Treaty of Amity and Commerce both nations pledged themselves to observe the rights of neutrals upon principles advantageous to small navy powers; to extend most-favored-nation treatment to each others' commerce; and to observe the usual amenities of allies, such as mutual protection of shipping and granting aid to shipwrecked mariners. Mutual residence of consular officials was agreed to, and France unilaterally made certain ports in the West Indies and in France free to American vessels.

Of central concern to each power was the Treaty of Conditional and Defensive Alliance (*alliance éventuelle et défensive*). Invocation of the treaty would begin when France and England went to war—thus the use of the word *éventuelle*. In retrospect, it is obvious that France and the United States were natural allies for they shared an identical overriding interest: achieving independence for America. Any other circumstance would have made an alliance treaty for America an extreme gamble. But in her hour of trial, when she had gone begging to the doorsteps of Europe's Great Powers, America was fortunate enough to secure a powerful ally who had a mutual interest in her cause. Article II was reassuring to America: "The essential and direct End of the present defensive alliance is to maintain effectually the liberty, Sovereignty, and independence absolute and unlimited of the said united States, as well in Matters of Gouvernement as of commerce."

France agreed that America was free to conquer the Bermudas, if she could, as well as all British colonies on the North American mainland. For her share of the spoils, France reserved British colonies in the West Indies. Article VIII bound both parties not

---

[12] Bemis, *Diplomacy of the American Revolution*, p. 65.

to conclude peace with England until the formal consent of the other had first been given; in any case arms were not to be set aside "until the Independence of the united states shall have been formally or tacitly assured by the Treaty or treaties that shall terminate the War." Article XI, later to be a source of anxiety for America, provided for the mutual guarantee of territory "from the present time and forever, against all other powers. . . ."[13] A separate and secret article provided that Spain could adhere to both treaties at some future convenient time.

Some students have wondered at American recklessness in concluding an old-fashioned alliance with a power able to make a satellite of her. Others have expressed surprise that Americans would abandon their ideals so freely and adapt to the supposedly debased international system that thrived on balancing power through knavery or war. Such comments reveal more about the authors' thinking than that of the Founding Fathers. They were desperate men, reaching out to grasp the strong hand of France. But beyond this they realized fully that America was part of an international state system. As the war graduated from the heroic stage to the grim, little was heard about preserving American purity; rather, how to manipulate the state system to America's advantage became the central question. Willingness to promote a general European war so that America might go free reveals the level of American thinking. But why, some asked, did Americans allow the word "forever" to be placed in the treaty? Wasn't this wedding America permanently to France and the European state system? Origins of the "forever" clause are obscure, but one thing is certain: within the context of cynical eighteenth-century politics, "forever" meant "as long as is mutually convenient" or "as long as is convenient for either power." In practical terms, it meant until the conclusion of the peace treaties. To argue otherwise compliments the hearts of the Founding Fathers but not their heads. Long before the Social Darwinists spun their theories, Americans realized that competition and struggle were an accepted part of the state

---

[13] See David Hunter Miller, *Treaties and Other International Acts of the United States of America* (Washington, 1931), II, pp. 35–40 for the complete texts of the treaties.

system. Those who stumbled and fell generally paid a heavy price; France would witness that. As wise stewards of government, therefore, American statesmen would do what needed to be done to protect America's position.

*   *   *   *   *

Concluding an alliance and making it work are two quite different matters. Keeping a coalition working harmoniously in time of maximum danger is a taxing enough assignment; when the pressures are lifting and peace is in sight, the temptations to pursue one's own objectives are overwhelming. Adding a third partner to an alliance, such as Spain, who was totally unsympathetic to the central purpose of the original coalition, immeasurably complicated the military and diplomatic situation.

France's position in the developing war crisis was not an enviable one. She had made her move to support America knowing it would provoke a war having world-wide repercussions, one that would be fought with desperation and bitterness on both sides. Also sobering was the anger and disgust she had aroused in Spain. Charles III and Don José Moniño Floridablanca, his Foreign Minister, believed Spain had not really been consulted on France's step toward war, only informed. The dignity of the court, therefore, required considerable deliberation and negotiation before Spain would join her family ally in combat. Due deliberation would also make the French sweat blood and soften them to Spanish terms for entering the war. Across the Atlantic, France saw her West Indies possessions threatened by British sea power and a needy American ally pleading for money, supplies, and a powerful naval supporting force. In Europe there was uncertainty in 1778 whether a war would spark from competing Austrian and Prussian ambitions in Bavaria.

Spain was a problem common to both France and America. Spanish officials fed American agents a steady diet of snubs, delays, and insults. Although the Spanish Court did give the United States a subvention of 1,000,000 livres in 1776, the direction of Spanish policy was anti-American. Wishful thinking and unfamiliarity with Spanish rationale on American colonial questions continually misinformed American approaches to Spain. Arthur Lee, and later John Jay, remained rather puzzled that Spain did not perceive its interests in American independence to be similar to those of America or even France. Spain, however, took a world view of a possible clash with Britain and trembled at her own vulnerability. From long experience, Spain also sensed that an independent American neighbor, uncontrolled by the conservative and steadying hand of England, would mean continual harassment for Spain's North American empire. This view of America as being guided in its frontier policy by bloodthirsty aggressive barbarians naturally escaped Jay and the Second Continental Congress, thereby partially explaining their myopic view of Spain's policy.

Circumstances finally combined to thrust France, Spain, and America into a temporary working partnership, a devil's bargain from the Spanish viewpoint. Spain actually never intended to enter the war. If England had bribed her with Gibraltar, Spain would have been content to take a siesta while her family ally sank beneath British blows. But England would not offer the bait. Accordingly, Spain turned to France to see what spoils could be arranged if they mutually defeated England. France saw no objection to Spain gaining Gibraltar if other booty arrangements were satisfactory. In the secret Franco-Spanish Convention of Aranjuez, signed on April 12, 1779, the two powers devised a stratagem to bring Spain into the war and concurred that hostilities would not be suspended until Gibraltar was restored to Spain. There were other agreements touching territories around the world: the river and fort of Mobile, Florida, the Bay of Honduras, and Minorca were to be gained for Spain. For France, the recovery of Newfoundland from England, unhindered trading liberties in the East Indies, recovery of Senegal, and possession of Dominica were deemed desirable.[14]

Much has been made of the clever phrase that American independence was chained to the Rock of Gibraltar when France

---

[14] Richard B. Morris, *The Peacemakers: The Great Powers and American Independence* (New York, 1965), pp. 14–17. Also useful is Jacques J. Engerraud, "The Anglo-French Policy of Floridablanca (1777–1783)," Unpublished doctoral dissertation, University of Michigan, 1935.

signed the Convention of Aranjuez; by agreeing to continue fighting until Spain had gained Gibraltar, France thereby bound her American ally to Spanish desires. Although the witticism has an element of truth, it is largely misleading. The war's outcome makes that clear, for when the last peace treaties had been ratified, America was independent and Spain Gibraltar-less. It would be more accurate to say that France assumed multiple interests when she signed the Convention of Aranjuez, interests that were not compatible with those of her American ally. But the dynamics of war have a way of making treaties irrelevant. Well-laid plans and good faith agreements quickly become archival filler when arms fail the state. So it was with Aranjuez. It posed a hidden complication in constructing an American settlement, but there were other complications equally troublesome.

Before peace could be made, a war must be fought. From the American side the French alliance seemed at first to guarantee victory and independence. Visions of invading Canada once again, but this time with a powerful French naval supporting force, danced in the heads of persons as practical as George Washington. France would stabilize the American currency through massive aid, France would woo Spain to assist America, France would faithfully protect America's national interests in the councils of Europe—these were the themes of hymns sung to America's great ally. Disillusionment set in rather quickly, however, mainly because no French navy appeared in force. "Where are the French forces?" became the bitter American cry. The French Minister to America, Conrad Alexander Gérard, was hard pressed to give Philadelphia a satisfactory reply.

Actually there was an excellent answer, but Americans were too self-taken to realize that England might be crushed in other than the American theatre. Unknown to Americans, France and Spain were amassing an armada whose purpose was to invade and smash England. The size and ambition of the plan quite justifies comparing it with the Great Armada of 1588. Vision, sound planning, poor execution, and extraordinary bad luck characterized the modern Armada. Shortly before the fleets of Spain and France were to join for common action, a disastrous outbreak of smallpox and putrid fever decimated the ranks and scratched the invasion plan. In September 1779 the French fleet sailed into Brest, its mission unfulfilled. Spain was immensely disappointed, having conditioned her entrance into the war upon this massive early strike. Almost at once she began to explore just how the war might be brought to a close; Spain might be capable of one great convulsive effort, but she faced a war of attrition with justified foreboding.[15]

If the invasion had succeeded—as in theory it should have— the diplomatic· and military consequences would have been far-reaching. France and Spain would have clearly become the new arbiters of Europe. As for America, it would have become only a minor problem in a general reshuffling of interests and power. So while Americans chafed at the dilatoriness of the French in giving them assistance, lady luck secretly struck a massive blow for American independence and a generous settlement. Spain in a commanding position would certainly have meant quite a different peace settlement for America even if France had discharged her pledge to guarantee American independence.

Americans had not been entirely without French assistance up until the Armada disaster. One year before the Armada sailed, in fact, a French fleet of eleven ships had appeared to assist General John Sullivan in an attack on the British garrison at Newport, Rhode Island. The attack never jelled partly because of a fierce storm in mid-August that scattered the French fleet as it was engaging the British navy. General Sullivan publicly accused the French and the fleet under Comte d'Estaing of abandonment when d'Estaing took his fleet into Boston Harbor near the end of August. In Boston the local population expressed its feelings about d'Estaing's withdrawal by provoking armed combat with his men. Although Sullivan retracted his statement, American indignation became widespread. As one patriot expressed it, if the "French fleet has a right to fight when they please & run when they please & leave Genl. Sullivan when they please & his Armey on a small island where a brittish fleet can

---

[15] The best brief account is found in Morris, *The Peacemakers*, pp. 27–42.

surround it when they please which we expect every hour, I do not understand the Alliance made with France."[16] Newport, a small campaign undertaken to demonstrate the military potential of the alliance, revealed how easily it could be damaged by disappointment and wagging tongues.

Other incidents occurred to anger Americans. In September 1779, for example, when the fleet of Comte d'Estaing joined the troops of General Benjamin Lincoln for an attack on Savannah, new provocations took place. D'Estaing outraged the American army by giving British forces an opportunity to surrender not to American but to French forces. When d'Estaing's fleet withdrew prematurely (as Americans saw it) and the attack failed, mutual recriminations were voiced. Were faint-hearted and glory-seeking naval officers all that France could send to assist America, many asked.

The very presence of the Marquis de Lafayette was answer enough to that question. Legends surround Lafayette's role in the Revolutionary War much as they surround Franklin's. He was certainly a dedicated and capable staff officer for General Washington and we know Washington loved him as a son. If Lafayette was impetuous and overly ambitious, he was also imaginative and enthusiastic in his adopted cause. All his energies were poured into the American war. He returned to France where his family was powerful and well-connected at court and wrote letters to his countrymen to urge support of America. He participated in numerous military campaigns, he poured oil on troubled Franco-American waters, and he gave personal support to George Washington during his darkest days. Such devotion and persistence warmed the hearts of those Americans who knew him best; in due time Lafayette came to symbolize the melded hearts of France and America, allies in crisis, friends in peace.[17]

---

[16] Quoted in Stinchcombe, *The American Revolution and the French Alliance*, p. 51.

[17] The literature on Lafayette is sizable. The best account of his revolutionary activities is found in Louis Gottschalk's *Lafayette Joins the American Army* (Chicago, 1937) and *Lafayette and the Close of the American Revolution* (Chicago, 1950).

Late in the spring of 1780 Lafayette returned from a visit to France with particularly welcome news. Very soon, Lafayette announced, a French fleet would arrive accompanied by fifteen thousand soldiers. This force would be stationed permanently in the American theatre. Although Congress expressed gratitude for assignment of the fleet, there were mixed feelings at the thought of foreign troops operating on American soil. Were the French returning to reclaim Canada, some asked. Others were concerned lest a foreign army make America a complete satellite of France with no will tolerated but that of Paris. Young Alexander Hamilton complained in June 1780 that Americans were "determined not to be free and they can neither be frightened, discouraged nor persuaded to change their resolution. If we are saved France and Spain must save us."[18] French power and American inertia could combine to fasten a new yoke, a Gallic yoke, upon American necks.

The arrival of the Comte de Rochambeau's army was not greeted with much enthusiasm when it sailed into Newport on July 11. Nor did it ever gain much popularity until after the battle of Yorktown in October 1781. One reason was that it never received its promised complement of men but remained at 5000, a disappointing figure after Lafayette had mentioned the imminent arrival of 15,000 troops. Also, for many months the army remained immobile. Rochambeau would not move until a project worthy of his forces could be readied. And Rochambeau complained that America had promised to support his troops but had welshed. There was nothing to do, he concluded, but wait for money from France; an army could not move on bare coffers and empty stomachs. Logic supported Rochambeau's position, but Americans were not in the mood for debates. They wanted action and they saw 5000 immobile troops of their wealthy ally sitting on their hands, complaining of American nonsupport. It was particularly infuriating when the army of General Cornwallis was making spectacular gains in South Carolina, North Carolina, and Virginia.

But all turned out well. From its first day on American soil,

---

[18] Quoted in Stinchcombe, *The American Revolution and the French Alliance*, p. 134.

Rochambeau's army was a model of decorum and discretion. In spite of their ancient prejudices, Americans found the Frenchmen positively delightful. As the French army started to move over the countryside in cooperation with Washington's, every report confirmed the initial favorable impressions of New Englanders. Rochambeau also worked well with Washington; their mutual regard soon extended throughout their respective staffs, down to the foot soldier. By the time that the West Indian fleet of Comte François de Grasse cooperated with Washington and Rochambeau to trap Cornwallis on Chesapeake Bay, Rochambeau's army had done more to cement the alliance than all the French monetary grants and all related naval actions. This was an extraordinary circumstance considering the usual impressions foreign troops make on alien peoples. Rochambeau and his army deserve better in American annals than they have been given.

America was less fortunate in the ministers sent to represent the French government. Conrad Alexander Gérard, who arrived in Philadelphia in July 1778 as France's first minister to the United States made an excellent first impression on his hosts. And well he should have, for he was an experienced diplomat and was highly knowledgeable about American affairs. Yet when he boarded ship for France in 1779, he left the Congress factionalized over French policy and a radical bloc convinced that every French action or policy recommendation should receive thorough scrutiny.

What went wrong? His instructions introduced elements of tension, particularly since France insisted that America should avoid actions that might alienate Spain. Although nothing was said about conflicting Spanish-American aims over the Mississippi River, the thrust of the instructions was clear; France would not support American territorial ambitions when they clashed with Spain's.

Difficult instructions were not the source of Gérard's difficulties, however. The problem centered in his attitude toward the alliance and in his unfortunate intervention into American politics. Where Americans interpreted French support as a self-interested action designed to support the broad aims of French foreign policy, Gérard liked to think in terms of French international philanthropy at work. France was helping the weak but meritorious America against a powerful and wicked England. Gérard's rather warped view led directly to his position that America should be eager to accept French suggestions. When a wise, experienced, generous and powerful nation offers help to a diplomatic nonentity, it is the proper role of the nonentity, he believed, to accept that help humbly and with tipped cap.

Revolutionary sparks are not struck by quiescent little men; this Gérard failed to appreciate. Abrasive revolutionaries such as Samuel Adams had already rejected the overlordship of England. Why would they now be content to follow in the wake of a French man-of-war? Examination, criticism, explanation of various lines of policy—these were the duties of politicians seeking to establish the freedom of a struggling constituency. If France wanted a silent satellite instead of a lively ally, then America must be on guard as much against its friends as against its avowed enemies.

These differing views of the alliance and its duties were bound to result in conflict, particularly when Gérard decided to take sides during domestic political infighting. Gérard chose to embrace the cause of Silas Deane and found too late that Deane was not a patriotic jewel but a sturdy millstone. Deane had been recalled by Congress in November 1777 so that he could give an account of his financial and officer recruitment activities while in France. Arthur Lee, as noted earlier, had accused Deane of corruption and conflict of interest. Although Lee had not actually substantiated his charges, there were enough surface irregularities to arouse apprehension even among Deane's friends. The Deane case then appeared superficially to involve the accountability of a minister to the Congress and to the public as well. But like the Dreyfus case in France one hundred years later, and the debate over Senator Joseph McCarthy in midcentury America, the Deane case became central to many fundamental public questions.

Just how this happened is a complex story. Questions of family status, sectional interest, alliance politics, and war and peace policy became intertwined in ways still confusing to historians. Putting the best face on matters, honest differences of opinion over public policy led to divisions in Congress. Should a reconciliation with England be considered? To what extent should sectional interests be recognized in granting commissions to the Continental army? How could the war best be financed? Should independence be declared? When, and on what terms, should an alliance be proposed to France? How important to the establishment of American independence was acquiring rights on the Mississippi River? What sacrifices should America be prepared to make to acquire a foothold in the fisheries? Vital questions such as these were bound to elicit different answers from thoughtful men.

As time moved on, the crucial questions all somehow related to France and French policy. This growing dependency on France increasingly alarmed one faction who sensed the dangers of over-reliance upon a powerful patron. Deane, a man trusted by the French Court and responsive to its wishes, therefore symbolized toadyism to those apprehensive of French policy. To others Deane was a realist who sensed the extent of American dependence on France and who rightly adopted an attitude of proper deference toward French viewpoints. Family status impinged on this legitimate debate over toadyism, or sensible patriotism, when Gérard decided to undermine Arthur Lee, then on a mission to Spain. Gérard made it clear that the cynical and paranoid Lee did not have the confidence of the French Court. He even openly advocated Lee's recall. This action was a frightful affront to the powerful and sensitive Lee family of Virginia, and to their staunch Adams family allies from Massachusetts. Was Lee to be recalled, they queried, simply because he was an independent thinker and a staunch patriot? Were others who dared to cross French desires also to be disgraced publicly? Anyone who valued national dignity and independence would never stoop to such a measure.

When Gérard chose to support Deane in his fight, even as he knifed Lee, the storm broke. Fortunately for the alliance, Gérard became too ill to discharge his functions and was recalled at his own request. Richard Henry Lee, offended by Gérard's attitudes, yet still a firm supporter of the alliance, made an interesting assessment of Gérard's major error: "It is very remarkable that those men who from the beginnings of the contest have been the most decided friends to the Liberties of

America and the firmest opposers of British Tyranny, and who in the hour of Trial will be found most true to the Alliance, are the men whom Gérard has shewn the least desire to deal with. Another sort of Men have shared his friendship and familarity."[19] To Lee it appeared that those Gérard least trusted were the most ardent in defense of American interests. Lee may have mistakenly juxtaposed temperamental fervency and impetuosity with true patriotism. What is surprising is his apparent assumption that a minister representing France should find ardent American nationalists congenial company and natural allies. Gérard's preference for American "moderates" at least underscored the necessity to assume that basic conflicts between French and American peace objectives would soon surface.

* * * * *

Once the alliance was concluded, discussion arose in America about the shape peace would take. This occurred partly because different sections of the country would have varying interests once independence was won. Obviously the interest one took in acquiring the Floridas, in gaining access to the Mississippi River, or in bargaining for the fisheries depended partly upon one's location and financial involvement. Beyond this, Americans assumed that independence might come in 1779 or 1780, or even beyond, but come it would. Prudence therefore dictated that America's desires be articulated at once and communicated to France. If peace were to come suddenly—and unexpectedly—France would be in a position to write the peace terms unhampered by American advice.

France, too, foresaw this possibility. But even if peace came late, France did not wish to be overly troubled by American demands. Vergennes knew that minor allies could be annoying when the Powers sat down to write the peace. With the new minister to America, the Chevalier de la Luzerne, Vergennes

---

[19] Lee to Arthur Lee, May 23, 1779, in Edmund C. Burnett, Ed., *Letters of Members of Continental Congress* (Washington, 1921–1936), IV, pp. 227–228.

shared his hope that Congress would not send extensive and precise instructions for the peace to its negotiators. Encourage the Congress to be more flexible, he urged. If possible, have the Congress instruct its negotiators ultimately to abide by the advice of France.

Gérard had already wrestled with this issue but with little success. Congress decided that the United States should claim all territory westward to the Mississippi and south to the 31st parallel. Spain would be pressed to grant navigational rights on the Mississippi south of the 31st parallel. Gérard was most distressed over the American fixture on Canada and American determination to stake a claim on the Grand Banks fisheries. On the fisheries the debate in Congress was particularly vigorous. New England representatives felt strongly that no peace ultimata should be composed without arguing American rights in the fisheries. France was so jealous on the fisheries claims and Gérard so persistent in opposing a fisheries clause in the peace plan that Congress in July 1779 finally decided to compromise: American rights in the fisheries would be made a necessary condition for a commercial treaty with Great Britain. New Englanders were disheartened to think that the peace treaty itself could easily be written without a fishery provision. In their eyes this compromise significantly devalued the French alliance and made them determined that negotiators would be appointed who properly appreciated American rights in the fisheries.

The prolonged eight-month debate in America over peace terms distressed Vergennes. It was apparent to him that the present Congress had a mind of its own and that it would not rush willy-nilly to accede to French demands. Yet it must be admitted that Gérard had been successful in limiting American demands: the United States did not make Canada, Nova Scotia, and Newfoundland fundamental objectives of the peace; it did not claim the Floridas; and it did not take an inflexible stand on the Mississippi River question.

Why then was Vergennes so concerned as Luzerne prepared to assume his new duties? For one thing, John Adams had been named sole negotiator of the peace treaty by Congress. Vergennes found Adams repulsive, independent, and aggressive. What kind of a peace could be written with this assertive New

Englander constantly lecturing him on the rights owed to a great and sovereign America! Someone else must be found to negotiate the treaty, preferably Franklin. When Russia offered in the spring of 1779 to mediate the war, Vergennes seized the opportunity to ask that American peace ultimatums be reconsidered and that a halter be placed on John Adams.

Luzerne went to work quickly and was as successful in fulfilling his instructions as any minister ever sent to the United States. Congress, said some critics, did everything for Luzerne except pay him open obeisance. Four additional peace commissioners were named to work with Adams, thus diffusing the fishery issue. Most significantly, the commissioners were instructed ultimately to be guided by the advice and opinion of France on all matters except independence. Such instructions were humiliating to many ardent patriots; it must be admitted that nations seldom voluntarily place themselves so completely in the power of another nation.

There are several explanations for Luzerne's success. He was a charming, polite man who quickly became the social lion of Philadelphia. For those who believe the wheels of diplomacy are best lubricated by liquor and chatter, Luzerne's conquest of Congress is easily explained. One can also point to the congressmen Luzerne suborned through payoffs, more politely called pensions or loans. It is very likely that these payoffs were influential in purchasing votes. Others credit M. Barbé-Marbois, Luzerne's private secretary, with an astuteness in handling congressmen unexceeded by the Minister himself. But these explanations, even if combined, do not really explain congressional subservience to French desires. Rather, amenability to French policy increased proportionately to America's growing military and financial dependence on France. When the ship is sinking amidst raging waves, those on board do not generally press the rescuer to name his terms. One is inclined to trust that the same providence that brought the rescue ship to the scene will see the rescued safely into port. So it was with American leaders. As France repeatedly shored American finances with loans, and as it became apparent that British forces could be defeated only with French assistance, it was natural to lean ever more heavily on France.

When the treaty instructions of 1781 had been posted, Congress had virtually placed the fate of America in the hands of her commissioners and of France. To work with Adams, the Congress named Benjamin Franklin; John Jay, then on a mission to Spain; Henry Laurens of South Carolina, whose current address was the Tower of London; and Thomas Jefferson, who decided his talents were of better use in Virginia. Laurens did not participate as the major decisions were being made, so Franklin, Adams, and Jay comprised the American delegation. An abler, tougher negotiating team would be difficult to imagine. All were men of vision and tested patriotism. Franklin provided the suaveness and sense of probity; Adams and Jay supplied the needed cynicism and the determination to see their side triumph no matter who else suffered. Of the three, only Franklin felt a sense of gratitude toward France. He also firmly believed that France would be America's guarantee of respectability among nations in future years. Adams and Jay appreciated the significance of French assistance but their accumulated impressions and information indicated that France would rob America of her territorial birthright at the first convenient moment.[20]

In his outstanding study of the peace negotiations, Richard B. Morris has shown that Jay and Adams were uncomfortably close to the bullseye. To say this is not to condemn France. Her major goal in the war was England's diplomatic and military humiliation. Within that guideline, achievement of American independence was important to France. But independence could be defined in various ways and France was certainly under no obligation to support the real independence desired by Americans. France, in fact, had an important stake in America gaining a barebones peace. If America acquired all she wished at the peace settlement, she would soon find little need for the French attachment. Vergennes was quite correct in believing that the future vitality of the alliance depended on the kind of settlement England made with America. Generous terms, he knew, would signal a probable end to the French-American alliance.

Congress had assumed that peace negotiations with England

---

[20] Jay's attitudes are well described in Frank Monaghan, *John Jay* (New York, 1935).

would be a joint undertaking of the allies, with America following the lead of France. Negotiations did not proceed in this way
mainly because the American commissioners thought it would
be disadvantageous to their cause. When Franklin began a
separate negotiation with an agent of the British government in
April 1782, a negotiation soon dominated by Jay and Adams,
Vergennes did not protest. Why did Vergennes not bring this
British-American peace effort to a stop, as he had the power to
do, and insist that American affairs be handled through his
office? One reason, perhaps, was that he never dreamed England
would be so generous with America. This was a careless slip on
his part, for England virtually destroyed the French-American
alliance in negotiating its contract with America. Too, like most
men in public life, Vergennes' energies were channeled toward
solving immediate crises. Of these he had an abundance, and all
seemed to point in one way or another to see the necessity of
getting the war stopped. Reverses in the war, financial crisis at
home, an unstable situation in Central Europe, a faltering American effort, and an unreasonable Spain all argued for ending
the war.

Spain was a particularly troublesome problem for Vergennes.
Although he placed a proper value on maintaining the family
alliance, Vergennes stood aghast at Spain's dogged insistence
on conquering Gibraltar. As France strained to support the war,
seeing her success ever more tenuous, Spanish fixation on the
rock pile seemed positively reckless. How long France should
continue to fight on so that Spain could gain Gibraltar from en-
trenched British forces became an agonizing question. One way
to bring heavy pressure on Spain to relent, Vergennes reasoned,
would be to start the process of peace negotiations. It would
then become clear to Spain that neither America nor France
would postpone indefinitely arranging a general peace in the
hope that Gibraltar would be surrendered.

America's separate negotiations with England, therefore,
proceeded with French blessing. But Vergennes made it clear
to England that France did not support either America's extensive western boundary claims or her claims to the inshore fisheries. Nor did Vergennes favor England recognizing American
independence before the treaty was concluded. By the time that

serious negotiations got underway (May 1782), it is fair to say that Vergennes believed France had done all she should to help America. There was even a distinct possibility that France had done too much, that America was in a position to gain a peace that threatened Spanish ambitions in the Southwest and French plans for the fisheries. With this attitude prevailing in the French Foreign Office, what America gained in the peace treaty depended on British attitudes, American negotiating skill, and luck.

The story of British-American negotiations has been told often and well. Fortunately for America, a man of vision and practicality guided British policy in the early stages of negotiation. Lord Shelburne perceived that American trade and friendship could be won if a liberal peace were written. Much dickering and compromising went on before the preliminary treaty was drawn, but the final terms represented an astonishing American victory. For America was granted the vast trans-Allegheny hinterland south of the Great Lakes, a full share in the fisheries, and the right to navigate the Mississippi on an equal basis with England.

Vergennes was not consulted on the terms of the treaty, despite the explicit contrary instructions of the Congress. When Franklin forwarded a copy of the treaty to him the evening before the agreement was signed, it came as a disagreeable shock. English concessions, he wrote to a friend, "exceed all that I should have thought possible. What can be the motive, that could have brought terms so easy, that they could have been interpreted as a kind of surrender?" As the brilliant opportunism of the American negotiators sank in, he wrote bitterly to another friend: "If we may judge of the future from what has passed here under our eyes, we shall be but poorly paid for all we have done for the United States and for securing to them a national existence."[21] Yet Vergennes, even at this disappointing moment, authorized a new loan of six million livres to America. Some have credited the suave Franklin with securing the loan. More likely, the French government didn't want financial catastrophe

---

[21] Quoted in Van Alstyne, *Empire and Independence*, pp. 222–223.

to overtake America at the last moment, an event that might immediately throw her into eager British arms.

For America, the alliance with France had been a godsend. It is difficult to dispute that American independence would have been won at a later time, and probably in quite a different context, had France not chosen to intervene. But she did and her aid was essential. For France, the alliance with America was at best a limited success. America's political break with England had been ratified but whether American trade would now be channeled to French ports was quite uncertain. Spain was noticeably angry that France had not controlled American treaty terms more in keeping with Spanish designs. Moreover, French finances were in a distressed condition partly because of resources directed America's way. It is easy to sympathize with Vergennes' feelings of frustration as the war ended. Drastic measures to humiliate England and elevate France had met with only limited success.

*   *   *   *   *

Months before peace had been secured even loyal Gallophiles began to wonder if their trust in France had been misplaced. There was, as always, the hard core of cynics who argued for trust only in God and a good right arm. But John Jay disturbed the waters when he wrote from Madrid that Spain was intransigent on the Mississippi question chiefly because she had full French support. Since Jay had been considered a "moderate" in Congress and a supporter of close cooperation with France, his assessment was not easily dismissed. Other random evidence accumulated after Yorktown disturbed open-minded men. Why would Luzerne not support enlargement of the American navy? Critics believed that France wanted no American competition in the Newfoundland fishery and they were right. Letters arriving from Paris during the peace negotiations contained hints of French duplicity and intrigue.

When the final treaty arrived in America and the story of the negotiations became known, two conclusions were reached by many: England had been generous and opened the door to reconciliation; France had tried to undermine American objectives and thus revealed her true colors. Such an assessment had utility for many groups. Old Tories, Francophobes, and merchants with English connections could sound this theme with enthusiasm. For congressmen who had sold themselves to France, some denunciations of France could rebuild their self-respect and their political standing. Outright nationalists, burning with zeal for their new country, were naturally reluctant to admit how crucial French support had been to winning the war. In his final address to Congress, George Washington failed even to mention the alliance, a marked discourtesy but nevertheless understandable. America's desire to enhance her own self-esteem, if nothing else, determined that she would not give France her due. And from those who believed America should have no political connection with Europe, little would be said to indicate that the alliance had conferred benefits upon the struggling states.

And how did the French regard this slight? Vergennes at least seemed willing to blot America from his mind, much as one does a bad experience. Gratitude, he soon determined, was a sensation as unknown to Americans as it was to himself. Vergennes was willing to disabuse anyone who believed a new and higher type of man was being bred in America. His experiences had shown them to be cynical, calculating, and contemptuous of friendly actions—very much in the mold of European politicians he had known all his life. They were also brazen and demanding, asking for loans and access to France's trading empire even as the war ended.

Both France and America realized that any meaningful relationship after the war would depend upon developing extensive commercial relations. These ties did not develop in the 1780s for many reasons. American preference for English goods, and need for credits that only English merchants could provide, tells much of the story. Lack of French aggressiveness in penetrating American markets and the reluctance of vested French interests to see American produce invading empire markets also explains much. Neither government was inclined to take the actions necessary to rechannel the trade. To have tried would probably have been foolish anyway. Language, consumer tastes, ancient trade connnections, and profitability all argued for a resumption of Anglo-American trade. France was disappointed, but she recognized the naturalness of this development.[22]

What then was left to give substance to the alliance? Very little except shared sentiment based on mutual suffering. Washington and Lafayette might love each other as father and son, but even this compelling symbol of hands-across-the-sea was inadequate to give life to the alliance. Pressing mutual needs had written the alliance. After 1783 it was natural that each nation would go its own way.

---

[22] Henri Seé, "Commerce between France and the United States, 1783–1784," *American Historical Review*, XXXI (1926), pp. 732–752. Also, Vernon G. Setser, *The Commercial Reciprocity Policy of the United States, 1774–1829* (Philadelphia, 1937).

CHAPTER III

Tensions, War, Resolution
1789-1815

> O FRANCE! the world to thee must owe
> A debt they ne'er can pay:
> The rights of man you bid them know,
> And kindle reason's day.
> COLUMBIA, in your friendship blest,
> Your gallant deeds shall hail,
> On the same ground our fortunes rest,
> Must flourish or must fail,
>
> Anonymous, 1793

Dragon's teeth have been sown in France and came up monsters.

John Adams 1793

Tremendous times in Europe! How mighty this battle of lions and tigers! With what sensations should the common herd of cattle look on it? With no partialities, certainly. If they can so far worry one another as to destroy their power of tyrannizing, the one over the earth, the other the waters, the world may perhaps enjoy peace, till they recruit again.

Thomas Jefferson, 1803[1]

S TUDENTS OF INTERNATIONAL RELATIONS can demonstrate conclusively that nations act in accordance with their perceived interests. If governments do indeed make decisions that appear beneficial to the state, we can at least be comforted that rationality and logic, if not philanthropy, are operative on the inter-

---

[1] *North-Carolina Journal*, cited in Jones, *America and French Culture*, p. 536; Adams to his wife, Philadelphia, Jan. 14, 1793, in C. F. Adams, Ed., *Letters of John Adams Addressed to his wife*, 2 vols. (Boston, 1841), II, p. 120; Jefferson to Benjamin Rush, October 4, 1803, in Andrew A. Lipscomb and Albert E. Bergh, Eds., *The Writings of Thomas Jefferson*, 20 vols. (Washington, D.C., 1904), X, p. 422.

national scene. However, determining what is advantageous to a state in a given situation is often a knotty problem. Long-term and short-term interests sometimes conflict. Too, the march of events has a way of making today's acclaimed policy soon appear tenuous or even absurd. And fallible men make decisions, which is to say that rationality will not always prevail even when the interest of the nation seems clear to experienced statesmen. It is therefore quite possible for states to follow policies apparently anchored to the solid rock of self-interest, only to have that rock crumble at the commencement of internal or international tremors. Even when the international situation is relatively stable, policymaking can be a risky business. Passions of the moment have a way of warping the judgment of even the most astute and dispassionate statesman. This is true today; it was true as well for the Founding Fathers.

At best the new American nation seemed headed for uncertain times. As officials of the new government assembled in Philadelphia in 1789 many important questions were yet to be answered. Having a constitution does not guarantee that a government will function satisfactorily, or that it will function at all. So it was in 1789. Decisions on how the prescribed institutions were to be organized and the ideas of concerned men on how, and for whose benefit, government should operate were yet to be poured into the lifeless document. Whether the states would yield to central authority in practice was unknown. Great questions of finance and taxation had yet to be analyzed and policy guidelines recommended. Would Britain to the north and Spain to the south be accommodating to the new government or would they be openly combative on border, port, and financial matters? Would the peoples of the western settlements remain loyal to the new government? With such problems initially confronting the Washington administration, its desire for a peaceful international situation was understandable. What the nation seemed most to need was tranquillity, expanded trade, calm leadership, friendly neighbors, and time for some national social cohesion to develop.[2]

---

[2] A fine survey of the Washington years is John C. Miller, *The Federalist Era, 1789–1801* (New York, 1960). A lucid analysis of the political and social situation in 1789 is found in chapter one of Forrest McDonald, *The Presidency of George Washington* (Lawrence, 1974).

Quite unexpectedly it was France who destroyed these sanguine hopes. Internal upheaval and revolution in France soon
metamorphosed into violent and long-lived conflict among the
nations of Europe. As American constitutional foundations were
being laid, those of France were suddenly thrust into a state of
distress and flux. Interaction between these two developments
was inevitable partly because of hopes shared by Frenchmen
and Americans to build a republic for their peoples. But nations
at war, particularly when they are desperately threatened, cannot be governed in their international policies by the niceties of
good feeling or ideology. France was no exception to the rule.
In her hours of need she wanted friends and friends were those
who served her interests. For many reasons America did not
choose to place her resources at the call of France. Accusations,
mutual recriminations, intrigue, and war were the result. France
emerged from this era bitterly disappointed in America. Perhaps
Americans did not fully reciprocate that feeling because they had
come through this time of troubles intact and with the awe-
somely large Louisiana territory added to the national domain.
The upsets and wars of France and Europe were truly regretted
by most Americans but French troubles, as in the decade of the
1770s, again proved to be America's opportunity.

*   *   *   *   *

It was the contention of the previous chapter that the diplomatic alliance of 1778 ended *de facto* in 1783 with the conclusion
of peace. This evaluation is not accepted by many historians nor
was it commonly understood by Americans and Frenchmen in
1783.[3] In fact the alliance did not officially end until the Treaty
of Mortefontaine was ratified in 1801. If many contemporaries
did not believe the alliance had legally ended in 1783, few
doubted that it would atrophy as America gained strength and
was increasingly able to set her own course. And since, as
Thomas Paine had stated so clearly in *Common Sense*, it was in

---

[3] Alexander DeConde discusses differing perceptions of the alliance in
Entangling Alliance: Politics and Diplomacy Under George Washington
(Durham, 1958), pp. 11–16.

America's interest to trade freely with all, it seemed unlikely to the reflective that America would choose to have a special relationship with any one nation, particularly with one whose trade was not crucial to America's prosperity.

In the early days of the Washington administration it appeared possible that America might remain unentangled politically with Europe, even as commercial relations and contacts were encouraged. Such an arrangement, from the American standpoint, would be ideal. The centrality of trade to America's foreign relations became more pronounced early in the 1790s than in previous years. Paradoxically, America's need for expanding markets led to political decisions that embroiled America in Europe's strife. Even trade has political overtones and those who find their prosperity dependent upon it must prepare to pay the piper.

Secretary of the Treasury Alexander Hamilton understood this principle, but he did not find it disagreeable. This brilliant and imaginative improviser has been given his meed of praise for having devised financial programs that would support the government, give it an enviable credit rating among the financial centers of Europe, and bind the hearts and pocketbooks of America's well-to-do to the new federal government. Nor has it escaped notice that Hamilton's program had its international political objectives as well. Hamilton believed that the most dependable and most easily collected resources to support the new government would come from trade revenues. Government finances would therefore prosper in a fairly direct relationship to the expansion of trade. Since the bulk of America's trade was carried on with England and her dependencies, a special relationship must necessarily be developed with England. This arrangement was not painful to Hamilton for he had long admired British institutions, in particular the British practices associated with the persistence of a social hierarchy. Hamilton fully understood the social and governmental implications of closer relations with England and was hopeful that some amelioration of America's democratic orientation would occur as the nation rubbed shoulders with a stable, sensible, and prosperous England. It is probably fair to say, therefore, that the second—and perhaps decisive—blow to the French alliance occurred with the adoption of Hamilton's fiscal program in 1791–1792. The pursuit of trade was placed before legal or moral obligations to France and in such a way that France did not mistake the trend of American policy.

Monarchial France would probably have made some reasonable adjustment to this direction of American policy. But France was experiencing a social and political revolution that made obsolete certain norms of international practice of the *ancien régime*.

In the early days of the French revolution, of course, nearly all Americans thrilled to the exciting news pouring out of Paris. It all seemed so grand and glorious that the people of France had finally decided to emulate America in breaking the chains of tyranny. Where Americans had had their Bunker Hill, Frenchmen stormed and destroyed the hated Bastille (July 14, 1789). Where France had adopted a Declaration of the Rights of Man (August 27, 1789), Americans attached a Bill of Rights to their Constitution in 1791. And it was inspiring to see Lafayette once more on the public scene, this time as commander of the newly established National Guard. But for some, many dangers lurked just behind the curtain. George Washington wrote to one friend of both his appreciation and fear of the situation late in 1789: "The revolution which has been effected in France is of so wonderful a nature that the mind can hardly realize the fact. If it ends as our last accounts to the first of August predict that nation will be the most powerful and happy in Europe; but I fear though it has gone triumphantly through the first paroxysm, it is not the last it has to encounter before matters are finally settled. In a word the revolution is of too great magnitude to be effected in so short a space, and with the loss of so little blood. . . . To forbear running from one extreme to another is no easy matter, and, should this be the case, rocks and shelves, not visible at present may wreck the vessel."[4]

To Thomas Jefferson, who had served as American Minister to France following Franklin's return and who had participated

---

[4] Washington to Gouverneur Morris, New York, October 13, 1789, in John C. Fitzpatrick, Ed., *The Writings of George Washington*, 39 vols. (Washington, D.C., 1931–1944), XXX, p. 443.

as a consultant in the early days of revolution, Washington's comment would have seemed wise. In his book on *Jefferson and France*, Lawrence S. Kaplan has written of Jefferson's ambiguous feelings toward the Revolution. On the one hand he did not believe the French people were politically ready to enjoy liberty American-style. On the other he was moved by the advance of liberty in a country central to Europe's political and cultural life. Jefferson repeatedly urged moderation on his revolutionary friends; change, he argued, would be placed on a more solid foundation if judiciously instituted. No matter which way the Revolution drifted, whether left or right, Jefferson kept steadily in view that France would be useful to America. As a counterweight to English influence, America had a vested interest in maintaining cordial relations with revolutionary France.[5]

Jefferson's blend of enthusiasm and pragmatism toward France during her early revolutionary developments was perhaps typical of responsible American politicians. The almost rabid enthusiasm of the American masses is difficult to recapture or even to explain. Only readers who can recall Victory in Europe (VE) and Victory in Japan (VJ) days in 1945 will truly appreciate the American response to events in France. It really seemed possible, both in 1789 and 1945, that mankind was being given a new chance. Tyranny, though not abolished, had been thrown on the defensive and would now be increasingly held accountable to the sovereign people. Exultation, prayerful gratitude, the catch-in-the-throat, high hopes—these marked American feelings in 1945 but probably were even more pronounced during the early days of the French upheaval. God and man, it now appeared, were working to introduce a whole new era in history. Freedom and social justice would be the hallmarks of this new Adamic age. And in this innovative enterprise America and France, the old allies of '78, had joined hands and hearts.

But it soon became apparent that American merchants were to gain no freer access to French empire ports under the new regime; if anything, trade restrictions were to be even more

---

[5] Lawrence S. Kaplan, *Jefferson and France* (New Haven, 1967). See especially Chapter 2, "The Revolutionary as Diplomatist."

severe. Democracy and a more pronounced nationalism had evidently become partners in revolutionary France. It was also disturbing to observe revolutionary justice at work. The seeming irrationality of the terror and the use of the guillotine made many, particularly those who identified themselves with the American oligarchy, wonder whether France had gone politically mad. It was also frightening to hear rumors from the European courts that vengeance would be taken upon France if Louis XVI himself were marched to the guillotine. If France did provoke or stumble into war, in what ways would America become involved? Prudence might suggest that America dampen its enthusiasm for France and adopt a more neutral stance.

Revolutions have a way of making men and nations run up their colors, whether for or against them. Events and circumstances certainly made America's involvement inevitable. In 1792 the march of events seemed particularly ominous. France declared war against Austria late in April, with Austria soon joined by Prussia. Five months later, as the combined anxieties of war and revolution gripped France, political prisoners were marched from the prisons of Paris, Lyons, Rheims, Meaux, and Orleans and put to death. In the same month the National Convention voted to abolish monarchy. France was declared a Republic on September 21; with that fervency typical of new revolutions, and as a war measure, the Convention offered, on November 19, to assist all tyrannized peoples wishing to overthrow their government. As the Christmas season approached, Louis XVI was placed on trial before the Convention for his various "crimes." On January 16, 1793, a majority of the Convention voted his death sentence, a sentence that was carried out five days later. An outraged England, Holland, and Spain immediately joined the coalition to crush France. To most observers it seemed a question of how long France could survive. Few seriously doubted that republican France would soon bend its knee to monarchial Europe.

Even before the decapitation of Louis XVI, the Girondin-controlled National Assembly had taken steps to interlock French and American destinies. It was during the months of Girondin ascendance, in the late summer and fall of 1792, that the Tuileries was stormed and the Swiss Guards massacred

(August 10), resulting in the deposition of Louis XVI. These events were followed by the call for a national convention based on manhood suffrage. Shortly after the Republic was proclaimed, on September 21, the Convention met to assume its duties. Within the Convention, the Girondins, ardent defenders of the Rights of Man, were the directing influence. Without really meaning to do so, the Girondins precipitated a great crisis in French-American relations with the appointment of Edmond Charles Genêt as minister to the United States.

Genêt's appointment and instructions were really the product of Girondin foresight, vision, and naiveté. As the French Assembly followed the mounting hostility of the European courts to the establishment of the republic in the heart of Europe, a premonition developed that France might soon have to face all Europe in armed battle. Instead of trying to still the waters, the Girondins issued that provocative challenge of November 19, offering assistance to people wishing to shake off the fetters of their present government. On the very day the proclamation was announced, Edmond Genêt was notified of his appointment.

Thus Genêt and the purposes of his mission are best understood when viewed as part of the Girondin challenge to monarchial Europe. In this challenge the Girondins naturally expected France to have the active support of her sister republic, the United States. The old alliance of 1778 would now be rebuilt on the solid rock of common ideology and the vision of a new world. America would accordingly want to lend its harbors to support French maritime efforts in the coming war. Likewise, America would wish to see both Spanish power destroyed in the Floridas and Louisiana territory and the British driven from Canada. America's own interests dictated these desires. If seen as part of a struggle against monarchy and the forces of despotism, and with promised French support, the Girondin ministry felt confident that America would enthusiastically join France in these actions against England and Spain.

Genêt's instructions, approved in Executive Council on December 27, 1792 told much about the Girondins and their widening ambitions. Symbolizing the more open diplomacy of the coming age, Genêt was commissioned not only as a representative to the American government but to the American people as well. Apparently because Congress symbolized best the will of the people, Genêt was accredited to the Congress instead of to the executive power. His government assured Genêt that he should spread democratic propaganda and employ secret agents when necessary to fulfill the objects of his mission. As Genêt sailed from France, new war clouds had gathered over Europe. France would probably soon be engaged in a desperate struggle to defend her territory—and the rights of man. M. Genêt, therefore, must do his best to consolidate good relations with republican America so that her economic and military resources would be thrown into the scales of France when the trumpet signaled the onset of battle.[6]

While Genêt was at sea, Louis XVI was beheaded and the anticipated war begun. Shortly after landing at Charleston, South Carolina, where he was warmly received, Genêt perceived that the Washington administration was not welcoming his overtures to join France and America in a new and revitalized partnership. Genêt, for example, had assumed that American ports would be available to support the French war effort. In particular he believed that French men-of-war and privateers should be permitted to bring their prizes into American ports where, as French property, they could be condemned and sold by French consuls. Beyond this, he planned to use American ports to arm and equip vessels that would prey on foreign powers. In his actions Genêt was taking advantage of Articles XVII and XXII of the Treaty of Amity and Commerce (1778) but in such a way that England and Spain might have good cause to accuse the United States of belligerent activities. Genêt even began to grant military commissions to American citizens, a clear infringement of American sovereignty.

If Genêt's and the Girondins' larger plans had been known, the Washington administration would certainly have moved more quickly to make its position clear. News of the outbreak of war on February 1 was enough in itself to precipitate a debate within the administration. Everyone agreed that America should be "neutral." Jefferson, with his sympathies for France, and

---

[6] Albert H. Bowman, *The Struggle for Neutrality: Franco-American Diplomacy During the Federalist Era* (Knoxville, 1974), Chapters II and III.

Hamilton with his predilection for England, could both agree that neutrality would be wise. The real question was neutrality in favor of whom? Since real impartiality is all but impossible to achieve, how a nation shapes its neutrality becomes the test of where its sympathies lie. And since wars generally produce winners and losers, casting a nation's lot one way or the other is bound to have momentous consequences. Washington's advisers were playing no parlor game as they debated America's course *vis-a-vis* the war.

So many imponderables were weighed in the decision-making process that even the steady Washington was visibly affected by the pressures. Were the Treaties of 1778 still operative, he asked. Jefferson and most Americans answered with an emphatic yes, but Hamilton raised doubts since the treaties were concluded with the monarchy. If operative, did France have the legal or moral right to invoke American aid? France's magnificent aid during "the times that tried men's souls" answered that question, many replied. But, said those reluctant to aid France, the treaty of alliance was a defensive treaty whereas France was waging an aggressive war. France had therefore voided her invocation rights. What then should be the tenor of American neutrality? Pro-France or Pro-England? France's past succor and America's obligation to embrace the cause of free government made American aid to republican France a moral necessity, said the Jeffersonians. But what about America's financial dependence upon England, replied Hamilton. Supporting a fanatical, regicidal, and imperialistic nation was at best a hazardous undertaking. To do so when the very financial foundations of government would be subverted seemed both blind and suicidal.[7]

Largely unarticulated in this debate, but always present, was the vital issue of what direction American government and society would take in succeeding years. To many Americans, the egalitarian tendencies of the French Revolution and the apparent rule of King Mob were matters for alarm. America's conservatives believed that French directions constituted a form of social cancer and that those nations who associated themselves with France would most likely fall victim to the dreaded disease. Re-

---

[7] DeConde, *Entangling Alliance*, pp. 185–195.

spect for government, the deference of the lower classes for their betters, authority itself might all be subverted in America if she took the fateful step of identifying her interests with those of France. Jeffersonians too were keenly aware of the significance of international relationships for domestic social policy. Many scenes in France pained the Jeffersonians; but the larger picture of men trying to shape their own destiny, to break the shackles of the past, was a thrilling one. To withdraw one's sympathy from the Revolution because of unjust executions or misguided French international policies seemed like historical nit-picking to the Jeffersonians. As Jefferson expressed this viewpoint in 1793: "In the struggle which was necessary many guilty persons fell without the forms of trial, and with them some innocent. These I deplore as much as any body & shall deplore some of them to the day of my death. But I deplore them as I should have done had they fallen in battle."[8] The apparent alternative—of virtually taking one's stand with England—was patently ridiculous and traitorous to the cause of '76.

Washington's Proclamation of April 22, 1793 was not entirely satisfactory to either viewpoint but was in substance a victory for the Hamiltonians. Minister Genêt would be received, the treaties of 1778 would be recognized as valid, and America would do what was possible to avoid angering France. But American neutrality would lean to the strict side, a blow to France since she was the naval inferior in the war and needed access to American bases plus resources for her campaigns in the West Indies. This basic stance of granting equal favors to all belligerents made Genêt terribly angry. Without some change on Washington's part, he foresaw there would be no attack on Spain in Louisiana, no expedition against Canada, no new commercial treaty to give life to the alliance, and no American bases or manpower made available to France. Old Washington, Genêt concluded, must learn that he was out of touch with the sovereign people; he must hear the voice of the Master and be forced to reshape federal policies.

What ensued over the next few months was one of the most

---

[8] Quoted in Louis M. Sears, *George Washington and the French Revolution* (Detroit, 1960), p. 161.

extraordinary scenes in the early national era. Historians have argued that a great national debate was held on American foreign policy. Students of the Constitution see these as crucial months in determining the power of the executive branch to conduct foreign policy. Political scientists contend that the great debate over national policies helped to define the two emerging political parties, Republican and Federalist. Whichever part of the elephant one describes, a crucial government policy was challenged by a majority of Americans who believed that gratitude, ideology, and interest should predispose America to France. Brawling, parades, broadsides, speeches, newspaper articles, and meetings of interested groups to pass appropriate resolutions were the common modes of expression. In the center of the storm stood Edmond Genêt, symbol and partial abettor of this challenge to the administration's policy.[9]

In retrospect, Genêt's cause was doomed. If not all, at least most of the newspapers were edited by men friendly to the administration. Washington's great prestige was also used to intimidate the protestors into silence. Would George Washington advise his fellow countrymen to follow a course that was unwise or antirepublican? To ask the question was to answer it. Washington even entered the lists himself, implying that the Whiskey Rebellion in western Pennsylvania was caused by the same elements supporting a pro-French neutrality.

After due deliberation the administration decided to ask for Genêt's recall. Even Jefferson was disgusted with this impetuous, imprudent man who had helped to dash so good a cause. But Genêt's short tenure had actually helped to crystallize a number of issues. Under Federalist leadership, for example, it was clear that no policies would be adopted that would alienate England or provoke her into a declaration of war on America. Federalist administrations would be helpful to France only within that guideline. France need, therefore, give no thought to invoking the alliance of 1778 (which obliged America to protect France's West Indies possessions), since this act would probably lead to an American denunciation of the alliance. Self-interest, defined

---

[9] Harry Ammon's, *The Genet Mission* (New York, 1973) is an excellent summary essay of the problems surrounding the mission.

largely in economic and maritime terms rather than in terms of ideological identification and territorial expansion, would also guide the hands of Federalist statesmen. Most historians of American diplomacy have approved of Washington's course though recognizing that his major supporters profited most by his commercial diplomacy.

Perhaps the soundest justification for the administration's course related to the new nation's need for time. Washington and many other Founding Fathers deeply felt the wisdom of evading external conflicts until the nation's new political institutions had had time to mature. And besides, common sense forbade this ocean-oriented republic from provoking a war with the world's greatest maritime power. France understood the rationality of America's course, but she had her interests to protect as well. She was not asking America to go to war, only to live up to the spirit of the alliance of 1778. This meant that America should practice benevolent neutrality toward France and vigorously defend American rights as a neutral carrier against the encroachments of England. Impossible, replied Hamilton, without a grave risk of war with England; French requests might sound reasonable on paper but if adopted by America would almost certainly result in war. Nations had no right to demand suicidal actions of their allies.

From the end of Genêt's mission well into James Madison's first administration, America's basic position did not change: she would remain neutral, trade with all nations, and only give succor to belligerents insofar as it did not threaten to engulf America in war. Nor did France's attitudes undergo major changes; honor, history, and the rights of men struggling for freedom, she felt, obliged America to take a stand. If America chose to support the old order, then she must be persuaded to change. If persuasion did not work, then America must be chastised until she realized where her true interests lay!

America made minor gestures to appease French anger. James Monroe, a public enthusiast of recent events in France replaced Gouverneur Morris, minister to France and an articulate anti-Revolutionist. Monroe gratified France's need to feel that it had a transatlantic friend. In his public reception, Monroe embraced the President of the National Convention to the prolonged applause of the delegates, and then addressed the Convention with rhetoric sympathetic to the Revolution. It was natural for many Frenchmen to believe that the appointment of Monroe signaled a new direction in American policy. In this belief they were completely mistaken. Monroe's appointment was essentially a diplomatic trick, a blind to France while America conducted its essential diplomatic business with England.

The Washington administration's wish to maintain its ties with England whatever the cost elsewhere, received a severe test in 1793 and early 1794. It justifiably disturbed England to find that although she had swept French shipping from the high seas, those commercial jackals, the Yankees, were still supplying France's West Indies possessions. By a series of Orders-in-Council, issued in June and November 1793 and January 1794, the British government tried to squelch this burgeoning trade. Commerce that had been forbidden to America in peacetime, the new rule stated, would not be allowed during war. That is, neutrals would not be permitted to trade during wartime in parts of the French empire that had not been open to them in peacetime (Rule of War of 1756). British warships in the Caribbean immediately swept down on American merchant vessels, confiscating ships and cargoes and impressing seamen. British officers often exceeded instructions and interfered with even the legitimate trade. This problem, together with apparent British interference among Indian nations in the Northwest, alarmed the administration and aroused Americans against the old enemy of '76. Defense preparations for a possible war with England were soon in train, with marked enthusiasm for the enterprise at the grass roots level.[10] In the background France was pressing America to defend her neutral rights, to defend the treaty principle that free ships make free goods. When America proved unwilling to take this step, France retaliated by seizing American ships transporting goods to England, a plain violation of her treaty obligations to America.

After considerable deliberation, Chief Justice John Jay was

---

[10] Alfred L. Burt, *The United States, Great Britain and British North America from the Revolution to the Establishment of Peace After the War of 1812* (New Haven, 1940), Chaper VII, pp. 141–142.

sent as a special envoy to England to negotiate a commercial treaty, to adjust grievances arising from the peace of 1783, to gain British recognition of America's neutrality principles, and to obtain compensation for seizures of American ships. France was angry at the appointment of this extraordinary mission, sensing an American sellout to England. Unwitting decoy Monroe tried to calm French apprehensions and assured the government, upon information he received from minister Thomas Pinckney in London, that the treaty concluded by Mr. Jay contained nothing contrary to the treaties of 1778.[11]

When terms of the Jay Treaty became known France saw that her fears had been confirmed. The treaty was silent on the impressment of American seamen. America virtually acquiesced in the Rule of War of 1756 and further agreed that even property and food on board American ships could be seized if the British paid for them. These latter agreements France considered an outrageous violation of the commercial treaty of 1778; America had pledged itself to uphold naval principles she now proposed to abandon by treaty. If America could not realistically be expected to vigorously defend her merchant marine against the might of England, at least she need not be so unconscionably eager to sign away her principles. It was obvious to France, and to her many American friends, that America had sold its soul to crafty England. Such betrayal provoked many Frenchmen to claim that the alliance was now ended. Since France was no longer America's ally by treaty, she would now be free to plunder American commerce and to demonstrate that England was not the only power able to injure America.[12]

The tremendous struggle in America over whether to ratify the Jay Treaty demonstrated to France that Federalist policies need not be permanent ones. Exhibiting a political myopia characteristic of inexperienced governments, France believed that American politics and political parties were dividing over issues

---

[11] The standard work on the Jay Treaty is Samuel Flagg Bemis, *Jay's Treaty: A Study in Commerce and Diplomacy* (New Haven and London, 1962). Also useful is McDonald's, *The Presidency of George Washington*, pp. 140–157.

[12] DeConde, *Entangling Alliance*, pp. 497–499; Bowman, *The Struggle for Neutrality*, pp. 238–253.

centering on France. Those apparently wishing friendlier relations with France were soon viewed as "pro-French" or "the friends of France." Jeffersonian Republicans, perhaps a majority of the electorate in America, were obviously hostile to the Jay Treaty or to any friendly association with England. Perhaps, the French government reasoned, with a few threats, increased maritime pressure on American commerce, and support of the Republicans in all feasible ways, it would be possible to see Thomas Jefferson elected President in 1796 and those despicable Anglophiles, the Federalists, disgraced and driven from office.

This decision to intervene in American politics, the second in three years, was an incredible blunder. Through the French minister, Pierre Adet, activities were directed to discredit the Washington administration and the Federalist Party. As the campaign became heated, Republicans and Federalists hurled the most serious charges at one another, charges of being in the pay of England or France, or of having sold one's country so that monarchy or mob despotism could be established in America. Adet's threat to rupture relations with America unless political changes were made enraged Federalists and in part provoked publication of Washington's Farewell Address. Partly an electioneering pamphlet, partly a distillation of his experience, Washington warned his nation in rather pointed terms that

a passionate attachment of one nation for another produces a variety of evils. Sympathy for the favorite nation [France], facilitating the illusion of an imaginary common interest in cases where no real common interest exists, and infusing into one the enmities of the other, betrays the former into a participation in the quarrels and wars of the latter without adequate inducement or justification. . . . Real patriots [the Federalists] who may resist the intrigues of the favorite are liable to become suspected and odious, while its tools and dupes [Jeffersonian Republicans] usurp the applause and confidence of the people to surrender their interests.

The great rule of conduct for us in regard to foreign nations is, in extending our commercial relations to have with them as little *political* connection as possible. So far as we have already formed engagements let them be fulfilled with perfect good faith. Here let us stop.

Jefferson's followers and the French government can be excused if they received the Address as a partisan political document. Whether or not it was effective in swinging votes to John Adams and the Federalist Party is unproven. Washington's appeals could at least be described as motivated by higher patriotism; Adet's maneuvers could only be viewed as great power interference in the domestic politics of a disobedient satellite.

As Washington left office, French-American relations were under great strain. France, believing that America had made her decision to embrace England, was determined to punish America for that decision. From the American side, the situation was agonizing; America's chief interests were to enlarge her trade and to stay out of Europe's wars. How these policies could best be achieved without sacrificing honor or long-term national interests (such as neutral rights) formed the core debate. Washington's decision to tack in favor of his country's best customer and potentially its most powerful enemy can hardly be faulted. His heritage on the matter of political alliances was thus threefold: avoid them if possible; conclude only short-range alliances for dire situations; circumvent or ignore the terms of any alliance that threatens to involve America in a war against its interest. If echoes of the cherry tree fable are but faintly heard in this advice, it still comported well with America's geographical position, economic interests, and Washington's extensive experience. Although France found such an opportunistic policy abominable, her own record in dealing with allies, even as a Republic, hardly entitled her to strike a self-righteous pose.

Even before leaving office, Washington made a last minute effort to better relations with France. To demonstrate the importance with which America regarded its ties with France, the administration sent Charles Cotesworth Pinckney of South Carolina as minister to replace James Monroe. Pinckney, a leading member of the South Carolina oligarchy and a noted friend of the French Revolution, was summarily expelled from Paris late in January 1797 under threat of immediate imprisonment. France made it clear that substance, not symbolism, was what she wished to see.[13]

---

[13] The Pinckney mission is discussed in Marvin R. Zahniser, *Charles Cotesworth Pinckney: Founding Father* (Chapel Hill, 1967), pp. 136–147.

Pinckney's rejection threw the newly inaugurated Adams administration into a dilemma. It wanted better relations with France but was not prepared to pay the price. What then should be done? The basic strategy was to stall France with conciliatory words and gestures while mending political fences at home. Those fences were tended by appointing a three-man commission to negotiate with France, a commission supposedly representative of the three great sections of the country and of the two political parties. Pinckney was named to head the commission, an unwise move on Adams' part since France now perceived Pinckney as a committed enemy. With him were associated John Marshall of Virginia, the future Chief Justice, and Elbridge Gerry of Massachusetts, a close friend of Adams and a future vice president. If this commission of distinguished men was threatened with imprisonment and ejected from France as Pinckney had been earlier, France would lose a significant part of its popular support in America. On the other hand, Adams would have placed a sizable feather in his cap if France did negotiate with the commission and conclude a satisfactory agreement.[14]

This shrewd tactic was not missed by the five-man Directory, a collective executive provided for in the French Constitution of 1795. Nor were they pleased by the instructions given to the ministers plenipotentiary; the essence was that America would make no loans to France for the duration of the war, would maintain its neutrality, and would adhere to the Jay Treaty. It was also difficult for the Directory to be tolerant of American desires when Napoleon's brilliant campaign in Italy had demonstrated how French power could destroy its enemies. Austria had been beaten, the Pope cowed, and European onlookers thoroughly frightened by French victories and territorial gains. Who, then, was this puny and treacherous transatlantic power to withstand French will?

France's determined mood was no secret to the three American commissioners. They believed as well that every friend of

---

[14] Appointment of the commission is discussed briefly in Stephen G. Kurtz, *The Presidency of John Adams: the Collapse of Federalism, 1795–1800* (Philadelphia, 1957), pp. 284–288.

America had been expelled from the French government in the *coup d'etat* of September 4, 1797 (18th Fructidor). John Quincy Adams predicted to his father that America would receive nothing but "unqualified injustice, under the Machiavelian mockery with which they have so long duped the world. Everything that envy and malice, both against our country and against you personally, can suggest, they will attempt."[15] When the treaty of Campo Formio was concluded on October 17, just three weeks after their arrival, the commissioners realized that this newest French triumph meant difficult times for themselves and their country.

Nor was foreign office head Charles Maurice de Talleyrand-Périgord any encouragement to the envoys. An exile from the Revolution in 1792, Talleyrand made his way to America where he subsequently spent an unpleasant thirty months. He departed believing Americans were a simple, crude people whose first and last wish was to acquire the almighty gold piece. Why Talleyrand didn't thrive in such a gross environment is surprising since his own reputation for greed was soundly established. Talleyrand saw no good reason why skillful diplomacy should not be embroidered by artful shakedowns. With the arrival of the American Commission he envisioned a prime opportunity to practice both arts.[16]

For the next several months a diplomatic farce, subsequently known to Americans as the XYZ Affair, was acted out in Paris. Through assorted agents, Talleyrand teased and provoked the American commissioners with cajolery, threats to their country, promises, and demands for a *douceur*, a bribe. What the Direc-

---

[15] John Quincy Adams to John Adams, Sept. 21, 1797, in Worthington C. Ford, Ed., *The Writings of John Quincy Adams*, 7 vols. (New York, 1913–1917), II, p. 211.

[16] For Talleyrand's American experiences and his views of America see George Lacour-Gayet, *Talleyrand, 1754–1883*, 4 vols. (Paris, 1928–1934), I, pp. 181–206. DeConde, *Quasi War*, p. 41, makes the point that Talleyrand had little direct power; he clearly was the servant of the Directory. Mirabeau said of Talleyrand: "For money he has sold his honor and his friends. He would sell his very soul for money, and he would be right too, for he would be bartering excrement for gold." Quoted in Echeverria, *Mirage in the West*, pp. 196–197.

tory wanted most from America during these months was apparently a loan and the continuing opportunity to plunder American commerce. While Pinckney, Marshall, and Gerry were distracted with Talleyrand's maneuvers, American commerce was suffering real distress from French depredations. Even as negotiations were being carried on, the Directory issued a decree on January 18 that could only be interpreted as a slap in America's face: a ship's cargo, the decree stated, and not the flag that the ship flew, would now determine if a ship were to be treated as a neutral. Anything of English origin on board— clothing, equipment, goods—would subject the ship to seizure. Even a compass of English manufacture would place the ship under hazard!

Under real pressure and provocation the American commissioners held steady. No loan was promised to France on the ground that it would violate American neutrality. The delegation would not apologize for certain remarks President Adams made to the Congress concerning French conduct, remarks the Directory found highly objectionable. Nor was a bribe paid, although the Americans were willing to part with a sizable sum if French attacks on American commerce were stopped. France refused to pay so dear a price. From the bribe negotiations America did at least gain a slogan pleasing to American nationalists. To one of Talleyrand's negotiators who insisted that the diplomatic wheel must first be greased, Charles C. Pinckney blazed back "No, no, not a sixpence!" His reply was later imaginatively transposed to "Millions for Defense but Not One Cent for Tribute" by Robert Goodloe Harper, a South Carolina Federalist.

To the envoys it soon became evident that France was asking changes in American policy that were virtually impossible to fulfill. Although France needed American neutral trade, and needed it desperately, she wanted to force her concepts of neutrality upon America. If America had allowed this, the Jay Treaty would have had to be renounced and serious problems, if not war, would have arisen with England. How then could American trade have helped France? The answer is that it could not. Since America refused to repudiate its neutrality policy, France then decided to punish America for its "betrayal." Ironically, American resources were probably more readily available to France under the Washington and Adams neutrality policies than they would have been if France had embroiled America in war with England.

France's true interest was peace with America, but she persuaded Pinckney and Marshall that she would soon declare war. As the mission drew to a close, they wrote to Secretary of State Timothy Pickering relating in convincing detail the indignities heaped on them and their country and cautioning that France respected nations in exact proportion to their military strength and internal stability. Weak, spiritless naions, they warned, soon found themselves bowing the knee to imperious France.

When the Adams administration released the XYZ correspondence by order of Congress, the nation reveled in a patriotic binge appropriate to the exaggerated emotions of a wartime era. At no time in America's national history have her people so heatedly denounced or so thoroughly detested France. Part of this feeling arose from national indignation and part of it was staged in order to destroy the Jeffersonian Republicans. It seemed possible to annihilate the party by associating the Jeffersonians with a pro-French policy. The eagle never screamed louder or flapped his wings more vigorously than in 1798. President Adams, short, paunchy, and balding, suddenly became a hero of sorts and felt flattered to receive widespread tributes to his courage and patriotism. Even Adams, who prided himself for a cynical detachment when lesser mortals were aroused, talked of the impending war in fervent tones. To an assemblage of Boston youth he cried out dramatically: "To arms, then, my young friends,—to arms, especially by sea." At another public meeting he warned, "The finger of destiny writes on the wall the word: War."[17]

Invasion jitters seized the country. Men pointed to the south as France's logical invading point, for there was a possible ally —the black slaves—who would be anxious to receive their freedom, arms, and a chance to take vengeance on white masters.

---

[17] DeConde, *Entangling Alliance*, p. 81. Adams' brief moment of popularity is described in Page Smith, *John Adams*, 2 vols. (New York, 1962), II, pp. 962–965.

From the end of March to mid-June 1798, Congress reflected the national fears as it enacted some twenty measures in preparation for war. A department of the Navy was created; Adams was initially given discretionary power to increase the regular army's strength; all French ships were forbidden to enter American ports unless in distress; and on June 13 an embargo with France and her dependencies was enacted, to be effective on July 1. Additions to the army were also provided for in June and July; Adams was authorized to call 80,000 militia to active duty at the appropriate moment.

Less praiseworthy aspects of the Quasi-War era began on June 18, 1798 when Adams signed the Naturalization Act, the first of four laws that are known in history texts as the Alien and Sedition Acts. Federalists, often stimulated by motives they considered patriotic, decided that the war crisis provided a fitting opportunity to erase all Jeffersonian and French influence from the nation's political life. This was the clear intent of the Alien and Sedition laws. Frenchmen, for various reasons, left the country in droves. "Right-think" became necessary for newspaper editors who wished to avoid both persecution and prosecution. All who did not view France as political wickedness incarnate were denounced as traitors or unwitting tools of France. Even as Federalists indulged their political paranoia, they sounded their own death knell. In trying to capitalize on a genuine national crisis to crush their opposition, they succeeded only in disgracing themselves before the electorate.[18] As a cap to their activities, the Federalists pushed through a measure formally abrogating all treaties with France; a few days later, through executive action, French consuls were forced to suspend their activities in America. Formal ties with France were now practically severed.

President Adams sensed that the most extreme Federalists were committing political suicide, and more personally, were undermining his chance to secure reelection. Other factors also served to rein Adams in. It slowly began to dawn on him, for example, that Alexander Hamilton was trying to use the crisis

---

[18] James Morton Smith describes how the Federalists discredited themselves in *Freedom's Fetters: The Alien and Sedition Laws and American Civil Liberties* (Ithaca, 1956).

for purposes with which Adams did not sympathize. Although Adams was not fully aware of Hamilton's larger purposes—to join with Britain in an attack on the Floridas and Louisiana and possibly other parts of Spain's American Empire—he feared the consequences if Hamilton's determined intrigue to become Commander-in-Chief of the American army were successful. Adams had sense enough as well to realize that France's interests would not be served by war. He recognized that France trembled for the fate of Saint Domingue if the navies of Britain and America joined in an attack. He knew that France should be concerned for the fate of her ally Spain's American empire. What he did not know was the extent of Talleyrand's concern, for Talleyrand looked forward to the day when Louisiana would once again be part of France's empire. Adams was also aware of how vital American commerce was to the French West Indies. He was not surprised, therefore, when in July 1798 Talleyrand sent peace feelers through various American officials, particularly through Adams' son Thomas and through William Vans Murray, American minister to the Batavian Republic.[19]

Against the advice of many extreme Federalists, Adams decided to treat France's peace feelers as sincere, not as insidious attempts to divide the American people further. His judgment was sound and the course he took was right for the country though ruinous to himself and his party. Even as America and France were carrying on a half-hearted war at sea, an undeclared war that lasted two and one-half years, a three-man commission was appointed to negotiate the issues at dispute, really to terminate the alliance on terms satisfactory to both parties. Adams and his cabinet did feel that in justice France should compensate despoiled American commerce and should relax its regulations in determining the neutrality of a ship's cargo. The commission was also instructed to promise France no loans or aids whatsoever, nor was it to write a treaty allowing French consuls the wide privileges granted them in 1778.

While envoys Oliver Ellsworth and William R. Davie were en

---

[19] See Alexander DeConde, "William Vans Murray and the Diplomacy of Peace: 1797–1800," *Maryland Historical Magazine*, XLVIII (March 1953), pp. 1–26.

route to join William Vans Murray, an event of consequence took place on November 9, 1799: young Napoleon Bonaparte engineered the Directory's overthrow and established a three-man Consulate, with himself as first Consul. Neither Bonaparte nor Talleyrand were happy with the thought that America wanted to slip free of French claims. It appeared logically ridiculous to them that America had annulled the old treaties with France but still intended to claim compensation from France for violating certain articles of those treaties. If the treaties were valid, France would discuss indemnities and claim her rights. If they were not, there would be no talk of indemnities and a new treaty would be discussed. Which position did America wish to take? Napoleon did not choose to press America too hard, for he was trying to encourage the formation of a League of Armed Neutrality to resist British maritime principles and practices. If treated properly, America might even join. But at least he should demonstrate that France smiled on nations who defended their neutrality. This could be done by exercising leniency with America.

Talleyrand urged other reasons for peace upon the Consulate: peace would be helpful to the Republican party in America; a possible American-British alliance would be aborted; peace would deter Americans from declaring war on a weakened Spain and then seizing the Floridas and Louisiana; finally, peace and a moderate policy toward America would encourage her development as a competitor of Great Britain. Bonaparte thought Talleyrand's viewpoints judicious and France therefore moved rapidly toward an accommodation with America.

In essence, the Convention of Mortefontaine, officially dated September 30, 1800, opened the road to peace. Indemnities and the treaties of 1778 were postponed as topics of discussion while recognizing that the treaties were not in operation. France relaxed her requirements for American ships to prove their neutrality. Mutual restoration of captured vessels was to take place. Measures were stipulated for the payment of debts owed by nationals of one nation to the other. And as a special bonus to the United States, the Americans were allowed to write into the agreement maritime stipulations similar to those in the commercial treaty of 1778. Contraband, for example, was narrowly defined. Neutral ships would neutralize the cargo except when contraband was on board. Although the American Senate ratified the Convention, it did so reluctantly and with difficult stipulations added: an indemnity was demanded, the Convention was to run only eight years (and not perpetually as first stipulated), and a definite abrogation of the Alliance of 1778 and related treaties was called for. Back the document went to William Vans Murray who subsequently renegotiated the treaty more in keeping with the Senate's wishes. The old alliance was now legally ended.

*   *   *   *   *

It was mainly the United States who experienced the unpleasant effects of the dissolving partnership in the late 1790s. A ripple in France provoked tidal-wave effects in America. Until its fighting navy reached a respectable size in 1799, America was sadly vulnerable to every adverse maritime decree of succeeding French governments. Worst of all, American diplomacy was helpless to correct the European situation from which French policy was shaped. The tides of war swept to American shores bringing impressments, commercial depredations, naval humiliations, foreign intrusions into American politics, and threats of retaliation. The apparent chain linking America to France was in reality a millstone since America's true interest was commerce.

This chain need only have been a rope of sand if France had not found herself so desperately challenged by the various European coalitions, and if a sizable American political group had not found it expedient to maintain the alliance. It is not difficult to argue that the Jeffersonian Republicans were patriotic Americans first and Gallophiles second. But it is hardly deniable that many Jeffersonians expressed sentiments that encouraged French politicians to meddle in American politics and to regard the Jeffersonians as the "friends of France." In transmitting these unofficial expressions of support to the French governments, the Jeffersonians played a very dangerous game. And in a sense they were irresponsible, for they would never have supported the consequence of a pro-French policy, namely expanding the navy to protect American commerce against inevitable British harassments. So the domestic repercussions of the dying alliance were harsh. Exploitation of the alliance issue became standard procedure for both parties as they struggled for power and self-definition.

As succeeding decades read the history of these early years, of their struggles and bitterness, it was natural to conclude that America should always avoid political alliances. Washington's farewell advice was twisted to suit the emerging orthodoxy. Where he had counseled concluding only short-term alliances in moments of national crisis, in the higher truth of national mythology he thundered against all "entangling alliances." Yet it can be argued that the alliance with France made very little difference in the substance of French-American relations during the 1790s. With or without the alliance, American and French interests would have remained unchanged. In repeated cases they supported or ignored the alliance depending on what forwarded those interests. Perhaps it would be sound simply to view the alliance as a complicating factor in a very complex international picture. It was little wonder that most Americans breathed a sigh of relief when the alliance was formally ended. Better days with France surely lay ahead.

*　*　*　*　*

Napoleon Bonaparte and Thomas Jefferson, so different in personality, background, and social values were nevertheless quite similar in certain ways. Both were empire builders, believing that nature or destiny had somehow ordained their nations to expand territorially so that the genius of their peoples would be fulfilled or their "natural" boundaries achieved. Each leader could be quite unscrupulous in certain situations. Jefferson's scruples tended to weaken when his nation's advantage was at stake, whereas Napoleon was more catholic in choosing situations where political dexterity seemed fitting. Each man also had the common experience of exercising persuasive leadership within his own nation. Bradford Perkins has noted that Jefferson never suffered defeat in the Congress on a single major piece of legislation.[20] Such success domestically naturally stimulated Jefferson and Bonaparte to wish equal success abroad, a wish that was only partly fulfilled for both.

But Napoleon's genius was war and Jefferson's passion was peace. In his vision of empire Jefferson was continental and territorial. Napoleon's vision was on a greater scale and encompassed French hegemony in Europe as well as a·French world-wide trading and territorial empire. Possibilities for empire in the western hemisphere strongly attracted Napoleon; thus it was in pursuing this ambition that he dangerously complicated French-American relations. Although Napoleon's interest in reestablishing a new French empire was partly an inheritance from preceding French governments, his was the first French government since the Revolution with the energy and military capacity to make the hope materialize.

The huge Louisiana territory, owned by a weak and tottering Spain, seemed to Napoleon a necessary acquisition before France could begin rebuilding her American empire. France already possessed the valuable Caribbean islands of Saint Domingue, Guadeloupe, and Martinique; if Louisiana were now acquired, it could supply these islands with timber and such necessary provisions as flour and salted meat. Louisiana, too, would flourish for its merchants would have a guaranteed market and American merchants would be severely limited in their trade with the French West Indies. If Spain could somehow be denied the Floridas, France would indeed be in an impressive position. She would have a vast and fertile base in the continental interior, she would control American commerce dependent upon the Mississippi and Ohio River systems, she would control the major American trade outlets through Florida's ports, and with a powerful navy, she could make the Caribbean a French lake. With a little skillful intrigue and some attractive bait it even seemed possible that France might woo the western American states into a union with French Louisiana.

At the very time the Treaty of Mortefontaine was being negotiated, Napoleon was secretly pressuring Spain to yield

---

[20] *Prologue to War: England and the United States, 1805–1812* (Berkeley and Los Angeles, 1963) p. 45.

Louisiana and the Floridas in exchange for an Italian kingdom for the Duke of Parma; while he was soothing America with one hand, he was taking measures that were bound to provoke a profound American hostility with the other. Louisiana (and particularly New Orleans) in the hands of a decaying Spain was not objectionable to the American government. With Europe wartorn, tantalizing opportunities to snatch Louisiana always seemed a distinct possibility. But Louisiana and possibly the Floridas in the hands of Europe's greatest power, a nation headed by a brilliant and unscrupulous general—that was quite a different matter.

If Napoleon's vision of a new French empire in America seems a reasonable or lofty one at first glance, that impression fades upon analysis. Acquiring a huge and unsettled area next to the aggressive and expansion-minded American people should have struck Bonaparte as a losing project. This was particularly so because France, the occupying power, would be several thousand miles away. With France in Louisiana it might reasonably be projected that America would link arms with Great Britain, an embrace that would soon prove menacing to French naval activity in the Caribbean. With migrating Americans thrusting into the Louisiana territory by the thousands each year, with the American government determined to keep the Mississippi River and New Orleans open to the flow of frontier trade, and with the possibility of a British-United States alliance cutting off French naval activity in the Caribbean, Napoleon's project seemed not only risky but also a little foolish. Perhaps that is why Jefferson reacted relatively calmly when he first heard rumors that France had acquired Louisiana. Jefferson was a firm believer in the principle that you take advantage of foreign nations when their fortunes are low, and with the wars *en projet* in Europe he foresaw opportunities to rain hard blows upon France.

France did acquire Louisiana in March 1801, but to Napoleon's great disappointment Spain would not yield the Floridas. Nevertheless, Napoleon proceeded to subdue Saint Domingue, an island that had experienced revolts and civil war since early in the 1790s. Toussaint L'Ouverture, the Black Napoleon of the Antilles, must be conquered and affairs mended on traditional and orderly lines. With Saint Domingue settled and firmly under French control, and the Louisiana territory occupied by several thousand French regulars, the work of empire building could go forward.

Unfortunately for Napoleon, the blacks would not cooperate, primarily because they believed he intended to restore slavery. Although L'Ouverture was subdued by trickery and shipped off to his death cell in France, fanatical resistance to French lordship was carried on. Nature herself struck devastating blows at French hopes when yellow fever decimated the army of General Charles Leclerc. A brother-in-law of Bonaparte, Leclerc finally succumbed himself to the dreaded disease. Fifty thousand men were quickly consumed in the Santo Domingo furnace. In the meantime, Napoleon prepared an expedition to occupy Louisiana, an expedition, as it turned out, that never left its port of embarkation near Rotterdam. Before the army could be properly provisioned the water of Helvoët Sluys froze over, and by the time of the spring thaw the British had blockaded the port.[21]

So the blacks would not assume their assigned role as slaves of France. Entire armies had been swallowed up. Bad luck had plagued the planned Louisiana expedition. These events gave Napoleon pause; he had also come to the conclusion that the preliminary Peace of Amiens (signed October 1, 1801) was only a truce, that the Tiger and the Shark must soon resume their combat for trade and empire. How then would he protect Louisiana from British seizure, particularly when America would likely support British aims? To ask the question was to answer it. Then the Spanish, by suddenly suspending American rights to land cargo in New Orleans before transhipment overseas (in October 1802) in violation of the Treaty of San Lorenzo of 1795, helped Napoleon to see the danger in which he would place France if she occupied Louisiana. Americans were demonstrably wrathful, war talk was rampant, and Spain faced the threat of 80,000 militia descending on her New Orleans base. Although Napoleon might scoff at America's lack of military strength, he knew the weight of numbers and logistics would

---

[21] E. Wilson Lyon, *Louisiana in French Diplomacy, 1759–1804* (Norman, 1934), pp. 129–144.

favor an American effort. Should France prepare to face American anger in a similar situation when so much was still unsettled in Europe? Napoleon thought not and events proved him right.

Bonaparte had had the American position on French acquisition of Louisiana impressed upon him by the American minister, Robert R. Livingston of New York.[22] Livingston was in a difficult position for the French Foreign Office denied it had acquired Louisiana almost to the time of the American purchase. But the message that the United States strongly opposed French acquisition of Louisiana was registered. To reinforce that message, and perhaps to persuade Napoleon to sell New Orleans and West Florida to the United States, Thomas Jefferson decided to send James Monroe to Paris. He authorized Monroe, the diplomatic fireman of the early national period, and Livingston to offer $10,000,000 for the Floridas and New Orleans. "On the event of this mission," Jefferson warned his diplomats, "depend the future destinies of this Republic."[23]

Through deduction Napoleon came to the decision that Louisiana would only benefit him if he were able to sell it. Funds from the sale could well be used to prepare his armies for the next round of European combat. To his finance minister he suddenly announced on April 11, 1803:

Irresolution and deliberation are no longer in season. I renounce Louisiana. It is not only New Orleans that I will cede, it is the whole colony without any reservation. I know the price of what I abandon. . . . I renounce it with the greatest regret. To attempt obstinately to retain it would be folly. I direct you to negotiate this affair. . . . Do

---

[22] Livingston's role in the Louisiana Purchase is thoroughly explored in George Dangerfield, *Chancellor Robert R. Livingston of New York, 1746–1813* (New York, 1960), pp. 352–394.

[23] Other proposed terms of the agreement were: to request France to guarantee the free navigation of the Mississippi to Americans and Frenchmen; America to give French vessels south of the 31° boundary equal treatment with American vessels together with a right of deposit of goods; France to receive most-favored-nation treatment in ports of East and West Florida; and if absolutely necessary, the United States would guarantee forever to France the remaining area of French Louisiana on the west bank of the Mississippi.

not even await the arrival of Mr. Monroe: have an interview this very day with Mr. Livingston. . . ."[24]

Livingston was astounded that same day to have Talleyrand inquire what America would offer for all of Louisiana. When Monroe arrived two days later and learned of France's decision to sell, he quickly agreed with Livingston that their instructions were irrelevant. Although authorized to pay up to $10,000,000 for New Orleans and as much territory *east* of the Mississippi as was obtainable, they quickly obligated their nation to pay $15,000,000 in cash and claims for all of Louisiana, a vast wilderness located west of the Mississippi.

Precisely what the purchase included was not clear. Texas or West Florida might or might not be included, depending on how one chose to interpret the treaty and past treaties relating to the area. Nor were the western and southeastern boundaries given a satisfactory definition. According to some historians, Napoleon believed that unstaked boundaries made bad neighbors; America would therefore find herself preoccupied in lengthy boundary disputes with Spain and Great Britain, presumably to the benefit of France. Just as likely, he did not wish to prolong the negotiations while a diplomatic abstract and title deed were drawn up. It was quite to America's advantage anyway to avoid boundary delineations. Talleyrand sensed America's opportunity when he said rather pointedly to Livingston: ". . . you have made a noble bargain for yourselves, and I suppose you will make the most of it."[25]

Much has been made of Jefferson's dilemma when he learned of the purchase. Since he had argued for a narrow—or literal— construction of the Constitution for over ten years, and since the Constitution nowhere specifically provided for acquiring territory not in the national domain in 1789, Jefferson suffered some

---

[24] François Barbé-Marbois, *The History of Louisiana* (Philadelphia, 1830), pp. 274–275. E. Wilson Lyon argues that Napoleon's "primary motive" in selling Louisiana "was to break up the growing Anglo-American *rapprochement* and to secure the good will of the United States for France and her allies." *Louisiana in French Diplomacy, 1759–1804*, p. 202.

[25] Livingston to Secretary of State James Madison, May 20, 1803, in *American State Papers: Foreign Relations*, II, p. 561.

temporary embarrassment over the Louisiana purchase. But he was not a man to let "metaphysical subtleties" or an "act beyond the constitution" stand in the way of a land purchase that would double America's size; principles were important but national opportunities had a nice way of shrinking them to proper size.[26]

Jefferson was accused by jealous Federalists of lending himself to land piracy. It is true that Bonaparte had no legal right to sell Louisiana given his unfulfilled contract with Spain as well as his promise to Spain that Louisiana would not be alienated. It is also true that Jefferson knew that France's legal title was faulty. But Jefferson had no mandate to act as international advocate for Spain, nor should he have. Powers unable to defend their interests or territory often lose both and Spain was to be no exception. Her decaying stance in the Western Hemisphere was visible to all. Any action that quickened the process was not necessarily cruel or untoward.

Some implications of the purchase were dimly but correctly perceived by contemporaries. America had suddenly received seemingly limitless room for expansion westward. The wealth of resources in the area would provide economic benefits to America for unnumbered generations. With a huge strategic base in the Mississippi Valley, it was but a giant step to Texas, California, Oregon, and the Pacific. Spain's ultimate loss of the Floridas was all but certain. America had truly become an "empire."

* * * * *

Cruel days were still immediately ahead for American-French relations. France resumed hostilities with England on May 18, 1803, a brief two weeks after Napoleon had sold Louisiana. This contest, waged with great intensity and with every nerve ultimately exposed, was to last twelve long years. Only with Napoleon's exile to the distant island of St. Helena could the

---

[26] Jefferson's dilemma is explored in Merrill D. Peterson, *Thomas Jefferson and the New Nation* (New York, 1970), pp. 770–776.

powers attempt to construct an order where peace was the norm.

Viewed in perspective, these were prosperous years for America. Europe's bitter struggles provided rich opportunities for American trade expansion. Spain and France, unable to supply their hemispheric colonies with the necessary goods, turned eagerly to America for help. No real solicitation was necessary since Yankee merchants were usually on the doorstep before the welcome mat had been well placed.

Both British government officials and merchants looked askance at America's burgeoning trade but little was done to interrupt that trade for two years after the renewal of hostilities. Even restrictions that were enforced upon America following the *Essex* decision of 1805 were not conclusive in shutting off American trade to England's enemies.[27] British impressment of American seamen was far more disturbing to most Americans than were hindrances placed on the expansion of American commerce, although any stoppage of trade was bound to and did provoke serious controversy.

America's situation deteriorated rapidly once Britain and France determined to force all neutrals into their own respective trade channels. In mid-May 1806 London announced a blockade of the European coast from the fortified city of Brest in France to the Elbe River in Germany. Six months later Napoleon proclaimed the British Isles blockaded, a rather wishful decree since part of the French navy was itself blockaded. Nevertheless, Napoleon moved quickly toward a policy of permitting Great Britain to trade on the Continent only upon terms favorable to France. In pursuing his Continental System Napoleon instructed vassal states, allies, and neutral powers as well to unite in strangling British commerce if they wished to retain their good standing with France.

The impact of this commercial warfare upon American trade was momentous. According to Napoleon's Berlin Decree, for example, any American ship even allowing itself to be searched

---

[27] In the *Essex* decision of 1805, the Lords Commissioners of Appeals in London made it considerably more difficult for American ships to establish the neutrality of cargoes they carried. A careful discussion of the decision is found in Bradford Perkins, *The First Rapprochement: England and the United States, 1795–1805* (Berkeley and Los Angeles, 1967), pp. 177–181.

by British cruisers was fair prey for French privateers. Given the circumstances, England's decree was stringent but not entirely unreasonable; vessels intending to trade in ports under Napoleon's control must first visit an English port to acquire permission. Failure to follow this rule made neutral vessels liable to British capture.

American-British relations now took center stage for the next several years, mainly because of Britain's ocean ascendancy and her determination that American commercial "jackals" should not fatten on the troubles of Europe. Bonaparte could only encourage America to resist British regulations, which he did by threatening and destroying American commerce at opportune moments. When Jefferson reached the point of desperation with England and retaliated with a trade embargo in December 1807, Bonaparte applauded from the sidelines. Like Jefferson, Bonaparte believed that Britain was dependent upon the American granary for her daily bread. Napoleon even did his part to enforce the embargo. By the Bayonne Decree of April 17, 1808, he ordered seized all American ships in French harbors. Since the embargo was in effect, he said, ships flying the American flag must be British ships in disguise! By this transparent act of highwaymanship Bonaparte netted over $10,000,000 for the French war chest.

In most ways the embargo was a decided failure. It was certainly one of the most divisive measures of the early national period. Ostensibly designed to protect American commerce, merchants found the measure ruinous. Supposedly inaugurated to protect American neutral rights, these rights were virtually surrendered by the stoppage of commercial activity. Three days before Jefferson left the presidency, a rebellious Congress substituted a Nonintercourse Act for the embargo; this new act legalized trade with all ports except those under French and British control. Exactly how this provision was to be enforced was beyond the wisdom of Congress. President James Madison, soon driven to desperation by the nation's plight, was to take steps that were even more foolish than Jefferson's embargo, steps that threw America into Bonaparte's arms and led to the War of 1812.

American foreign policy between 1806 and 1812 is instructive to the historian but not very scintillating to the nationalist. James Madison was not the kind of chief executive best suited to crises conditions. Although possessing a brilliant mind he appeared more a chief clerk in an established business than the head of a troubled, dynamic nation. No one ever called him an outstanding leader. And, like many really well-informed men, he had difficulty in making choices. His choices, of course, were often not very attractive: shoals to one side, an apparent precipice to the other. Worst of all, Madison was unlucky. No miraculous doors opened by which America could escape involvement in Europe's Armageddon. At every turn Madison found deliberate infringements on American rights and great powers determined to force America to do their bidding.

The Congress provided even less inspiration in these years. Very few Congressmen were willing to pursue policies toward either France or England that would impress upon those powers America's intention to protect her rights. Congressional indecisiveness was the product of military weakness, commercial avarice and weak executive leadership. Congress rightfully opened America to British and French contempt. Ultimately, America's erratic and often craven policies between 1806 and 1812 helped to precipitate the war with England; when a change in temper and direction occurred in the American government and the talk became tough, England unwisely counted heavily on American greed and pacific inclinations to avert a crisis.

Napoleon had even less respect for the American government and people than did the changing English cabinets. He believed Jefferson and Madison were timid, visionless men who responded better to cuffs than to caresses. His distorted view inspired an extremely unwise bullying policy toward America. If Napoleon had persistently wooed American trade with a liberal maritime policy, both France and America would have benefited. American trade would certainly have flowed in increasing quantities into French ports. But he chose to adopt tactics that were harsh and overlaid with cynicism. Even without a sizable navy to prey upon American commerce, he so alienated America by his various decrees and subterfuges that Americans were puzzled in 1812 whether France as well as England ought not to be attacked.

Congress opened the door to considerable misunderstanding with the Nonintercourse Act of March 1, 1809, when it authorized the President to renew trade with those powers that ceased violating American rights, even as it closed all trade with the British Empire and ports controlled by Napoleon. The Act also forbade armed French and British ships from entering American ports. Napoleon found this act particularly objectionable since it damaged chiefly French interests. To give American merchantmen access to the high seas, while warning them against trading in British or French ports, was really to throw their trade to England. Once out of American waters, the ships would go where there were trade possibilities and where the powerful British navy would allow—straight to English ports. And since French ships had few shelter points in the Western Hemisphere, whereas British ships had many, closing American ports to all worked serious hardship upon France.

Napoleon did see one possibility for mischief. If he could make the Madison administration believe he had revoked his edicts violating American shipping, according to Macon's Bill No. 2 (passed May 1, 1810) the President could prohibit all trade with England. At best England might ultimately be forced to liberalize her maritime policies; at least he might sow considerable discord between England and America. To American minister John Armstrong, Napoleon sent word via his foreign minister, the Duc de Cadore, that his earlier decrees (issued at Berlin and Milan) would be revoked *on condition* that America resume nonintercourse against Great Britain unless British Orders-in-Council were withdrawn. On that very day, August 5, 1810, he secretly ordered sold all sequestered American vessels that had called at French ports between May 20, 1809 and May 1, 1810. Secretary of the Treasury Albert Gallatin, who subsequently procured a copy of this Trianon decree in 1821 noted the "glaring act of combined injustice, bad faith, and meanness as the enacting and concealment of the decree exhibits."[28] Although Madison could not know of the decree, he did receive news of the Trianon tariff, enacted the same day the Cadore

---

[28] Perkins, *Prologue to War*, p. 247.

letter was sent. The tariff made it quite clear that no privileges would be extended to American commerce even if the Berlin and Milan decrees were revoked.

With this indication of French policy plainly before him, Madison still chose to take the greatest gamble of his political life; he decided to assume that the French decrees had in fact been revoked. Madison then approached Great Britain with this French "revocation" and threatened Britain with a nonintercourse sanction unless she too revoked her noxious Orders-in-Council. The British government caused Madison increasing embarrassment by demanding proof of the French revocation order. Madison then turned to the French government for confirmation, purposefully overlooking that the French revocation was contingent upon similar British action. Naturally, he obtained no confirmation from France. But in the meantime the American government resumed nonintercourse with England (March 2, 1811) in keeping with the provisions of Macon's Bill No. 2. Madison was in a terrible predicament. His political enemies raised the loaded question of whether he was the conscious tool of Napoleon or only his dupe. Madison was neither but he had decided to play high-stakes politics with low cards; his gamble was ill-advised, and in the wake of American anger and frustration at British firmness, the Congress moved on a zig-zag course toward a war declaration.

Madison despised Napoleon; he still saw certain advantages, however, in clinging to the Corsican's coattails. He hoped, as was natural, to use France as a counterweight to England. In this his success was generally minimal. Yet Madison did wish to use French influence in American attempts to regain her lost Latin American markets, markets lost to British merchants during the embargo days. British merchants naturally rejoiced when American merchants abandoned their growing portion of Latin American markets. As the Spanish and Portugese New World empires staggered from internal revolution and from lack of direction from the embattled parent states, British power and British products moved in to fill the vacuum. Once Spain had been invaded by France, Britain found it easy to pose as the true protector of Spanish interests. One sign of friendship was to supply Spain's Western Hemisphere colonies with British goods.

Jefferson's embargo thereby provided British merchants with unanticipated opportunitiès.

How could America thus regain her old markets when Britain had taken over so decisively, Madison queried. One answer seemed to be that if democratic revolution spread in Latin America, governments hostile to Great Britain would probably arise. In 1810, therefore, Madison moved toward cooperation with France in Latin America for the purpose of undermining governments friendly to the old regime. Great Britain was aware of America's intentions, and the tension created by French-American handholding in Latin America further helped to undermine the Anglo-American peace.[29]

This same hope, to use French resources against Britain, played a part in Madison's decision not to press for war against both France and Great Britain in 1812. Britain was no doubt more menacing to America because of her impressment practices and her presumed incitements of the western Indians, but French conduct also justified an American declaration of war. Rapacity, bad faith, open hostility, and contempt toward America had all been expressed in Napoleon's policies. It has been argued that the Madison administration's intent to use French ports and facilities as bases in the coming war influenced the decision to pretend that Napoleon had complied with Macon's Bill No. 2, and further that this desire to capitalize on French bases influenced the administration to grant France a special status in the pre-war days. Why then did the administration not move toward an alliance with France? For one reason the domestic consequences would have been fearful. Federalists had charged since the mid-1790s that Republicans were France's New World puppets; an alliance with Napoleon would have seemed to be conclusive proof. Too, having recently escaped one alliance with France, it would have been foolhardy to embrace another unless the circumstances were utterly desperate. America and France, Madison and Secretary of State James Monroe assumed, had parallel interests. This was adequate security for France's benevolent conduct toward America in a war situation.

---

[29] Arthur P. Whitaker, *The United States and the Independence of Latin America, 1800–1830* (Baltimore, 1941), pp. 79–84.

In any case, once France invaded Russia, America could see the end of the war in sight with France triumphant. When Russia fell the Continental System would be completed. Britain's trade with the Continent would thus be totally at Napoleon's whim, with disastrous consequences for Britain. As the Congress moved toward a decision for war it seemed very likely that America was casting her lot with a winner. France and America, while fighting for dissimilar objectives, might at least aid each other in their hours of crisis with a common enemy.[30]

In their neat little analysis Madison and Monroe failed to consider America's role from Napoleon's viewpoint. Why he should be especially considerate of American interests escaped Napoleon. As he viewed it, American power was marginal in that it promised France very little aid in the immediate future— and as Napoleon saw his empire collapsing in 1813 and 1814, the immediate was his only future. Also, the American government took no effective steps to stop the Iberian trade, a trade of enormous value in supplying the British army's campaigns in Spain. Napoleon also resented America's continuing insistence that France owed her sizable indemnity monies. Even as he granted American ships the unique privilege of bringing their cargoes into French ports and selling them there, he had to endure harassment about indemnities from this opportunistic nation with a shopkeeper's mentality. So during America's struggle with England in the War of 1812, America found her commerce under attack from France as well as England. Insofar as he could, Napoleon interrupted the Peninsular grain trade. Nor would he discuss the subject of indemnities. American sailors languished in French prisons, the mute casualties of continuing maritime warfare. New violations against America's mari-

---

[30] This theme is developed in Lawrence S. Kaplan, "France and Madison's Decision for War, 1812," *Mississippi Valley Historical Review*, 50 (March 1964), pp. 652–671. Richard Glover argues that newspaper reports of a growing French fleet may have predisposed Madison and his cabinet to believe that England would soon be defeated and that France would then attempt to retake Canada. "The French Fleet, 1807–1814; Britain's Problem; and Madison's Opportunity," *Journal of Modern History*, XXXIV (1967), pp. 234–251.

time rights were perpetrated without regard for American protests.

When Napoleon's last supreme effort to defeat the coalition arrayed against him was unsuccessful and he was forced to abdicate in April 1814, Madison found his hopes to use France in ruins. He had picked a loser and was now facing a triumphant if weary English enemy. Fortunately for America, England's physical and financial condition argued for an end to the American war as did the logistics problems necessary to bring the war to American soil. Madison's chagrin and bitterness toward Napoleon and France are understandable even if it is difficult to sympathize with his feelings. Madison, apparently so sophisticated and learned in the ways of political behavior, had shown himself a rather wretched amateur in calculating great state policies in a war crisis; he had to learn through experience that a common enemy did not make French and American interests parallel.

*   *   *   *   *

Beginning in 1789, America had gradually been sucked into the swells generated by the French Revolution. While America suffered from Europe's intermittent wars she also profited in spectacular ways. The Louisiana Purchase, to name but one, was a gift of the Revolution. Founding Fathers such as Jefferson realized that there were mixed blessings to America from Europe's warfare. Jefferson tried to take advantage of Europe's crises in 1806, for example, when he proposed to bribe Bonaparte so that he would force Spain to cede the Floridas to America. Napoleon's need for money and Spain's desperate weakness seemed the perfect opening to fulfill American acquisitiveness. Though Jefferson abhorred war, he entertained mixed feelings toward Europe's strife. While he would not wish war on Europe, he nevertheless was fully prepared to take advantage of Europe's agony for his nation's benefit. Madison shared these viewpoints. That Europe's distress was America's advantage, a theme stressed in the distinguished works of Samuel Flagg Bemis, was well understood by that realistic generation of Founding Fathers.

France and the Revolutionary aftermath not only provided America with territorial and commercial opportunities. Through contacts with the French experience America also gained self-definition and a sense of its proper role in the international system. A fledgling nation in 1789, America was easily imprinted as she interacted with France. American revulsion against alliances, her opinion that Europe was the seat of corrupted men and politics, and the conviction that America could best work out its future facing westward were products, in part, of French-American relations in the Washington and Jeffersonian eras.

French culture had a definite yet modest impact on America in this era. Refugees from revolution-torn Saint Domingue considerably enlivened the cultural life of seaboard cities, particularly in the South. French theater, language, and social manners temporarily became the vogue. The Roman Catholic Church was noticeably strengthened by the émigré influx.[31] But political controversies with France quickly evidenced themselves in displeasure toward French nationals and the culture they represented. In one of those ironic contradictions, while France stimulated America to move in a more egalitarian direction, horror stories told by refugees from Saint Domingue and Haiti helped to fasten the slave system on the nation. Massacres of whites by enraged Saint Domingue blacks persuaded American slave owners and others involved in the slave system that even limited freedoms were heady wine for slaves. Tighter control, a more determined oppression seemed the only possible policy if social control of the transplanted Africans was to be maintained.

Despite the antagonisms created during the Napoleonic era, it was during these years that the political foundations were laid for a lasting special relationship between France and the United States. The fact that both had shared in the experience of constituting republican governments and had watered the tree of liberty with their blood created a bond that lasted far beyond the bitter memories of a violent chapter in American and European history.

---

[31] Jones, *America and French Culture*, p. 150; Winston C. Babb, "French Refugees from Saint Domingue to the Southern United States, 1791–1810," Unpublished Ph.D. dissertation, University of Virginia, 1954, p. 265.

CHAPTER IV

Disappointments, Challenges 1815-1860

These people [Americans] seem to me stinking with national conceit; it pierces through all their courtesy.

Alexis de Tocqueville, 1831

If a universal monarchy is bad for the Old World, a universal republic would be equally bad for the New.

François Guizot, 1846

> And down the happy future runs a flood
> of prophesying light;
> It shows an Earth no longer stained with blood,
> Blossom and fruit where now we see the bud
> Of Brotherhood and Right

James Russell Lowell[1]

IT IS RATHER INTRIGUING to hear politicians or holiday speakers warm to the subject of a special and friendly relationship that has existed between France and America through the years. This myth of benevolent intertwining destinies is, of course, quite at odds with the facts. Conflict, mutual suspicion and mistrust, rumors of wars, and verbal missives have been the common stuff of French-American relations.

From 1815 to 1860, certainly, French-American relations present a rather melancholy picture. The only great interest France and the United States shared was the desire to maintain peace.

---

[1] Tocqueville's comment came in a letter to his mother, dated May 14, 1831, and is quoted in George W. Pierson, *Tocqueville and Beaumont in America* (New York, 1938), p. 68. Guizot's remark was made in a speech on January 12, 1846, quoted in Frederick Merk, *The Monroe Doctrine and American Expansion, 1843–1849* (New York, 1966), p. 88. The lines by Lowell are taken from his "Ode to France," c. 1848.

Every other area seemed to present added zones of friction: claims arising out of the Napoleonic era, tariff competition, trade rivalry in Latin America, American expansion, and competing political ideologies. Many bitter words were exchanged over these issues and occasionally the two nations seemed headed for a collision.

France emerged from the wars beaten but ambitious, anxious to regain her accustomed place among the world's greatest and most prosperous powers. She demonstrated her peaceful intentions to a wary Europe by becoming an ardent defender of monarchy and of the "system" established by the Congress of Vienna. Potential new areas for the expansion of French influence must however be exploited, French statesmen believed, if French respectability and power were to be established in Europe. Rivals to the expansion of French trade and influence, in whatever area of the world, must be challenged by those means France had at its disposal. As one historian has commented, the French government was restored to the rule of the old landed nobility and the new industrial class. An alliance between the industrialist and the agriculturalist "secured the establishment of a commercial policy more rigid than that of the previous governments." As France sought to expand her influence and to protect her commerce and industry, "American commerce was given no special treatment, but was fitted in with a larger foreign trade in a commercial policy which sought a protection for all fields of industrial endeavor."[2]

America too saw its role in world affairs expanding but not in such immediate terms. Before the United States could expect to exert great weight in world affairs, its continental destiny must first be fulfilled. The vast Louisiana purchase territory had now to be digested, settled, and exploited. Other continental territories also exerted a pull on American imagination; but time, fate, and skillful opportunism would settle their destiny. In the meantime America must make certain that future possibilities for expansion not be foreclosed. Immediate commercial expansion was possible, however. Growing trade in Europe, in

---

[2] W. H. Walker, *Franco-American Commercial Relations, 1820–1850* (Hays, 1931), p. 4.

the Western Hemisphere, and in the world at large would underwrite American prosperity, giving notice to all powers of America's enlarging economic role. Infant industries that had sprung up during the war years clamored for protection when peace dawned, and the government saw no compelling reasons to ignore these demands.

Both France and America thus emerged after 1815 determined to enhance their trade and influence and to protect those industries considered essential to maintaining economic growth and independence. There was little chance for a vigorous, direct French-American trade developing, if for no other reason than the commercial policy adopted by France in mid-December 1814. France either forbade foreign manufactured goods made from iron, wool, or cotton entrance to the country or saddled them with prohibitory duties. Sugar, coffee, spices, cotton, and wool also carried high duties. As for tobacco, a prime American export, Restoration France regulated its import and sale much as had the Régie Impériale under Bonaparte. The French merchant marine was encouraged by granting to it a monopoly on the colonial and coastwise trades, and by reducing tariff rates on goods imported in French vessels. French protectionism was thus very explicit; in its assessment of national needs, France expressed "little need for the commerce with America either in its import or export trade."[3]

American commercial policy immediately after the war followed a somewhat different course. By legislation enacted on March 3, 1815, the United States announced a policy of trade reciprocity. That is, if any European nation would agree to remove discriminatory duties on American goods entering their ports, America would in turn remove its barriers. Since this offer was ignored, the old discriminatory duties were reassessed two years later on the vessels of nonreciprocating nations. France and America now entered a period of strained trade relationships and acrimonious discussions concerning liberalization of trade policy.

Poisoning the trade negotiations—and all other issues—for twenty years was the matter of American claims against the

---

[3] *Ibid.*, p. 56.

French government. These claims were an outgrowth of Napoleon's wartime attempt to control the trade of the Continent to France's advantage through imposition of the Continental System. As a result of the Berlin decree of November 21, 1806, the Milan decrees of November 11, 1807, the Bayonne decree of April 5, 1808, the secret decree of Vienna of August 1809, and the Rambouillet decree of March 23, 1810, American cargoes were seized and sold or simply burned at sea. Just how valuable these cargoes and ships were depended on who was calculating costs, but Napoleon's estimate of $7,000,000 was believed by Americans to be, at best, a rock-bottom figure.

Madison's administration began to press these claims upon the restored Bourbon government of Louis XVIII through its minister to France, Albert Gallatin. While Louis' ministry recognized the justice of at least part of the American claims, there was a tendency to procrastinate on this issue. This was due partly to the embarrassed state of the French treasury. Other issues seemed more important, and the French ministers never gained a proper appreciation of American concern about these claims until American politicians became threatening. Too, French ministers were cognizant that allowing American claims might subject the French government to sustained harassment by other nations with similar grievances arising out of Napoleon's wartime depredations.

French strategy then became to postpone serious discussion, to make counterclaims, and to charge that American claims were largely fraudulent. The Beaumarchais claim against the American government, arising out of the American Revolutionary War, had never been settled. Why should America be pressing the Bourbon government for the depredations committed by the Bonapartist regime, it was asked, when America had never made an honorable settlement with France on the Beaumarchais claim. France had compensated the heirs of playwright Beaumarchais who had bankrupted himself to help America establish its liberties, while America dishonorably denied its responsibility to assist the Beaumarchais family. Moreover, France pointed out, America did not have clean hands on this matter of violating international law. In the Louisiana Treaty of Cession, for example, the 8th Article clearly specified that the ships of France "shall be treated upon the footing of the most favoured nation" in the ports of the ceded territory. America had not in fact executed that clause and its justifications were not generally recognized in international practices.[4] If American grievances were just, those of France were no less so.

French charges were not without merit but her general reluctance to take positive action to ameliorate American grievances placed her in the wrong. Nevertheless, one must recognize that domestic circumstances often make it difficult to dispense evenhanded treatment to all nations; throughout the twenty years of the claims controversy the French legislature, particularly the Senate, expressed doubts about the validity or urgency of the American claims.

Steady American pressure through three administrations (those of James Monroe, John Quincy Adams, and Andrew Jackson) finally resulted in a treaty, signed in 1831, with a dominant motif of compromise. America was promised 25,000,000 francs in payment for damages. France was promised 1,500,000 francs to satisfy the Beaumarchais heirs and thirteen other claimants. As for American violation of Article 8 of the Louisiana Cession Treaty, France was to surrender all claims in return for substantial reductions in duties on French wines.[5] The treaty was sensible and promised to ameliorate the nagging irritations in French-American relations. President Jackson had every right to be pleased with the treaty and to reflect that he, the old soldier, had been able to consummate what his diplomatically astute predecessor, John Quincy Adams, had found impossible.

Vigor is a diplomatic virtue, however, only upon occasion; it was Jackson's misconception that it had constant value. In the treaty it was stipulated that the first payment from France would fall due one year from the date ratifications had been exchanged, February 2, 1832. Without bothering to ascertain whether the French Chambers had approved the treaty and funded monies

---

[4] Richard A. McLemore, *Franco-American Diplomatic Relations, 1816–1836* (Baton Rouge, 1941), p. 16.
[5] The treaty text is found in David Hunter Miller, Ed., *Treaties and Other International Acts of the United States of America, 1776–1863,* 8 vols. (Washington, D.C., 1931–1948), III, pp. 77–90.

to honor it, Jackson ordered the Secretary of the Treasury to draw a draft on the French minister of finance for the named sum. Since funds had not yet been legislated, the minister of finance refused to honor the draft pleading lack of funds. When the draft returned through the Bank of the United States, Jackson's ire was not placated when he discovered that the Bank, his sworn enemy, included a bill for 15% damages on the protested draft!

Under prodding the Chamber of Deputies began formal consideration of the treaty in March 1834. After five days of lively debate the deputies surprised themselves by rejecting the treaty 176 to 168. The ministry of the Duc de Broglie resigned in indignant protest against this irresponsible decision. President Jackson quickly resolved to take the issue to Congress despite French assurances that the treaty would be presented expeditiously to the Chamber for reconsideration. As Jackson wrote to Vice President Martin Van Buren, there "is nothing now left for me but a recommendation of strong measures, to protect our national character, and to procure justice to our citizens by compelling France to a prompt fulfillment of her treaty with us."[6]

Jackson's message to Congress reflected his sizable and growing indignation. If the French chambers refused to make the necessary appropriation at its next sitting, he would recommend to Congress "that a law be passed authorizing reprisals upon French property. . . ." This was not to be construed as a threat, Jackson assured the Congress, for French "pride and power are too well known to expect anything from her fears and preclude the necessity of a declaration that nothing partaking of the character of intimidation is intended by us." "I know them French," Jackson was supposedly heard to say. "They won't pay unless they are made to."[7]

While Jackson's supporters cheered his "firm and manly" position, the French chambers and people were chagrined and

---

[6] McLemore, *Franco-American Diplomatic Relations,* pp. 102–104.
[7] Jackson's message of December 1, 1834 is found in James D. Richardson, Ed., *Messages and Papers of the Presidents, 1789–1897,* 10 vols. (Washington D.C., 1907), III, pp. 100–107. Jackson's offhand comment is found in Charles Peck, *The Jacksonian Epoch* (New York, 1899), p. 248.

disgusted at the President's menacing statements and blustering demeanor. Nevertheless his words awakened France to the serious view the American government took of the treaty. Seen this way, Jackson's vigorous message to Congress and his alert to the navy served the cause of peace. Great Britain certainly came to attention, offering its good offices to mediate the dispute. And despite the French chamber's reluctance to approve the treaty under threat from the belligerent Yankee, the step was taken. There was one slight condition, however, attached to French approval; the American government must give a satisfactory explanation of the President's hard words to Congress about France.

"France will get no apology," cried the *Washington Globe*, "nothing bearing even the remotest resemblance to one." When the American legation in Paris was closed in November 1835 and the French chargé in Washington was called home, it looked as though neither side intended to back off. Jackson ordered the navy to a state of readiness and the French government dispatched a special squadron to the West Indies. Jackson now saw that he had pushed France too vigorously and that he must either press on or eat crow. Little as the "Hero of the Hermitage" appreciated that dish, in his next annual message to Congress, in December 1835, he swallowed hard and uttered phrases that sounded suspiciously apologetic. Or at least the French were so able to construe them. The eagle lowered his wings, French pride was soothed, and peaceful relations between France and America were preserved.

To an impartial observer the claims controversy, particularly in its crisis stage, must have seemed much like the proverbial tempest in a teapot. Talk of war, and even some preparation for it, was ridiculous given the size of the claims when balanced against the probable cost of even a very short war. Such large supplies of adrenalin released over such a relatively minor cause does, however, tell the student something about the nature and tone of French-American relations in this era.

There was, for example, a strain of contempt on the part of both toward each other. President Jackson's comment that he "knew them French" epitomized a general American feeling that Frenchmen were unreliable; unable to establish stable, democratic, and responsible governments; and likely to act as real men only when prodded by threats to their honor or existence. Jackson's approaches to France were surely representative of American frontier character of the day: aggressive, enterprising, boastful, cocky and quite direct. While these characteristics were generally camouflaged by a facade of traditional diplomatic techniques, the real thrust of American diplomacy was bared under threat or when the opponent's cause and methods were considered beneath contempt. French evasions finally cracked the American facade and revealed to France aspects of American character and the deep-seated American attitudes toward France.

Frenchmen and the government of France might be excused if this episode confirmed their rather negative assessment of Americans and their government. Americans first presented badly inflated claims and pressed them with all the vigor of a holy cause. French counterclaims were denounced as roguish, designed only to confuse the "real issue." When a treaty was finally concluded in 1831 the American government lacked even the courtesy to inquire how payments were to be arranged. The entire opera bouffé was consummated by hollow threats from a stump-orator president who had no navy or army to give his warnings substance. Such uncivilized behavior was certainly contemptible. France would perform a service to the international community by maintaining its dignity and proceeding with deliberation, thus demonstrating to the Americans that the brawling techniques of a frontier town were unsuitable to the world of refined men and international diplomacy.

*   *   *   *   *

France had good reason before the crises of the mid-1830s to suspect Americans of congenital over-aggressiveness. France, and the rest of Europe for that matter, stood agog when General Andrew Jackson burst into Spanish East Florida in April 1818 to punish marauding Indians. Jackson did not stop at chastising the Indians, but confiscated the royal archives, seized every major post in Florida except St. Augustine, placed an American in the governor's chair, declared American revenue laws in force, and summarily executed two British citizens he believed had incited the Indians. France was ready to mediate the dispute and to calm Spanish fury. But Secretary of State John Quincy Adams' long and ardent defense of American policy made it clear to all observers that American territorial ambitions had not been sated by the Louisiana purchase and that Europe's traditional role in the Western Hemisphere was now under challenge by this rising power.[8]

The American challenge was necessarily muted, particularly in the immediate postwar years. And that, of course, was the part of wisdom. There were so many uncertainties to perplex America. Would the great powers, for example, take effective steps to stem revolution in Europe and to maintain the great colonial empires? For America this could mean in practice that the powers might try to prop up the shaky throne of Ferdinand VII of Spain. One helpful measure (to Ferdinand at least) would be to secure for Spain her Western Hemisphere colonies, in a state of rebellion and upheaval since 1810. It occurred to many that a sterling manifesto of Europe's intention could involve reincorporating Spain's provinces into her unglued empire.

While we now see the visionary quality of those hopes, the threat seemed real enough to many influential Americans. The machinery and power to force this arrangement were apparently operative. In order to preserve the territorial and dynastic arrangements made in 1814-1815 and to prevent the Napoleonic dynasty from returning to France, Great Britain, Prussia, Austria, and Russia had formed the Quadruple Alliance. Article VI of the alliance treaty provided for periodic meetings of the four to discuss measures that would best contribute to the stability and repose of Europe. At the Conference of Aix-la-Chapelle (1818), to be sure, the conference's reflections upon Spain and Latin America should have quieted American fears; but even the agreement that the colonies should not be restored to Spain by force, only through mediation, left President James Monroe uneasy.

---

[8] Samuel Flagg Bemis, *John Quincy Adams and the Foundations of American Foreign Policy* (New York, 1956), pp. 326–327.

Events in 1820 gave some substance to the President's disquiet. When revolutionary uprisings in Spain, Portugal, Piedmont, and Naples caused anguish among the crowned heads of Europe, Prince Metternich of Austria suggested at the Conference of Troppau that the Quadruple Alliance assume the responsibility of restoring to good standing any member state experiencing revolution; that is, use force to crush revolution. Although Britain dissented, some meat was put on this particular skeleton when Austria invaded Naples in March 1821 and when France, now back in good standing as a member of the great power club, prepared to rescue Ferdinand VII from the Constitutionalist insurgents in Spain. Like any new club member France was eager to prove herself worthy of admission.

France was also anxious to export her trade and general influence outside Europe's boundaries in such a way that right political principles would be forwarded. In the Western Hemisphere this meant trying to recapture lost French markets (lost to Britain and the United States during the wars), particularly in the West Indies. She could accomplish this partly by restoring Spain's colonies to her by force, by establishing Bourbon princes on Latin American thrones, or by working with Great Britain to spike America's Cuban ambitions. If President Monroe had realized how strenuously France and Russia had worked at Aix-la-Chapelle to gain consent to some interventionist formula in Latin America he would have been more than merely uneasy.[9]

France thus had objectives in Latin America, but effectively pursuing those objectives was frustrating business. Unsettled affairs in Spain after the Revolution in 1820, the reluctance of Great Britain to support a reactionary policy for reasons of trade, the difficulties of surmounting a growing coordination between Great Britain and United States policies in Latin American affairs, the lack of solid support by members of the Quadruple Alliance other than Britain, and the tensions within France over the proper policy to follow exposed French thrusts to a series of rebuffs. But to the United States especially, France

---

[9] William S. Robertson, *France and Latin American Independence* (Baltimore, 1939), pp. 168–177, 211–216.

seemed to be plotting everywhere—in Haiti, Argentina, Colombia, Mexico, and the Rio de la Plata. And while statesmen both in France and in the United States realized that Latin American trade was the immediate objective, there was also a feeling that the survival of certain political principles might also be at issue. In 1822 French Foreign Minister Chateaubriand stated his larger view of the Hemispheric competition: "If the New World ever becomes entirely republican, the monarchies of the Old World will perish."[10]

When France invaded Spain in the spring of 1823 and within three months released Ferdinand VII from Constitutionalist captivity and restored him to the throne, it seemed possible that Spain and France, in tandem, might seek to reestablish Spanish authority in Latin America. Or at least they might launch a diplomatic offensive that could bring the revolted colonies back within the Bourbon orbit. President Monroe was distinctly disturbed and proposed to lecture France on the invasion of Spain in his message to Congress in 1823. Secretary of State John Quincy Adams was more sanguine. He urged the President not to anger France through a public challenge for, he said, ". . . I no more believe that the Holy Allies will restore the Spanish dominion upon the American continent than that the Chimborazo [an Ecuadorian peak] will sink beneath the ocean."[11]

Adams was right, mainly because the British navy would certainly be used to prevent a restoration of either Spanish or French power, and Adams knew it. The story of how British Prime Minister George Canning secretly pressured the French Foreign Office to sign a statement, the Polignac memorandum, promising not to support an offensive-by-force in Latin America has been told many times. Monroe's famous message to Congress in 1823, therefore, has an aura of irrelevancy. But to a generation that has experienced the Cold War, Monroe's expressed belief that different systems of government operating in proximity are incompatible and a danger to the common "peace and safety" is arresting. "The political [monarchial] sys-

[10] Quoted in *ibid.*, p. 211.
[11] *Memoirs*, C. F. Adams, Ed., 12 vols. (Philadelphia, 1874–1877), VI, p. 186. Entry: November 15, 1823.

tem of the allied powers is essentially different . . . from that of America. . . . We owe it, therefore, to candor and to the amicable relations existing between the United States and those powers to declare that we should consider any attempt on their part to extend their system to any portion of this hemisphere as dangerous to our peace and safety." What America expected, in practice, was that the European powers should keep their hands off those Latin American nations who had moved toward independence.

In a rather striking way Monroe's message—and advice—harmonized with the larger purpose of the Quadruple Alliance: to provide Europe and the world with a period of quiet and recuperation. Intervention in Latin America to restore a lost order would certainly throw America and Europe into a state of turmoil. Too, Monroe's message promised that if Europe followed a policy of abstention in the New World, the United States in turn would not intervene in European problems, such as the Greek War of Independence. Most historians have found this self-denying pledge faintly amusing since American physical power to intervene was nearly nonexistent. But the President was saying that the American government would not use even its rhetorical or diplomatic resources to upset the established order in Europe or to encourage revolutions already underway. This was an important commitment, especially for a nation that saw itself leading the world into a better, a republican way. Most European statesmen, in their indignation at American presumptuousness to speak for the Hemisphere and to lecture Europe on political principles, failed to see that Monroe was apparently standing sponsor for the status quo both in America and in Europe.

One Paris newspaper, stimulated by Monroe's message, nicely expressed the feelings of contempt and mistrust that lay so near the surface of French-American relations: "Mr. Monroe, who is not a sovereign has assumed in his message the tone of a powerful monarch, whose armies and fleets are ready to march at the first signal. . . . Mr. Monroe is the temporary President of a Republic situated on the east coast of North America. This republic is bounded on the south by the possessions of the King of Spain, and on the north by those of the King of England. Its independence was only recognized forty years ago. . . ."[12] Perhaps France and the other powers of Europe should be excused for not interpreting Monroe's declaration as a support for the status quo; republicanism per se was perceived as a decided threat to monarchial institutions. An aggressive and expansive republic with a maturing economy and a rising merchant marine was not to be dismissed lightly. Also, the hints of future American hegemony being established over the Western Hemisphere, so easily deductible from Monroe's tenets, made statesmen nervous as well as the nationals of every European country who coveted the opportunities for profit and trade in Latin American markets.

So the threat of France acting in conjunction with her Holy Allies helped to provoke one of the most significant of all pronouncements of American foreign policy. If most Frenchmen found Monroe's declaration bordering on the obscene, that was understandable. France felt she had an important cultural and economic role to play in the development of the Western Hemisphere; thus she perceived no sound reason why an upstart United States should presume itself qualified to warn off the Old World powers. In fact, to legitimize American hemispheric pretensions by unduly limiting France's adventures in the New World was distinctly frowned upon by a succession of French ministries.

Although Britain, with her great navy and vast trading contacts in the Western Hemisphere was the prime challenger to the Monroe Doctrine, France somehow managed to seem quite as threatening as Britain. Hardly had the ink dried on Monroe's message before Colombia (in July 1824) was knocking on America's door asking for protection, through a treaty, against France who was trying to establish a monarchy at Bogotá. One year later a French fleet was dispatched to Haitian waters for purposes of extortion and diplomatic pressure, frightening both Haiti and Mexico. Thirteen years later, in 1838, France blockaded both Mexico and Argentina in order to redress commercial grievances; in Argentina, France went much beyond blockade to

---

[12] *L'Etoile*, January 4, 1824, cited in Dexter Perkins, *The Monroe Doctrine, 1823–1826* (London, 1927), p. 30.

the point of landing troops on Argentine territory and intriguing with her neighbor, Uruguay. In none of these instances did the American government become terribly alarmed, for no vital American interest was involved. Nonetheless, the French were building a record in the Hemisphere that struck most Americans as being discreditable and irritating.

It was over the Texas issue that French policy seemed to Americans to become downright provocative and irrational. When Texas broke away from Mexico and proclaimed its independence in 1836, most Americans were convinced that American-Texas destinies would soon intertwine through Texas' addition to the Union. Negotiations were started that led in eight years to that goal, but the road was a winding one with French and British roadblocks dotting the terrain.

Britain and France saw no reason to rejoice at the thought of Texas joining the Union. Since neither enjoyed their uncomfortable dependence on cotton grown within the Union, they saw competing cotton from an independent Texas as one tool to lower American prices and to win concessions for their own products in American markets. It also bothered sensitive British consciences to be so dependent on slave-grown cotton; as an independent nation, and one highly amenable to British pressure, Texas might be induced to abolish slavery. France was not as taken with the possibility of reducing the area of slavery as she was with establishing a power able to withstand the enormous American momentum for territorial growth. For their own reasons, then, France and Great Britain were strongly motivated to offer Texas a guarantee of independence (which would scratch any reinvasion threat from Mexico) and to encourage Texan independence by dangling tempting commercial concessions before Texan politicos.

The bait was ultimately rejected and the Texas treaty of annexation with the United States concluded, but France was not tempted to think her principle of American containment any less valid for failure. "France has a lasting interest in the maintenance of independent states in America, and in the balance of forces which exist in that part of the world," Foreign Minister Guizot asserted in June 1845. As President James K. Polk contemplated the joint French-British naval intervention in the Rio de la Plata in fall of 1845, as he entertained visions of possible British and French intrigue to deny California to the Union, and as he reflected on the challenge sounded by Guizot, Polk decided that it was time to reassert and update the earlier declaration of President Monroe.[13]

In his message to Congress of December 2, 1845, Polk warned the nations of Europe who "desire the establishment of what they term 'the balance of power.' " This pernicious policy "cannot be permitted to have any application on the North American continent, and especially to the United States. We must ever maintain that people of this continent alone have a right to decide their own destiny. Should any portion of them [such as in Texas] constituting an independent state, propose to unite themselves with our Confederacy, this will be a question for them and us to determine without any foreign interposition. We can never consent that European powers shall interfere to prevent such a union because it might disturb the 'balance of power' which they may desire to maintain upon this continent."[14]

Guizot can be excused if he found Polk's assertions belligerent and in some ways contemptible. The notion that political principles of proven value in Europe were somehow rendered invalid or disreputable by an ocean voyage was enough to provoke sneers. But for the President to claim that the nations of Europe were out of bounds in maintaining normal relations with states of the Western Hemisphere when those relations inconvenienced the ambitions of America, was too extreme to be ignored. Guizot thus felt it necessary to issue the first public challenge to the principles of Monroe and Polk and he did so before the French Chamber of Deputies in early January 1846.

Guizot described Polk's contention that European powers were not to intervene in New World affairs "a strange one." Legally constituted states had every right to contract alliances, make treaties, or to take other actions in accord with their interests.

---

[13] *Histoire Parlementaire de France. Recueil Complet des Discours Prononcés dans les Chambres de 1819 à 1848 par M. Guizot*, 5 vols. (Paris, 1864), IV, p. 563. Entry: June 10, 1845. French interest in California is recounted in Rufus K. Wyllys, "French Imperialists in California," *California Historical Society Quarterly, 8* (June 1929), pp. 116–129.

[14] Richardson, *Messages and Papers of the Presidents*, IV, p. 398.

And proximity to the United States "cannot in any degree limit their independence or their rights." France had historic hemispheric rights and interests, and France intended to "maintain them without any feeling of hostility toward the United States, indeed, with the same sentiments of good will and friendship which we have long professed and practiced toward them; we will maintain them without giving the United States any just subject of complaint, but also without yielding to any unfounded pretension."[15] These were firm words and France demonstrated her intention to give them substance by her continuing intervention in Argentine and Uruguayan affairs, an action to which the Polk administration did not take exception.

Exchanging such mutually bristling phrases was to be expected given French-American economic and political ambitions. America was aggressive and growing but paranoid and insecure. Intrigue on France's part to stymie America's growth westward or to contain its influence to the South was construed as part of Europe's systematic and malevolent plan to stifle the growth of divinely-ordained Republican institutions. France's viewpoint about how peace was maintained (through balancing interests and powers) and France's assumption that lessons learned through European experience had relevance to nation-state relationships in the Western Hemisphere were never given proper consideration by American statesmen. If an idea or a policy was deemed inconvenient to American ambitions, that idea or policy must be considered either invalid or wicked; this was certainly the position of President Polk. France was thus placed in the unfortunate position of being unable to maintain amicable relations with the United States except through repeated capitulation. Because France believed the powers of Europe should play a large role in hemispheric policies and trade, and because she believed there should be some reasonable limit to American continental growth, she periodically became the *bête noire* of American policy. France did not relish this role, partly because her long-term hemispheric prospects were doubtful and, too, because she was overly dependent on British cooperation, par-

---

[15] Guizot, *Histoire Parlementaire*, V, p. 30.

ticularly when issues such as Texas, California, Cuba, and Puerto Rico were on the agenda.

*   *   *   *   *

The will to make French-American relations cordial in tone was generally lacking in this period. It was lacking both at the popular and at the governmental levels. This was due partly to American disappointment at the course of France's internal political development following the end of Napoleon's wars. Americans were not overly surprised that the Bourbons were restored by the powers of Europe, for sensible men recognized that the political climate demanded stability and order. Some Americans were even cheered that the monarchy had strong constitutional overtones and that Louis XVIII took measures to defang certain radical political elements. It was a distinct letdown, therefore, when Charles X (Louis' brother) succeeded Louis in 1824 and started France back toward absolutism and clericalism. Americans could only conclude that the seeds of liberty in France, watered by the blood of two generations of Frenchmen, had apparently not taken root. Charles' moves to reduce the electorate by three-fourths, to strike the number of deputies by 174, and to enlarge the influence of the Roman Catholic Church warned Americans of the Jacksonian era that ideological comity with France was not a reasonable prospect.

Hopes rose, of course, when in July 1830 Charles X was overthrown and the Bourbon regime was replaced by that unimaginative head of the House of Orléans, Louis Philippe. There was widespread rejoicing in America that a new day had dawned for Europe, when France and her Republican King would lead Europe toward the establishment both of order and enlightened political principles. Such a power would surely be a friend to America; together they would be a formidable instrument in advancing the cause of Republicanism. Lafayette's embrace of Louis Philippe at the Hotel de Ville (city hall) on July 31 not only delighted the observing Paris crowd but encouraged Americans to hope that the king, annointed by the "hero of two worlds," would treasure American friendship and republican principles. The whole scene soured very quickly, however, over the claims issue. And Prime Minister Guizot's well-articulated policy that American advances on the continent must be circumscribed infuriated more aggressive Americans. Guizot's desire to organize a coalition that would discourage America's threatening posture toward Mexico, and possibly stop America's march westward, showed that France did not intend to abdicate its position in the Western Hemisphere.

Yet Americans found some reasons to be pleased for the regime initially made concessions to the liberal spirit. It widened the electorate, lowered property qualifications for voting, abolished censorship and extraordinary judicial commissions, and ended the intimate relationship between throne and altar. But as months passed Americans concluded that those elements in society who supported the bourgeois ing were anti-republican and unsympathetic to democratic principles. Preservation of public order and guarantees of private property seemed the highest ambition of Louis Philippe and his ministers; but they had sought those goals in such a way that Republicans and democratic sympathizers were unable to win substantial numbers of converts. Order had triumphed over liberty. Yet if French foreign policy toward America was a disappointment, a body of American opinion developed that expressed hope that the monarchy was a step toward a moderate, constructive republican regime which would be a beacon to other like-minded nations, and ultimately a friend to America.

In mid-January 1848, citizens of Palermo in Sicily took to the streets in open rebellion against Ferdinand II of Naples. Just one month later the liberal opposition to the conservative government of Guizot in France announced its intention to hold a propaganda banquet on February 22; in panic, Guizot's government forbade the banquet. People poured into the Paris streets to demonstrate and by nightfall the barricades were up in the working class districts. These two incidents touched off popular insurrections which within the year sparked a series of revolutions all over Europe. Germany, Austria, Hungary, Italy, Switzerland, Belgium, and France were rocked by the disturbances and Britain was not left untouched. When the uprisings had run their course, it seemed clear that the conserving and balancing system of Prince Metternich, so central to European events since 1815, had been overthrown.

Americans were particularly fascinated by events within France, for they generally assumed that as revolution prospered in Paris, so it would fare in Europe. The rapidity of events within France, and the wild swings of the political pendulum were astounding to Americans who had little real knowledge of the unsettled state of French political affairs. At first, developments were encouraging. Louis Philippe's regime, overthrown in two days by Paris in rebellion, was replaced by a provisional government comprised of moderate liberals who hoped to establish constitutional parliamentary government. At one stroke of the pen this provisional government enlarged the electorate from 20,000 to 9,000,000. Restrictions on the press and on private citizens were removed. In order to relieve the suffering of the unemployed, "National Workshops" were established to provide jobs. But elections held late in April made it clear that an overwhelming number of Frenchmen were opposed to the new government. Not content to accept the national will, a Paris mob invaded the assembly and proclaimed a new emergency government at the Hotel de Ville. Louis Auguste Blanqui, Armand Barbès, and their socialist following were thus asserting their prerogative to act in defiance of the expressed will of France. But the National Guard refused to accept this new provisional government; the provisional assembly was cleared, Barbès and Blanqui were thrown into prison, and the Hotel de Ville was reoccupied.

Events took a violent turn in June when the government decided to abolish the national workshops. Mobs roamed the street in protest, often singing the *Marseillaise* as they smashed windows and erected barricades. The uprising, almost spontaneous in nature, was opposed by the army, the National Guard, and the new Mobile Guards commanded by the African veteran, General Louis Eugène Cavaignac. On June 24 and 25 pitched battles took place. Workers were mercilessly massacred. Even after the fighting ended on the evening of June 25, summary executions were ordered for those implicated in the rebellion. The ferocity of the "June Days" blurred all hope for a democratic republic and headed the government toward certain reaction. That direction was confirmed in elections for the presidency held in December 1848, when Louis Napoleon Bonaparte, nephew of the great warrior, received a total of 5,500,000 votes out of 7,500,000 cast. With a Bonaparte at the helm, it was assumed that France was not far from a more authoritarian regime, an assumption that was realized when Louis Napoleon made himself emperor of France in December 1852 by a *coup d'etat*.[16]

Without a working knowledge of French society and politics, it is understandable that Americans were dismayed by the convulsions in France. Fickleness, savagery, and a bent toward political immoderation seemed to characterize the French political scene. If Frenchmen were somehow to be considered brothers of Americans, they must surely be regarded as fallen brothers. The desire for moderation, compromise, and finding the middle way—so much a part of the American political tradition—apparently had shallow roots in France. It was easy to conclude that Frenchmen were political infants, a prime case of arrested political growth, more to be pitied than despised. At best they were certainly no fit partners in a struggle to enlarge the areas of freedom. French political influence, in fact, was likely to be pernicious to republican regimes and principles.

*   *   *   *   *

French-American trade, unfortunately, was never sizable enough so that great internal pressures could be generated for amicable relations. As stated earlier, after 1815 both nations were determined to protect infant industries against destructive British competition. This resulted in tariffs that not only regulated trade with Britain but also minimized exchanges with each other. David Thomson has commented that as late as 1830, "no large section of the [French] community was directly involved in foreign trade." And the entire foreign trade of France amounted in value to about $6.00 per head of the population in

---

[16] Perhaps the best brief history of the revolution is J. Dautry, *Histoire de la Revolution de 1848 en France* (Paris, 1948).

a given year.[17] Both nations were also largely concerned with the development of internal trade; it is in this era that the building of canals and roads in France and America proceeded at such a feverish pace. Tariffs on incoming goods not only protected industries considered vital to the national interest but also served as a source of limited revenue to enhance the possibilities of a burgeoning internal trade.

French attitudes toward the role of foreign trade in her economic development were revealed in the tariffs of 1816, 1820, 1822, and 1826; protection was repeatedly increased to please agricultural interests, and in coal, iron, and cotton goods to satisfy industrial pressure groups. On the American side, Henry Clay's "American System," with its emphasis on protection and internal development, was expressed in the Tariffs of 1816, 1818, 1824, and in the 1828 "Tariff of Abominations," where protection reached its apogee before the Civil War. Raw wool, in the last tariff, was given a general *ad valorem* duty of 50%, as well as a specific duty of four cents per pound; and duties on such items as hemp, and pig and bar iron were sharply increased. Thus as pressures were growing in Great Britain for the advance of international free trade, a movement encouraged by merchants such as Richard Cobden and William Bright, French and American interests were determinedly following exclusionist trade policies, but ones that seemed most advantageous to their total national interests.

One other area related to trade that was certain to enlarge the base of French-American friction concerned their mutual desire to strengthen each nation's merchant marine. Handsome profits were to be made by those firms engaged in transoceanic shipping. Too, seamen, a national resource in time of war developed their skills on commercial voyages. The appearance of a country's flag in foreign ports was also a way to enhance a nation's prestige. For those reasons French and American statesmen took seriously the need to create conditions favorable to the growth of the merchant marine. One way France approached this problem was to levy such a heavy import on foreign bottoms, or on their goods entering French ports, that foreign merchants would

---

[17] David Thomson, *Europe Since Napoleon* (New York, 1958), p. 139.

patronize vessels flying the French flag. Quarantine expenses and shipbrokers' expenses on foreign ships were also charges that a determined nation could use to give vessels owned by its own citizens an unfair advantage.

This was the course taken by France at war's end despite America's offer in 1815 to establish reciprocity with the vessels of France. Upon the recommendation of President Monroe and John Quincy Adams, Congress levied a special duty of $18 per ton on French bottoms beginning July 1, 1820. France retaliated in turn and the issue was not settled until the Commercial Treaty of 1822 was negotiated and ratified. The treaty provided for the abolition of the special duties within six years. While America and France were quarreling about these punitive duties, Great Britain and other powers were carrying three-fourths of the French-American trade in their vessels.[18] Nevertheless, both nations felt the need to be zealous and far-seeing about merchant marine matters.

So the context in which French-American trade developed after the war was not propitious. Both nations, economically, were largely oriented internally. And although their mutual trade was important to national economic development, it never became important enough to sway great political decisions, or to place a high value on amicable relations. Even those commodities that formed the bulk of their trade seemed to cause one or both nations continuing irritation.

Importation of tobacco into France, for example, was rigidly controlled by the Régie Impériale, a government corporation that Bonaparte had established. The Régie encouraged the domestic production of tobacco, mainly grown in the upper Rhine valley, and was therefore reluctant to see tobacco imported in quantity. America was granted 90% of the foreign tobacco quota but in the 1840s this amounted to only about 20,000 kilograms. During Louis Philippe's reign, the Régie did encourage America's tobacco owners by purchasing equal amounts of French and American grown tobacco, a policy which enlarged the American tobacco trade to France by 300%. But American tobaccomen did

---

[18] Vernon G. Setser, *The Commercial Reciprocity Policy of the United States, 1774–1829* (Philadelphia, 1937), p. 205.

not want a fixed level or quota; they wanted the chance to win the entire French market! Although the Régie consistently refused to consider allowing free trade in the tobacco markets, every American administration had hopes that it would do so. When the Régie stood fast, all too many Americans wrongly felt they had a legitimate grievance against France.

It was the cotton trade, of course, that formed the bulk of French-American trade. In certain years cotton constituted 85% of American exports to France. For a time some mutuality in the trade existed. While America produced the raw cotton, France produced textiles that were popular in seaboard America. France was uneasy, however, with her dependence on American cotton, particularly for the excellent sea island variety, and tried to encourage production in Brazil, Egypt, India, and later in Algeria. These efforts were not successful and added to this frustration was the fact that by 1850 American industry produced low-cost quality textiles whose prices France could not hope to match.

French exports to America consisted primarily of quality silk and other textile products and superb French wines. But the trade never began to match the size of French expectations. One reason was that the products were generally considered luxurious and most Americans were still struggling to pay for life's necessities. Nevertheless, between 1821 and 1850, French textiles exported to America increased almost 500%. But the favorable American import duties on silks were dropped, first to please the infant American silk industry and then to encourage the development of America's East Asian trade. French wines too could be taxed with little domestic repercussion; for although American consumption of alcoholic beverages was prodigious, the whiskeys produced by Jacksonian American distilleries were more to the nation's taste than the more delicate French table wines.[19] The United States was generally France's second best customer for wine; however, French producers always felt that an enormous market eluded their grasp chiefly because of un-

---

[19] Henry Blumenthal, *A Reappraisal of Franco-American Relations, 1830–1871* (Chapel Hill, 1959), p. 107; Walker, *Franco-American Commercial Relations*, pp. 219–221.

reasonable American import duties. Tastes, they reasoned, might vary according to price structures.

Because of its own economic policies France did not expect generous tariff treatment at American hands. But Frenchmen did expect that their capital investments in America would be protected by prudent government action. The depression of 1837 was therefore a great disillusionment for French investors and for others tied to American markets. Ruined banks, suspended payments, and commercial disorders brought economic disaster to sufficient numbers of Frenchmen that years later French consuls in America were warning their countrymen to place little confidence in the soundness of the American economy or the financial practices of the government.[20]

Trade and other financial relationships between France and America thus did little to insure more amicable diplomatic ties. Both France and America after 1815 were vigorously promoting their own economic salvation and caring little for damage done to the other. Some mutual profit and losses, and considerable irritation, were the unsurprising results.

Both trade and diplomatic relations between 1815 and 1850 tell much the same story about French-American relations. Mutual suspicion and distrust often keynoted the political relationship and for quite understandable reasons. Clashing political ambitions in the Western Hemisphere, rivalry in trade and shipping affairs, and a concern that the other nation was promoting political principles disadvantageous to its interests put the ragged edge to French-American relations. Trade patterns mirrored this unsatisfying but rather normal condition of the relationship. For example, while Louis Napoleon took steps in 1851 and 1852 to establish himself as Emperor Napoleon III, to a chorus of political catcalls from the western side of the Atlantic, French-American trade entered a period of relative decline.

French-American fears, antagonisms, sense of competition, and clashing ambitions found full expression in the 1850s. Whereas France had been doubtful about how to execute its containment policy as the United States advanced into Mexico, California, and Oregon, she was much more certain of her abil-

[20] Blumenthal, *ibid.*, p. 110.

ity to control America's ambitions in Cuba, Santo Domingo, Haiti, Central and South America, and even as far away as the Hawaiian Islands. The United States, on the other hand, was less anxious than France believed to acquire new territory, Cuba excepted, but France's determined stance on any new American advances convinced many that France was hatching New World territorial plots of her own.

From a French perspective, America by 1850 seemed extraordinarily aggressive and, if unchecked, a mortal threat to the establishment of any power balance in the Western Hemisphere. The "Young America" movement of this prewar decade, and its diplomatic expressions, left little doubt in French minds that America was a congenital aggressor and even a threat to the political systems of Europe. "Young America," a faction within the Democratic party with its base in the Mississippi Valley, openly lamented the failure of the Revolutions of 1848 and called for American political intervention to relight the lamps of Europe. The Democratic party platform of 1852 resolved that "in view of the conditions of popular institutions in the Old World, a high and sacred duty is devolved with increased responsibility upon the Democracy of this country." In the aftermath of 1848, nervous European governments did not take these expressions lightly. Substance was given to their fears when it was discovered that George N. Sanders, an active Young American and one who had earlier tried to sell 144,000 antiquated muskets to European republicans, was named consul at London by the Franklin Pierce administration. Sanders' home in London became virtual headquarters for the exiled revolutionary leaders of Europe: Garibaldi, Kossuth, Mazzini, Ledru-Rollin, Orsini, Arnold Ruge, and Alexander Herzen. America's minister to England, future President James Buchanan, who was hospitable to the exiles, wondered over dinner with them whether such "combustible materials . . . would explode and blow us all up,"[21] a thought shared by more than one European statesman.

George Sanders addressed a circular letter to Frenchmen early in October 1854 calling for revolution: "Hate Napoleon more

---

[21] Merle Curti, "Young America," *American Historical Review*, XXXII, No. 1 (October, 1926), pp. 34–55.

and you will fear him less. Hate this conqueror of France in whose political slave camps thousands of distinguished Frenchmen suffer a corroding death in Africa and Cayenne. . . . Men of France! Strike once more for the Republic. Europe—America expects it of you. Strike! . . . America will ever welcome the men who fight for liberty."[22] And Sander's colleague in Spain, American Minister Pierre Soulé, was suspected by the French government of plotting to overthrow Napoleon's regime by violent means, even of seeking to encourage Napoleon's assassination. The fact that a public demonstration was held in New York City to honor two men who had tried to assassinate Napoleon III argued that Soulé's activities had the approbation of the American people if not the unspoken support of his government.[23]

Needless to say, Napoleon III and his ministers did not regard America as the lamplighter either of the Old or New Worlds. Empress Eugénie expressed concern too that if unchecked the Yankees would not only make the New World Republican but Protestant as well. The extraordinary aggressiveness of American missionaries who had tried to exclude French and Catholic influence from the Hawaiian Islands during the late 1820s had demonstrated to France the religious and cultural influences that would prevail under Yankeedom.[24]

Feeling deeply that American power and influence must somehow be contained, the French government moved in the 1850s to support that view. In Hawaii, for example, when it appeared that the American government would accept Hawaii's offer to be annexed, France joined in a naval demonstration with Britain in the fall of 1854 to indicate it would not permit this consummation. The French government hinted as early as 1853 that France would help Mexico, a continuing source of American-French conflict, stave off further American aggressions.[25] In Central America, where a future canal would surely be built, France

---

[22] Quoted in Blumenthal, *Reappraisal*, p. 28. Sanders' letter was dated October 4, 1854.
[23] *Ibid.*, p. 29.
[24] See Harold W. Bradley, *The American Frontier in Hawaii: The Pioneers, 1789–1843* (Stanford, 1942), p. 270, 311–319, 418–420, 461–462.
[25] P. N. Garber, *The Gadsden Treaty* (Philadelphia, 1923), p. 99. The French role in Mexico will be discussed more fully in the next chapter.

made it clear that she would help Nicaragua, considered a prime canal area, to resist American filibusters who threatened the integrity of that country.[26] Haiti and the Dominican Republic were troubled waters in which France found the fishing promising; the Dominican Congress even offered itself to France as a protectorate as the decade opened. American influence was at least more easily countered on this island (upon which French naval pressure could be applied) than in such contiguous areas as Mexico.

It was American territorial ambitions toward Cuba that most alarmed France during this decade. American acquisition of Cuba, so openly discussed in American newspapers, would have threatened French commercial and territorial interests in the Caribbean in a rather direct way. Filibusters from American ports, mainly New Orleans, kept France in constant fear that Cuba would come under direct American influence. Secretary of State Edward Everett's decisive rejection in December 1852 of an Anglo-French overture to guarantee jointly Cuba's neutrality, and the joint recommendation in 1854 (the Ostend Manifesto) of the American ministers to England, France, and Spain, that attempts be made to buy Cuba from Spain, that it be seized if Spain refused to sell and circumstances warranted, confirmed French suspicions of purposeful American ambitions toward Cuba. Together with Great Britain, France made it quite clear that annexation would not be permitted. Although France's position was annoying, particularly to Southerners who envisioned carving Cuba into several slave states, Secretary of State William L. Marcy, for one, took the long view. Like his predecessor, John Quincy Adams, Marcy apparently believed that some form of Cuban political association with America was inevitable. If France and England chose to block that association for the present, one could resent that action without being alarmed by it.[27]

Marcy's countrymen were not generally as philosophical as

---

[26] J. Fred Rippy, *The United States and Mexico* (New York, 1931), p. 199.
[27] Robert L. Scribner, "The Diplomacy of William L. Marcy, Secretary of State, 1853–1857." Unpublished Ph.D. dissertation, University of Virginia, 1949, pp. 199–209.

he. French power, once again, was being used to set boundaries to the growth of American commerce, influence, and territory. Those Americans who loved France (and there were many) and considered it their second home grew alarmed by the rising incidence of French-American disagreements in the 1850s. Although no truly explosive situation was on the horizon in 1860, few doubted that it would be difficult for either government to resist injuring the other if the opportunity and means came to hand. Controlled, if polite, hostility was the dominating tone of French-American relations as America stepped toward its most anguishing national experience, the War between the States.

CHAPTER V

Civil War Years

But listen to what I say: whatever we do, let us be tactful with the North. I have a great deal of respect for them since I have seen what they can do. . . . It is truly astounding what their navy has achieved in the last year through its resources and the valor of its men. We must be friends with this people, all the more because they very much want that and because we do not know where their bellicose mood might push them.

Henry Mercier, May 1862[1]

We are the natural protectors of the weaker republics on this continent, and we will have the will and the means, and we will very soon have the opportunity, of expelling all foreign pretensions to government in America. The unwise action of France will hasten this decision on our part; for not only must the French go out of Mexico, but we will not tolerate them on this continent at all.

New York Herald, August 4, 1863

ELIX GILBERT wrote a cogent essay some years ago describing how the courts of 18th-century Europe tried to reduce the guesswork in formulating foreign policy. "Schools" were created to train bright young men in the various ways of nation-states. Shrewd rulers themselves contributed to this study through essays or through *bon mots* that summarized the wisdom of experience. Out of this extended study emerged certain useful ideas: that nation-states have certain definable (and honorable) interests, ones that emerge from their history, their geography, the inclinations of their people, or the preferences of their monarchs. Other than in highly unusual circumstances, nations can

---

[1] Minister Mercier's observations were written to French Foreign Minister Édouard Thouvenel from Washington, D.C. on May 12, 1862. Quoted in Daniel B. Carroll, "Henri Mercier in Washington, 1860–1863," Unpublished Ph.D. dissertation, University of Pennsylvania, 1968, p. 310.

be depended upon to pursue those interests and to pursue them by fair means or foul. It is the wise monarch, therefore, who devotes thought not only to his own foreign policies but to the interests and policies of other nations as well. For an adequate understanding of another peoples' history and aspirations would point with some certainty to the policies which that nation was likely to pursue.[2]

Although Lincoln's Secretary of State, William E. Seward, found merit in the "doctrine of the interests of the states," by 1865 he could have written an advisory addendum to concerned students. His experiences with France and Napoleon III had shown that a visionary, misguided, and temperamental monarch could redirect a nation's policy away from its channel of "interest," involve it in unprofitable overseas adventures, and threaten his nation with a war which would destroy its merchant marine and gain the enmity of a powerful and rising people. But this was Seward's view, of course, and Napoleon III can be excused if he saw his actions and policies in a rather more favorable light.

Napoleon III believed in France. He understood the significance of its central geographical position in Europe, he appreciated France's power relative to most other nations of Europe, and he cherished the idea that French culture and values should be exported to nations less fortunate in their heritage and practices. Louis Napoleon was also enamored with the concept of progress, and with the idea that technologically and politically advanced peoples had an obligation to humanity to export their know-how to less developed nations. Louis' desire to prove himself worthy of the Bonaparte name, both in civilian and military matters, was likewise an element in his thinking, as was his desire to please his devoted Catholic spouse.

Louis had some reason to be pleased with himself and with France in 1860, the year when the "liberal phase" of his rule was inaugurated. France was casting a lengthened shadow over European affairs, a fact attested to by the selection of Paris for the peace conference ending the Crimean War. If his role in the Piedmontese-Austrian struggle over Italian unification re-

---

[2] Felix Gilbert, *To the Farewell Address: Ideas of Early American Foreign Policy* (Princeton, 1961), pp. 89–100.

vealed him as an adventuresome weakling, the power of France to say yea or nay to major European settlements was acknowledged even by France's enemies.[3]

France's expanding horizons were illustrated by the rising volume of French capital seeking profits outside the nation's boundaries, particularly in railway, canal, and mining ventures. France's physical presence had been established in Algiers by 1857; after the capture of Saigon in 1859, France annexed the three provinces of Cochin-China and established a protectorate over Cambodia. Earlier conquests included New Caledonia, occupied in 1853, plus Tahiti and the Ivory Coast, which had been added to the French empire before 1850. Expeditions were sent to Peking in 1859–1860 and to Syria in 1861, even as explorers were probing the mysteries of West Africa and new settlements were being established in Dahomey and the Guinea Coast. Although England continued her mastery of the seas and Prussian ambitions to play a larger share in Continental affairs lurked as a threat, the France of Napoleon III was nevertheless regarded by most Europeans as the power best able to disrupt Europe's status quo in 1860. France in 1860 was prosperous, well populated, expanding, technologically advanced, governed in a reasonably enlightened way, and exercising its traditional place of leadership in European affairs.

The American crisis in 1860 disturbed the French government and people but it certainly did not preoccupy them any more than France's war with Austria in 1858 engrossed Americans. As the southern states seceded and gave substance to the break by forming a rival government, France had two causes for regret. In a general way she had counted on the United States as a check to British power and ambitions in the Western Hemisphere; although France was now cooperating closely with Great Britain on developing free trade policies (Cobden Treaty, 1860), the principle nevertheless endured. Two American governments would inevitably complicate that situation. Second, in the initial flush of secession, it seemed obvious to most Frenchmen that the South's main concern was to protect slavery. It seemed highly

---

[3] A study that illuminates this period in French political history is J. M. Thompson, *Louis Napoleon and the Second Empire* (New York, 1955).

anachronistic that as other nations moved toward abolishing slavery or serfdom, in the "home of the free" a new government had been founded with slavery as its cornerstone. Precisely how this separation would affect French-American trading patterns was a matter for speculation, but France saw no immediate threat to her cotton supply in the separation—indeed, there might even be certain advantages for industrial France as she dickered with an agricultural South traditionally opposed to high tariffs.

Trade questions were the least of Abraham Lincoln's worries as he struggled to organize his administration and to minimize the number of seceding states. At his side as Secretary of State was William H. Seward, a politician of high standing within the Republican party and Lincoln's chief rival for the party's presidential nomination in 1860. Seward rather understandably felt the wrong man had gained the nomination, particularly since he knew the crisis called for abilities beyond the ken of a prairie lawyer. Seward initially perceived himself as the new administration's *eminence grise*. The Secretary's high opinion of himself was justified. After an uncertain beginning, he gained Lincoln's confidence even as he outraged the nations of Europe by his occasionally brusque and preemptory tones.

Two of Lincoln's and Seward's chief concerns in the days immediately following the inauguration were to keep the border states from seceding and to prevent foreign nations from giving permanence to the division of the states through some diplomatic initiative. Some politicians, such as Seward, even hoped that the seceded states might be wooed back into the Union. A national convention of right-minded men, Seward suggested, might be able to reverse the fatal trend toward disunion.

With an eye on possible diplomatic recognition being extended to the Confederacy either by France or Great Britain, and with his hopes for reunion still not crushed, Seward prepared a memorandum late in March 1861, entitled: "Thoughts for the President's Consideration." Most historians have written off this memorandum as the irresponsible action of an imaginative but naive Secretary of State. The memorandum was more than that. Seward hoped, in brief, to externalize the domestic crisis; to focus eyes north and south on the scheming nations of Europe rather than on the drama being played out at Fort Sumter,

South Carolina; and to distract the nation from its obsession with disunion. Fortunately for Seward's purpose, news arrived on March 30 that Spain had annexed San Domingo and, with France's blessing, would soon absorb Haiti as well.

In his memorandum, Seward advised Lincoln to "demand explanations from Spain and France, categorically, at once." If "satisfactory explanations are not received from Spain and France," the President should "convene Congress and declare war against them." The government should also "seek explanations from Great Britain and Russia [apparently about their policy if a civil war broke out] and send agents into Canada, Mexico, and Central America to rouse a vigorous continental spirit of independence on this continent against European intervention." To emphasize the seriousness of American purpose, all ports in the Gulf of Mexico should be reinforced and the navy recalled from all foreign stations.[4]

In retrospect, of course, Seward's plan was quite unworkable and highly dangerous. It was unworkable because the South was determined on secession and unwilling to rejoin the Union to fight foreign enemies; indeed the powers termed "enemies" by the Union government might soon prove to be the Confederacy's lifeline. And for the Lincoln government to have adopted such a grossly antagonistic policy in the midst of disunion and uncertain loyalties would assuredly have been madness. In the supercharged political atmosphere of Washington in early spring 1861, however, Seward's desperate expedient might have seemed rather sensible to many politicians who had run out of plans. Seward's scheme, which leaked in time to the diplomatic corps, provoked one fortunate aftermath. Diplomats warned their governments that Lincoln's chief advisor was a bold, vengeful, and probably reckless man; it behooved all to move cautiously in dealing with the United States government. If Seward accomplished nothing else with his memorandum, his effort was richly rewarded.

France and Great Britain stood by helplessly as the Union and the seven seceded states moved toward armed conflict. Lincoln's

---

[4] See Frederic Bancroft, *The Life of William H. Seward*, 2 vols. (New York, 1900), II, pp. 131–137.

decision to provision Fort Sumter, under confederate guns in the harbor of Charleston, angered the Confederate government and it determined to reduce the fort before new supplies arrived. Guns blazed on April 12–13. Lincoln immediately announced that a domestic insurrection had broken out, one too powerful for the ordinary armed forces of the nation to suppress, and on April 15 called for 75,000 volunteers to join the army. The Confederate government responded by speeding its defenses.

Partly in order to reduce international complications arising from the conflict, Lincoln decided to maintain that the war was a purely internal affair, that the Confederate government was not a government in any proper legal sense but only a group of willful men leading a temporarily powerful rebellion. But in its eagerness to sever the South from any external supplies, the Lincoln government misstepped. One week after the firing on Fort Sumter Lincoln proclaimed a maritime blockade of Confederate ports. Since a government exercising sovereignty over a territory does not need to blockade its own ports, the proclamation was a virtual announcement to the world that an extraordinary combination of power had now challenged the United States government and that the government felt itself compelled to take unusual measures to suppress the insurrection. Beyond this, the proclamation's international legal significance was startling. Through issuance of the proclamation, the Confederacy became a belligerent, entitled to all the rights of a belligerent in the international community; included were the rights to commission privateers and commerce destroyers and to float loans abroad. This new status certainly encouraged Confederate diplomats as they prepared to seek diplomatic recognition from foreign governments.

Not realizing the international significance of its blockade proclamation, the Lincoln government was astonished when the British government announced on May 6 that it would issue a proclamation of neutrality. Such an action was necessary if for no other reason than that British shippers must be warned of the Union blockade lest they be seized. This British proclamation had the effect of recognizing the belligerent status of the Confederacy and thus extending to it all the rights of a belligerent power. About a month later France followed with a similar pronouncement. These actions the Union government interpreted as hostile ones, an indication that France and Great Britain might welcome the splitting of the Union.

This interpretation was certainly a perverse one but was understandable in view of the circumstances. Napoleon III, for example, protested on several occasions early in the war that he sincerely regretted the breakup of the Union. France was a satisfied power and in need of no benefits that might accrue from a disruption of the United States. In many ways he found the United States attractive. It was dynamic, democratic, and moving rapidly into the industrial age—progress was its keynote. To one auditor he stated that after his visit to America in 1837 Europe struck him as being asleep. Napoleon was also impressed that this rising power must weigh increasingly heavy in the scales against British power. There is every reason, therefore, to accept as sincere the statement of Thouvenel, Napoleon's Minister of Foreign Affairs: "Our sentiments, in line with the traditional policy of France, brought us to regret profoundly the disagreements which split the United States. We consider ourselves to be interested in the integral maintenance of the North American Union, and we sincerely desire to see reestablished the harmony which has unfortunately been disturbed. Far from contributing to a deplorable separation, from which we can expect no advantage, we should like to be able to ward it off."[5] In keeping with these sincerely held views, Thouvenel was a model of diplomatic decorum, much less inclined than Napoleon III to take ill-considered steps vis-à-vis America.

Seward's initially incorrect assessment of Napoleon's unfriendly attitude toward the Lincoln government began to take on substance over time. Louis, for one, had a sportsman's attitude toward the underdog. Also, it seemed inconsistent for a ruler who had favored national self-determination for Poland, Italy, Nice, and Savoy to deny that the Confederacy was not in fact a nation, and one with overwhelming popular support. Jefferson Davis, as Chancellor of the Exchequer William E.

---

[5] Thouvenel to Mercier, Paris, April 25, 1861, in Lynn M. Case and Warren E. Spencer, *The United States and France: Civil War Diplomacy* (Philadelphia, 1970), p. 30.

Gladstone was to say in Newcastle on October 7, 1862, had "made a nation" and to this assertion Louis believed most honest men must give their assent.

As the war in America developed and as his thinking matured, Napoleon III was inclined to think increasingly of the American separation in world strategic terms. Despite France's alliance with Britain, Napoleon III was anxious to sponsor a revival of Latin influence and power to check the Anglo-Saxon ascendancy—large and growing—of Great Britain and the United States. In the Mediterranean, for example, he was trying to counter British dominance by establishing closer ties with the Latin countries of Spain, Italy, and Rumania, and with other nations such as Egypt, Greece, and Turkey. His net, too, was being drawn ever tighter around Algeria and French power was being augmented through a buildup of the Mediterranean fleet. In the Western Hemisphere an Anglo-Saxon advance into the Caribbean and into Central and South America seemed much less likely with the Union split. Why so? First, the immense resources of the industrial North could not be used to suborn formerly contiguous territorial governments. And it seemed likely that the driving wheel of Southern expansion would be stilled once the need for new slave states to maintain a balance of power within the Union had disappeared. American disunion could therefore be France's opportunity; developing a Latin sphere of influence in Central America, an old dream of Louis', now seemed within grasp.

There were other reasons, too, why Napoleon III found himself drawn toward the South. His courtiers were notably more sympathetic toward the southern, the gentlemanly and more cultured way of existence. This predisposition might have been neutralized if the Lincoln government had been free to emphasize that the war's central issue was slavery. But Napoleon III and France repeatedly heard that union was the issue; and it seemed regrettable to the Court that the aggressive and bumptious Yankees should be seeking to destroy a government led by cultured and worldly gentlemen.

There was much more concrete pressure acting directly upon Napoleon III than the undigested views of his courtiers. Economic dislocation with its resulting misery appeared very soon on the French scene following outbreak of the Civil War. At first glance the cotton situation seemed most threatening for in 1860 France purchased 93% of its cotton from the South. But even before war broke out in America, quarterly reports were submitted by the district attorneys (*procureurs généraux*) to the central government that reduced exports to America were causing problems.[6]

Three months later reports of reduced orders increased notably. Lyons industries complained more sharply about the silk trade. Limoges' district China industry was suffering a depression. Men were being discharged in the dying industries. Silk and ribbon factory employees were suffering a like fate. Glove industry workers in the Dijon district were threatened with massive unemployment. Their orders had all come from America, and not only were orders being countermanded by American producers but some deliveries were even being refused.[7] Thus Napoleon III's early desire to see reconciliation had substance, for he was made aware even before the explosion at Fort Sumter that France would suffer if normal trading patterns were disrupted. If France was forced to inaugurate public relief before the war began—and she was—an American civil war could be an extremely costly affair for France as well as for America. As head of state Napoleon III had the obligation to avoid, or to soften, these impending economic blows for France. With the Lincoln government in distress, and with the wedge of Confederate commissioners knocking on France's doors seeking diplomatic recognition, Napoleon III believed France was in a favorable position to bargain effectively with the Union government on trade and economic policy.

But France was, nevertheless, in a distressing position for most of her import trade with America had been in a Southern produced commodity—cotton. If Southern cotton became un-

---

[6] Lynn M. Case, *French Opinion on the United States and Mexico, 1860– 1867; Extracts from the Reports of the Procureurs Généraux.* (New York, 1936), pp. 9–10. The *procureurs généraux* were agents of the ministry of justice in the twenty-eight districts of Imperial Courts. In effect, they were public prosecutors but the government relied on them as well to submit reports on the public mood within their judicial district.

[7] Case and Spencer, *United States and France,* p. 32.

available to feed the sizable textile industry of France, the long-range domestic consequences for France seemed staggering. France's need for cotton was the major reason that France blanched upon announcement of the Northern blockade. It also accounts for the consistent pressure that France placed upon Seward to capture or scavenge for cotton and send it on to France at once. France's need for cotton, in one way or another, was behind the major thrusts of French diplomacy through 1863.

*　*　*　*　*

"Cotton is King!" In this short slogan one finds summarized the Confederacy's hope for diplomatic recognition, the factor that would guarantee its desire for independence and its future economic security. At first glance it did seem that the industrial nations of Europe must have Southern cotton or face ruin and starvation in their textile districts. It was difficult for knowledgable Confederates to believe that any nation would long suffer cotton starvation without taking every means within its power to acquire its customary and needed supply. If the South therefore were to play this diplomatic trump in a skillful way, the road to independence seemed certain and swift. For if the South simply withheld its cotton from the world's markets, a desperate Britain and France would soon find some means to stop the Civil War. And an aborted war would mean that the South could establish its independence.

Once war commenced a great cry went up throughout the South that the quickest way to end the war was to destroy or embargo cotton in order to create an artificial scarcity that would bring Europe to its knees. Frank Owsley has described in detail the evolution and implementation of this "embers and embargo" policy of the Confederacy. While the pyres were being lighted or the warehouses stuffed with cotton, Confederate diplomats began to prepare their approaches to the courts of Europe; diplomatic recognition of the Confederacy in exchange for cotton would be the primary bargain with other arrangements to follow.

While Seward blustered and threatened France and Great Britain with unfortunate consequences if they received the Confederate diplomats, Napoleon III and Touvenel were trying to evaluate the diplomatic and economic position of France. A prime consideration in their policy was that France should follow the lead of Great Britain on American affairs. If war were somehow to ensue with the Union, France would need British naval power to protect her navy and merchant marine from Union privateers and the Union navy. France's general desire to keep her young alliance with Great Britain in a healthy state also indicated that lockstep with British policy would be wise.

Napoleon III was consoled by the thought that while France was dependent upon American cotton, Great Britain needed it no less. Thus Britain would be responsive to the deteriorating French economic situation. Fortunately for both, no immediate step to challenge the Union blockade was necessary for at the outbreak of war the warehouses of Europe were bulging with at least a year's supply of cotton. France had time, therefore, to evaluate the situation in America. Perhaps the Union, or the Confederacy, would win an early and smashing victory and the war would end quickly. Perhaps the Northern blockade would be so ineffective as to be illegal; in that case the powers of Europe might be compelled to disregard the proclaimed blockade in the name of upholding international law. Or if the blockade was as ineffective as Confederate diplomats claimed, enough cotton could probably be smuggled from Southern ports to postpone indefinitely any need for decisive French action.

Europe's one-year cotton cushion proved a godsend to the Lincoln administration and a curse to the Davis government. France and Great Britain were given time to deliberate, to see how the American drama would develop, before economic pressures would force them to hard decisions. This situation exactly suited the Northern program, for the North needed time to marshall its tremendous resources in materials and manpower, time to organize and train an effective and offensive-minded army, and time to prove that its blockade of Southern ports was effective. The year and one half of "cotton grace" gave the Lincoln government an opportunity to make egregious blunders but to recover sufficiently by late 1862 so that the war's outcome was doubtful enough to make intervention by France or Great Britain a highly questionable action.

* * * * *

Although cotton was in good supply in Europe when the Civil War began, France and Great Britain still found it necessary to look ahead to the day when the supply would be exhausted. And cotton was not the only economic concern of the French government. Those commodities, such as silk, that France had exported to the United States over many decades became low demand items in the war situation. British industry was relatively quick to adjust to the needs of a war economy and therefore prospered during the Civil War. French industry was not as adaptable to those needs and thus found the slack created by its underpatronized industries not taken up by new enterprises.

The cotton industry does illustrate nicely, however, the economic difficulties for France that were exacerbated by the Civil War. As the result of a trade treaty with Great Britain in 1860, French manufacturers were given eighteen months in which to prepare to meet British competition in cotton manufactures. Great outlays of capital were necessary to purchase machinery that would make the French cotton industry roughly comparable technologically to Great Britain. At the very moment when French factory owners and supporting capitalists were striving to drum up the resources for capital improvements, the cotton market was shaken by the American conflict. Prices shot up two or three times over prewar value. Of course there were alternative sources of cotton such as India and Egypt. There was always cotton available in France throughout the war, but at exorbitant prices. India cotton, however, had quite different working qualities than did American cotton. Adjustments were therefore necessary even in the recently purchased machinery. Little wonder that the cotton manufacturers of France were discouraged, or that they pressured their government to help end the war. And it is also understandable why unemployment grew rapidly in the cotton manufacturing areas and remained high throughout the war.

New competition from sophisticated British plants, unstable cotton prices, and adjustments to different breeds of cotton all combined to depress the cotton industry.[8] It may be argued that American cotton was more crucial to Britain than to France, if for no other reason than that the British textile industry was much larger than France's; however, a case can be made that the Civil War had a more disruptive total effect on the economy of France. Napoleon III had economic reasons that extended far beyond French need for cotton to bring the Civil War to a stop.

Diplomacy during the Civil War finds all the actors concerned with economic issues in some central way. France saw the Civil War as potentially striking a devastating blow to her economy, yet she feared to threaten intervention lest a war end all trade with the North, ruin the French merchant marine, and cut France off from the bountiful supply of Northern wheat which a poor harvest made necessary in 1861. Britain shared some of the same needs and fears but Northern need for British loans and the products of British industry promised enough profit that Britain was not obliged to pursue a cotton diplomacy.

Confederate diplomacy was quite openly economic. France and Britain were promised cotton for industrial needs of the immediate future as well as a longterm low-tariff market for their finished goods. Once freed of Northern manufacturing interests, Confederate diplomats emphasized, industrial nations would have a prize low-tariff market in the nonindustrial South. Union diplomacy was much more direct and threatening. War would certainly follow, Seward repeatedly stated, if France or Britain extended diplomatic recognition to the Confederacy or if they took any other significant actions to aid the South in its struggle. Privateers would be unleashed to destroy their merchant marine and no interest of theirs in the Western Hemisphere would be safe. Lasting enmity would surely result. If, on the other hand, they withheld aid from the Confederacy they would gain the friendship of this wealthy and rising American giant. American

---

[8] An excellent brief description of the war's economic impact on France is David Pinkney, "France and the Civil War," in *Heard Round the World: the Impact Abroad of the Civil War*, Harold Hyman, Ed. (New York, 1969), pp. 97–144.

raw materials would be available to fuel their industries and the American market would welcome their finished products.

With Britain pursuing a cautious and correct policy and with the Union government taking a very positive, albeit occasionally belligerent stance, Napoleon III decided to move forward slowly. But move he did. In retrospect, he may be seen to have explored three approaches to bring the war to a close and thus to relieve the economic pressure on France. First, he investigated very carefully whether the Northern blockade of Confederate ports was effective. If it was not, France would at least have a pretext for initial intervention through nonrecognition of the blockade.

In the Declaration of Paris of 1856, the European nations had agreed that to be legal a blockade must be effective. The catch was in defining what constituted effectiveness. In practice an effective blockade is what foreign powers recognize as an effective blockade. Professor Frank Owsley in particular has vehemently argued that for at least a year the number of vessels slipping through the blockade was so numerous as to render it a farce.[9] But Owsley could have made his computations in quite a different way. If he had acknowledged that the Union concentrated on stopping ocean-going vessels engaged in the international trade, and that Southern ports capable of handling such vessels were in short supply, Union blockade capabilities could have been viewed as quite substantial. They were in fact substantial enough to play some part in Britain's decision not to challenge the blockade as illegal. And while Napoleon wondered about the easy British acceptance of the blockade, he was confronted with the fact that little American cotton was coming into Europe. In this instance, therefore, it seemed best to keep in step with Britain.

Napoleon's next move was to exert pressure on the Union government to relax the blockade so that France could obtain fresh cotton supplies. This request, first made in October 1861, was renewed following the *Trent* episode, an affair in which France had been helpful to the Union government. In early November 1861, Captain John Wilkes of the Union warship

---

[9] Frank L. Owsley, *King Cotton Diplomacy: Foreign Relations of the Confederate States of America* (Chicago, 1959), pp. 229–267.

San Jacinto, without authorization from his government, stopped a British mail steamer, the *Trent*, as it steamed through the Bahama channel. On board he found two Confederate diplomats, John M. Mason and John Slidell, who were on their way to Europe to seek recognition for the Confederacy. With little ceremony Wilkes seized the two diplomats and transferred them to the *San Jacinto*. Wilkes immediately became the talk of the Union and was toasted as a bold and imaginative man who had brought honor to a government still without a military victory. Dangerous and wily diplomats had been taken out of circulation and in style, for Great Britain had been made to eat dirt. Captain Wilkes, it seems, had fired two shots across the *Trent's* bow while making her heave-to. The old enemy of 1812, Union patriots cheered, was finally being given the same medicine she had dished out to Americans during the Wars of Napoleon!

If the Union had wanted war with Great Britain it need only have refused to release Mason and Slidell. It was an agonizing decision for the Lincoln government to release the diplomats and thereby admit that the capture had been illegal, particularly when most people rejoiced in the joint chastisement administered Great Britain and the Confederacy. It was at a crucial point in the deliberations that French Foreign Minister Thouvenel sent a message to the Union government on the *Trent* affair that was so sensible, logical, and tactful that it became much easier than expected for the Union government to release the prisoners. In essence the note pointed out that Wilkes' manner of seizure, the time of the seizure (the *Trent* was in transit between two neutral ports), and the seizure of noncombatant personnel on a neutral vessel violated maritime principles that America had ardently defended in past decades and to which she was committed by treaty. "We believe," Thouvenel concluded, "we are giving proof of our loyal friendship to the cabinet of Washington" by giving this counsel and by urging the Union government to hand over Mason and Slidell.[10]

---

[10] Thouvenel to Mercier, Paris, Dec. 3, 1861, in Case and Spencer, *United States and France*, p. 104. Case and Spencer argue that evidence indicates Mason and Slidell were part of a diplomatic trap skillfully constructed by the Confederate government.

Thouvenel's letter, printed shortly after the *Trent* affair, made it clear how misguided and foolish the Lincoln government would have been to defy Britain. France's advice was therefore the advice of a friendly nation, one interested in helping the Union government to avoid a fateful misstep. When France returned to her earlier request that the Union blockade be lifted, temporarily at least, Lincoln and Seward could not lightly wave the request aside. What the Union government did was to open the ports of Beaufort, Port Royal, and New Orleans to French traffic, ports that had fallen under Union control. Seward had asked France to withdraw its recognition of the Confederacy as a belligerent in exchange for this favor, but France declined.

It is fortunate that France did decline for she found the Union favor worthless. Through firsthand experience, France learned that the Confederate government was withholding all cotton from the market as a means to expedite her diplomacy. The Confederate embargo and not the Northern blockade was therefore the source of an impending cotton famine. Whereas Seward thought he was demonstrating Southern perfidy, Napoleon III learned quite a different lesson in this episode: that France would only gain free access to cotton when the war stopped. This perception, which gradually found its way into policy, headed France in a direction that placed her on a collision course with the Union government.

If the war had taken a decisive turn fairly early and some end had been promised, Napoleon III would have been less likely to have thought in mediatory terms. But from Washington his diplomatic representative, Henri Mercier, was advising him how unlikely it was that a region as enormous as the South, with its manpower resources, interior lines of communication, high determination, and capable military leadership could be subdued by the Union. Battlefield reports in the early months of the war made it uncertain which power would ultimately prevail. What seemed likely in 1862 was that the war could drag on for a very long time, inflicting death and destruction on America and economic misery or recession on an observing France and England.

By mid-July 1862, as reports began to stream into Paris of mounting distress in the various industrial centers of France, Thouvenel was weighing joint Anglo-French mediation of the war. If mediation failed, he felt full diplomatic recognition should be extended to the Confederacy. Even as Napoleon III was sounding British support for the decisive step of joint recognition, events in America were rapidly pushing British foreign minister Lord Russell along the same path. The savage Seven Days' Battle (June 25–July 1) and the Second Battle of Bull Run (August 29–30) seemed to offset the earlier Northern capture of New Orleans (April 1862) and to indicate that the Americans were caught up in some infernal machine that only the nations of Europe could stop. In mid-September 1862, therefore, Palmerston and Russell agreed that joint Anglo-French mediation must be placed on the agenda, that it would be mediation on the basis of a separation, and if mediation failed, as Russell said, "we ought ourselves to recognize the Southern States as an independent State."[11]

However, Russell cautioned that another military contest was in the offing and that prudence dictated waiting its outcome. That crucial battle took place at Antietam Creek, Maryland, in late September. Never was the South so close to success as in that month; one last smile from Mars would probably have tripped Anglo-French mediation and the consequent diplomatic recognition of the Confederacy. Robert E. Lee's invasion was halted once again, demonstrating the staying power of the North. Napoleon III would still have found intervention entirely acceptable but Palmerston's cabinet cooled so quickly toward intervention that by late October only two members were willing to press ahead.

Announcement of the Emancipation Proclamation directly following Antietam was an interesting stroke on the part of the Union government though even liberal sentiment in France was puzzled how to receive the news. Was Emancipation merely a sign of the Union's desperation, an attempt to provoke a slave insurrection in the South? Or was it the first in a series of enlightened measures that would free the black man in America? Whichever was true, a celebration was hardly in order since the

---

[11] Russell to Palmerston, Gotha, September 17, 1862, in Spencer Walpole, *The Life of Lord John Russell*, 2 vols. (London, 1891), II, p. 361. Palmerston's agreement follows on pp. 361–362.

only slaves liberated were those under the jurisdiction of the Confederacy.

Reports of the *procureurs généraux* through 1862 make clear the rising pressures on Napoleon III to take action that would relieve area economic distress. Napoleon III paid particularly close attention to public opinion for, as one historian has observed, Napoleon "ruled the nation by no legal right of succession. . . . Napoleon's title and his authority rested only on force and on the sanction of popular endorsement by plebiscites."[12] Public distress and expressed discontents were therefore of real concern to him. Thus he was not content merely to follow the lead of Great Britain on the mediation question. Drouyn de Lhuys, his foreign minister, newly appointed in October 1862, was instructed to invite Russia and Great Britain to join France in a mediation offer to the Union and Confederacy. Although the French feeler was politely but quickly rejected by Seward, Napoleon III's move had at least strengthened his hand before the bar of public opinion, important to him particularly because of pending French elections early in 1863.

Just before the elections Napoleon III tried one last time to stop the war through conventional diplomacy. On his own, he offered the good offices of France to negotiate a conference between the North and South. At this conference the two parties would negotiate whether union or separation would be their destiny, even as the two armies continued to fight. In all likelihood such a conference would have raised hopes for peace so high that resuming the war in earnest would have been most difficult. Lincoln and Seward therefore saw the proposal as a virtual plan for disunion and rejected it with gracious murmurings for the concern of the Emperor about American affairs.

Although the French government won the elections in 1863 by a substantial majority, opposition opinion was much better represented in the new legislature than in the old. And economic distress continued to mount. Britain apparently was going to do nothing, she with her gross money bags and an opportunistic people who somehow managed to manufacture fortunes from

---

[12] Pinkney, *Heard Round the World*, p. 100.

every throat-slitting situation around the world! Yet Napoleon III felt that France dare not confront the Union alone no matter how badly France needed Southern cotton; by 1863 France needed cheap quality cotton acutely. He had suggested joint, triple, and unilateral mediation, all of which had been rejected by potential colleagues or by the Union government. What then remained to do?

Southern diplomatic agents were naturally grieved that Napoleon III had not moved from recognition of Southern belligerency to extending the Confederacy full diplomatic recognition. Nevertheless, they did suggest intermediate steps that sounded attractive to Napoleon III and to which he gave his support. John Slidell, for example, working through the House of Erlanger and Company, Frankfort, received the Emperor's permission to list Confederate bonds on the French bourse. The bonds, to be redeemable in Southern cotton at any Southern port six months after the reestablishment of peace, were also listed in London, Amsterdam, and Frankfort on March 19, 1863. European subscribers to the bonds gained not only an interest in peace but a peace in which Southern contracts would be honored. The loan, however, was a dismal financial failure with the Confederacy realizing only a fraction of its hopes. Yet Napoleon III had indicated that he was not averse to helping the Confederacy with positive steps.

One pressing need of the Confederacy was for commerce-destroying vessels, the instrument by which Northern commerce could be smashed. Lacking ship-building facilities of its own, the Confederacy had managed to have swift vessels built *sub rosa* in England. Three of those destroyers, the *Florida*, the *Shenandoah*, and the *Alabama*, accounted for sixty Union ships burned, sunk, or incapacitated. American shipping suffered acutely from these attacks, so much so that a real war crisis loomed with Great Britain unless she prevented these ships from escaping to the high seas. In March 1863 Congress even authorized the President to commission Union privateers, a threatening gesture at Great Britain since the Confederacy had no merchant vessels upon which to prey. Between March and mid-September 1863, the British finally took firm measures to stop the escape of any more commerce destroyers or the more deadly ironclad steam warships (rams) which could easily have smashed the Union blockade.

Even as British-American relations were approaching a crisis over this issue, M. Arman, France's largest shipbuilder, a member of the *corps legislatif*, and a confidant of Napoleon III, approached John Slidell early in January 1863 and offered to assist the Confederacy in its shipbuilding program. After obtaining permission from Eugène Rouher, Minister of the Marine, a contract was signed. Arman would build four corvettes (wooden cruisers) for the Confederacy. Six months later the French government even agreed that the cruisers could be armed. Arman even went so far as to contract to build two ironclad rams for the Confederacy. In time Bravay and Company of Paris, secretly acting as an agent for the Confederacy, even arranged to purchase the rams built by the Laird shipyards of Great Britain, the very rams that had brought on the war crisis between the Union and England. Although Napoleon III may not have known the details of each negotiation, they certainly had his blessing. It was Napoleon III himself who first suggested to Slidell in October 1862 that the Confederacy might buy ships built in France under the pretense that they were intended for the Italian government.

Napoleon III was playing a very dangerous, high-stakes game when he gave his sanction to these unneutral activities. He left himself a way out, however, for he had made it clear that if the shipbuilding activity were discovered he would divorce the government from it at once. As it turned out, he was unlucky. John Bigelow, American consul-general in France, was approached by a clerk, "Mr. X," who offered to transmit papers showing the government's collusion in the Confederate shipbuilding program. For 15,000 francs Bigelow and Minister William L. Dayton were given all the evidence they needed to prove positively that a vast conspiracy to build ships for the Confederacy was underway and that Napoleon III had sanctioned the project. What surprised them both was that the Foreign Minister, Drouyn de Lhuys, knew nothing of the covert plan and sharply disapproved of it.

Lincoln and Seward were naturally enraged at this perfidy of the Emperor. Article three of the French Declaration of Neutrality of June 10, 1861, clearly read: "It is forbidden to any Frenchman to take orders from either party to arm ships-of-war, or to accept letters-of-marque for privateering, or to concur in any manner in the equipment or armament of a ship-of-war or corsair, of either party." France's self-imposed neutrality obligation was pretty clear and Seward intended that France honor its commitments or face very disagreeable, punitive consequences. Knowing how slippery the Emperor was and, from experience with England, how many ways there were for ships to make their way into Confederate hands, Seward first instructed Minister Dayton to inform the French government that the Union government considered France's success in preventing the vessels from going to sea a test of friendship.[13]

For months the negotiations dragged on. Finally, all the implicated vessels were apparently disposed of to Prussia and Denmark. Union pressure on the French government mounted to the degree that Napoleon III finally called in M. Arman and promised him faithfully that unless all the vessels were *bona fide* disposed of to neutral governments, Arman would find himself behind prison bars. Seven days after this interview, Dayton told de Lhuys (on June 8, 1864) that if any of the vessels escaped "the exasperation would be such that the [United States] Government if so disposed (which I did not intimate it would be) could scarcely keep the peace between the two countries."[14] That such stern warnings were necessary demonstrates how attached Napoleon III was to the project and how far he was prepared to go to help the Confederacy establish its independence. Obviously, he had moved a long way from the sympathy he had first expressed for an enduring Union.

* * * * *

Perhaps the major reason for Napoleon III's change of heart can be summed up in one word: Mexico. Over a number of

---

[13] John Bigelow, *France and the Confederate Navy, 1862–1868: An International Episode* (New York, 1888), pp. 28–36.
[14] Quoted in Owsley, *King Cotton Diplomacy*, p. 426.

years Mexico became in part to France what Viet Nam became to the United States—a distant intervention carried on against the firm objection of a nearby power, an intervention pursued in the face of an apathetic or hostile local populace, a campaign that aroused domestic hostility to the government, an enterprise in which the national honor seemingly forbade a hasty withdrawal, and one where advisors deceived the government about local conditions. Both projects were approached with high hopes and worthy intentions; both recessionals were played against the background of recriminations and charges of bad faith.

Mexico had seemed to Napoleon III an outstanding opportunity where enterprise and West European know-how could put a poor, revolution-wracked country on the road to rapid improvement. Mexican émigrés at the French court continually whispered in his ear how the people of Mexico longed for stability, for a monarchy that would give authority and energy to the government domestically and dignity to its foreign relations. Napoleon III was aware as well that a strengthened Mexico could serve to contain the overflowing ambitions of American expansionists; what better time to move into Mexico than when America was absorbed with domestic problems. Mexico might even prove suitable for cotton growing. France would then have a reliable satellite as its cotton supplier.

Other reasons were less persuasive but played their part in inching Napoleon toward intervention. His wife Eugenie, for example, cherished an opportunity to preserve the Spanish culture of her ancestors against the Anglo-Saxons and to advance the cause of Roman Catholicism against the forces of agnostic republicanism, led in Mexico by Benito Juárez. Napoleon III needed some way to appease domestic Catholics, particularly after his intervention in the Italian unification movement had led to the Papacy's being stripped of certain prized territories. Another problem that might be eased by a Mexican intervention was his promise of 1858, made to Count Camillo Bensi di Cavour of Piedmont, that he would help Piedmont acquire Venetia as part of a new North Italian kingdom. Napoleon had betrayed his promise in 1859 when war with Austria had given him an opportunity to detach Venetia from Austria. But, thought Napoleon III, if he found a throne for the idle Ferdinand Maximilian, a younger brother of Emperor Francis Joseph, perhaps in gratitude Austria would consider releasing Venetia to Piedmont. Piedmont would be gratified, Austria somewhat compensated for her territorial loss, and Napoleon III freed of an embarrassing commitment.

Fortunately for Napoleon III, excuses for intervention in Mexico, torn by civil war between 1857 and 1860, came rather easily to hand. Mexican debts to foreign creditors piled up; Mexico promised to pay but could not. Mexico seemed unable to pay even the interest on her debts, an indication how low her fortunes had sunk. Just to make certain that Mexico would not escape his intentions, Dubois de Saligny, the French minister to Mexico, was instructed to make French claims against Mexico so excessive that Mexico would refuse to recognize the claims as valid.[15] France could then work up considerable public indignation as it prepared to intervene in Mexico.

Great Britain and Spain sympathized with France's general deprecation of conditions in Mexico and shared her conviction that Mexicans would only pay their debts when made to sniff gunpowder. Lincoln and Seward also sympathized with the powers but urged less severe solutions than intervention upon the Europeans. Seward even suggested that the United States negotiate a loan treaty with Mexico that would obligate the United States to pay 3 per cent interest per annum on the funded debt of Mexico, a debt Seward estimated at $62,000,000. The loan would be made retroactive to July 17, 1861, when Mexico suspended payment of its funded debt to foreign creditors for two years. All America would ask as security was a mortgage on the public lands and mineral rights of Lower California, Chihuahua, Sonora, and Sinalon! Under this plan, Seward argued, foreign powers would be spared a troublesome intervention, their creditors and bondholders would receive some minimum satisfaction, Mexico would be given a few years to stabilize the government, and Mexico would be placed under the benevolent protection of the American union.

---

[15] Carl H. Bock, *Prelude to Tragedy: The Negotiation and Breakdown of the Triparte Convention of London, October 31, 1861* (Philadelphia, 1966), p. 447.

France was more hostile to the plan than either Great Britain or Spain, seeing in the American plan an end to her ambitions. England and Spain agreed with France that the situation in Mexico was intolerable, that unilateral American intervention must not be allowed, and that some form of customs collection intervention was fully justified. America could hardly object to so mild a plan for even President Buchanan had asked authorization from Congress in 1859 to send a military force into Mexico to obtain "indemnity for the past and security for the future." So in October 1861 representatives of Spain, France, and Britain signed the Convention of London providing for a joint military expedition to collect the defaulted debts from Mexico. The United States was invited to sign the Convention, after it had been negotiated, but Seward demurred. Seward was anxious, however, that each signatory to the Convention be faithful to its pledge not to seek any "peculiar advantage" through the expedition.

Great Britain had the same concern having gained some early inkling of the Emperor's ambitions. While the Union and Confederacy necessarily watched from the sidelines, the intervention proceeded. The script pleased no one. Great Britain was disgusted by France's unseemly behavior toward the Juárez regime in seeking out grievances that would justify an intervention beyond the Mexican coastal areas. Spain was disappointed in the weakness of Mexico's conservative forces, which were unable to rally despite the encouragement received from the intervening powers. France grew discouraged with Britain's and Spain's determination to refuse her help in bringing down the Juárez government, instead adhering to the announced purposes of the intervention. Tensions among the cooperating powers quickly developed, tensions so severe that Britain and Spain decided to suspend the Convention of London and to abandon the intervention. Napoleon III became alarmed that French ambitions were so quickly bared and by his associates' warnings that Mexico was a quagmire more likely to suffocate than to exalt France.[16]

---

[16] Bock, *Prelude to Tragedy*, pp. 216–54, presents an excellent study of the opening phases of France's Mexican intervention.

What should Napoleon III do? To press ahead would likely gain considerable advantages, both long- and short-range in nature. To withdraw would not only forfeit those advantages but would also bring humiliation on himself and France. Napoleon III had made approaches to Maximilian even before the Convention of London had been signed and to a certain degree the honor of France had been pledged in the Mexican enterprise. The American Union was frowning, to be sure, but its future power and freedom of action was at best problematical. Storm warnings were up everywhere and public opinion was not enthusiastic, but could a descendant of the great Bonaparte scuttle the project when only a few Mexican banditos openly opposed his plans? Such were some of the considerations being weighed by Napoleon III when a military setback firmed up his decision to press on. On May 5, 1862 the rag-tag forces of Juárez soundly defeated a French army before Puebla. Only the deposition of Juárez could ease this humiliation. *L'honneur*, if nothing else, urged Napoleon III and his forces on to Mexico City. They formally occupied it in June 1863.

One step led to another. By French prearrangement a cooperative Assembly of Notables (composed mostly of priests and other political reactionaries) met and voted to offer the throne of Mexico to Ferdinand Maximilian, Napoleon III's hand-picked choice. E. C. Corti has described in detail why the offer was attractive to Maximilian, the role of his ambitious wife Carlotta, who desired much for her husband and the title of Empress for herself, and Maximilian's preparations for assumption of the newly created throne. Although by all accounts Maximilian was not overly endowed with intelligence, he did have enough sense to bind France to his cause through treaty, at least until 1867. In April 1864, six months after he had been invited to ascend the throne, Maximilian accepted the call. Carlotta's grandmother urged him to reconsider. This exiled former Queen of France repeatedly warned Maximilian, "They will murder you."[17] But like his mentor Napoleon III, Maximilian decided to believe what he wished to be true. Maximilian believed that while the Mexi-

---

[17] E. C. Corti, *Maximilian and Charlotte of Mexico*, 2 vols. (New York, 1928), I, p. 332.

can people were not at present overly enthusiastic about his position, his just and enlightened rule would soon convert and transform compliance into cooperation.

From the American side of the Atlantic the Mexican venture aroused quite divergent hopes and fears. To the Confederacy, France's intervention in Mexico was not entirely unwelcome. If Napoleon III's anxiety to establish the success of intervention could be parlayed into French diplomatic recognition of the Confederacy, a great *coup* would be scored. Confederate agents did in fact offer to support the intervention if France paid the right price but the Confederate approaches came as Southern military power was waning. Napoleon III was not willing to exchange recognition and all its potentially disastrous consequences for France for a mess of Southern pottage.

Washington's view of France's Mexican intervention was less than dim. France was flagrantly violating Monroe's dictum and subduing a sister nation's struggle to establish a viable republican government in order to establish a monarchy. This entire enterprise was being conducted by a nation that professed friendship for the United States but which took crude advantage of the American death struggle. Even worse, the French government repeatedly tried to mislead the Union government into believing that it had no ambition beyond the collection of honest debts. Such actions, and the accompanying lies of the French government were cause for considerable indignation in Congress, in the executive, and throughout the Union.

Seward shared that indignation, but unlike many hot-tempered newspaper editors he tried to keep a set of rational priorities before him. To threaten France, perhaps provoking her into recognition of the Confederacy, or to arouse European sympathy for France by adopting belligerent gestures, might hazard the first priority—winning the Civil War. Union diplomacy therefore played an elaborate game with France. All assurances that France had no far-reaching ambitions were accepted as good-faith statements, even when the context of events proved their hypocrisy. Seward never mentioned the Monroe Doctrine, for although it had some credit in America, its principles were considered quite absurd and pretentious in France. Even when the announcement of the invitation to Maximilian unmasked French ambitions, Seward reacted with a rather mild statement. He reminded France that in Mexico "the inherent normal opinion . . . favors a government . . . republican in form and domestic in its organization, in preference to any monarchial institution to be imposed from abroad." Seward even prophesied "that foreign resistance, or attempts to control American civilization must and will fail. . . ." Despite the measured tones of Seward's argument, the message came through very plainly that a continental French presence in Mexico, despite mutual good wishes, would almost inevitably lead to a French-American collision.[18]

Congress was not nearly as patient as Seward. Senator James McDougall of California introduced a series of resolutions in January 1864 which stated it was America's duty to demand that French troops evacuate Mexico and to expel them if they did not comply. Senator Charles Sumner commanded enough influence to have the McDougall resolutions laid on the table but he could do little to prevent unanimous passage of a stern resolution in the House of Representatives, introduced by Henry Winter Davis, chairman of the Committee on Foreign Relations. It was resolved: "That the Congress of the United States are unwilling by silence to have the nations of the world under the impression that they are indifferent spectators of the deplorable events now transpiring in the republic of Mexico; and that they therefore think fit to declare that it does not accord with the policy of the United States to acknowledge any monarchial government, erected on the ruins of any republican government in America, under the auspices of any European power."[19] This was not the language of a patient power. France was duly impressed that serious consequences lay not too far into the future.

Henry Winter Davis' resolution appeared to threaten Seward's well-orchestrated policy of slowly increasing pressure against France. "Do you bring us peace, or bring us war?" Drouyn de Lhuys queried Dayton shortly after news of the Davis resolution

---

[18] George W. Mallory, "The United States and the French Intervention in Mexico, 1861–1867," Unpublished Ph.D. dissertation, University of California, Berkeley, 1938, pp. 74–75.

[19] 38 Congress, 1 session, *Congressional Globe*, April 4, 1864.

reached Paris.[20] Dayton was able to assure Lhuys that the Union government's position remained unchanged; it was neutral toward the Mexican embroglio, it still recognized the Juárez regime as Mexico's *de jure* government, and it hoped France would continue to assess its position and possibilities in Mexico. In the background, nevertheless, was the spectre of a powerful, experienced, and well-equipped Union army that might soon be free to pursue foreign adventures. There was even a rumor making the rounds that the North and South would bring their conflict to an end in a common activity that would reunite heart and hand: booting the French out of Mexico. In June 1864 Vice-President Andrew Johnson was indiscreet enough to harangue an enthusiastic Nashville audience about the impending fate of France in Mexico: "The day of reckoning is approaching. It will not be long before the Rebellion is put down. . . . And then we will attend to this Mexican affair, and say to Louis Napoleon, 'You cannot found a monarchy on this Continent.' (Great applause) An expedition into Mexico would be a sort of recreation to the brave soldiers who are now fighting the battles of the Union, and the French concern would be quickly wiped out."[21]

When General Robert E. Lee surrendered to the forces of Ulysses S. Grant early in April 1865, the Union government immediately had room to maneuver on Mexican affairs. A firm course toward France would certainly receive united support from a divided people. Napoleon III had managed to make both sections feel he had betrayed their interests which was, to a limited extent, quite true. Seward's tone toward the French government now began to rise in shrillness. What Seward wanted from France, he now emphasized, was a definite date when all French troops would be withdrawn from Mexico; until he received a schedule of withdrawal, the screws would continue to turn.

France did not miss the significance of Seward sending General John Schofield to Paris on a special peace mission in November 1865. Schofield was a confidant of Ulysses S. Grant, a known

---

[20] Mallory, "United States and French Intervention in Mexico," p. 198.
[21] Speech of June 10, 1864, quoted in Dexter Perkins, *The Monroe Doctrine, 1826–1867* (Baltimore, 1933), p. 471.

proponent of intervention in Mexico, and was himself a believer that a little expedition into Mexico would be a fine way to inaugurate the postwar era. Seward explained in a nutshell what he expected of Schofield: "I want you to get your legs under Napoleon's mahogany and tell him he must get out of Mexico."[22] Through normal diplomatic channels Seward sent the same message. On February 12, 1866 he asked in very short tones for "definitive information of the time when French military operations may be expected to cease in Mexico."[23]

After their own Korean and Viet Nam experiences, contemporary Americans should find it easy to sympathize with the Emperor's predicament and to admit his courage in the face of severely conflicting pressures. There were many reasons for withdrawal and he did not shrink unduly from recognizing them. American power was a factor in his decision, but the Emperor found it difficult to believe that Americans were eager for combat after their recent bloodletting. In this judgment he was probably correct. Just as serious and disconcerting was the failure of Maximilian to rally sufficient support to maintain his throne; the extent of his authority corresponded rather precisely to the areas controlled by French troops. Juárez's guerilla forces could neither be annihilated nor bought off. So Maximilian's future looked rather bleak even if France continued its support beyond the treaty date of 1867. Too, Napoleon III was cognizant that a throne held up by bayonets would never have the vitality to block American expansionism or to provide the order and sense of well-being that would help to modernize Mexico and make it a valuable trading partner of France.

Events in Europe also argued for withdrawal from Mexico. Partly because of his involvement with Maximilian, Napoleon III was unable to exert much influence when Prussia and Austria went to war with Denmark in 1864 and quickly deprived Denmark of the duchies of Schleswig and Holstein. Otto von Bismarck, named prime minister and foreign minister of Prussia in 1862, was also maneuvering in 1865 and 1866 to provoke a war

---

[22] J. M. Schofield, *Forty-Six Years in the Army* (New York, 1897), p. 385.
[23] Seward to Montholon, February 12, 1866, *House Executive Documents*, 39 Congress, No. 93, p. 34.

with Austria. Bismarck believed the war necessary to unify Germany in such a way that Prussian leadership would dominate any German confederation. Napoleon III miscalculated badly when he assumed that a Prussian-Austrian war would be a standoff and that France might step in to mediate and exact her price. Even before the war started he promised Austria that France would remain neutral. Austria promised in return to cede Venetia to Piedmont, whatever the war's outcome. This promise naturally relieved pressure on Napoleon III to support Maximilian, for he had originally chosen a Hapsburg as Mexican emperor partly to induce Austria to cede Venetia to Piedmont. But Napoleon III's pledge to remain neutral in the coming contest was a doubtful piece of statecraft. Austria was thoroughly trounced and forced to accept humbling terms in the Treaty of Prague (August 1866). Prussia gained a treaty right to organize a new federal constitution for Germany north of the Main; this would parallel an association of southern German states "with an independent international existence." Modern Germany was thus in the making. And France, rather than playing some lead part in events so portentous for her future, seemed paralyzed by the rapidness of change and the political wizardry of Bismarck.

Public opinion in France was another factor in Napoleon III's decision to withdraw from Mexico. From the first there was no strong support at large for Napoleon III's New World adventure. And as the project grew more risky and costly, opinion swung decisively against a continuation. Besides the venture's consequences for France's European diplomacy, the public objected on the ground that America was being needlessly alienated. Napoleon III had made the error of not explaining his higher purposes in Mexico to the public at an early date. Once the intervention became pock-marked with failure, the public was in no mood to listen. No disquisition on "containment" or platitudes on the duty of the advanced to help the underdeveloped nations would have found a receptive audience; failure closes the public's ears even to a politician's most constructive visions.

Much like his decision to enter Mexico, Napoleon III's decision to withdraw was based on a number of important factors. The arguments for withdrawal were finally so compelling as to be irresistible. Napoleon still hoped to make his troop withdrawal gradual enough to give Maximilian adequate time to organize the government and to firm up its shaky support base. Even here Napoleon III was unfortunate for Maximilian did not possess the political wisdom necessary to put together some minimally satisfactory programs and government. So while Napoleon III continued to bring home the troops—the last leaving Mexico in the spring of 1867—he left with the assurance that he had built on sand. Mexico became a personal humiliation for Napoleon III. When the persistent but politically blind Maximilian was shot on June 19, 1867 by the followers of Benito Juárez, the French public was reinforced in its opinion that the Emperor's political judgment was deteriorating. Mexico was not only a defeat for Napoleon III but a large nail in his political coffin as well.

Reverses for one nation have a way of being a triumph for another. Dexter Perkins, the foremost historian of the Monroe Doctrine, has stated that French withdrawal from Mexico under intense American pressure "marks a great and vital step in the affirmation of the principles of 1823."[24] France's setback was America's gain, at least in immediate terms. Taking a longer view of the incident, it served to alert France that American power was no longer "potential," that the United States was an international actor who would soon be center stage. The relationship could never again be the same. American power was in its adolescence, but even so it was awesome and France would do well not to ignore it.

Perhaps France's Mexican adventure should not be viewed so much a humiliation as a lesson in the political education both of France and America. America learned not only that its power on the world scene was now respectable and respected, but also that power is often best used in restrained ways. Seward, keeping in mind the consequences President Andrew Jackson reaped when he tried to bully France, was cautious but firm with France. Acting in this way he avoided wounding the pride of a sensitive and notably proud people, yet achieved the purposes of his government. France learned something about the cost of New World interventions of such magnitude, and something of the

---

[24] Dexter Perkins, *A History of the Monroe Doctrine* (Boston, 1963), p. 138.

growing role which the United States would now play in the Western Hemisphere and in the world at large.

* * * * *

The Civil War years to 1867 were unfortunate ones in French-American relations. It would be easy to blame Napoleon III for everything that went wrong but this would be unfair. World power relationships were changing in these years. Too, the American Civil War presented legal, financial, and domestic problems to the statesmen of France and Great Britain that were complex and without satisfactory solutions. If most Americans were angry with the French government in 1865 or 1867, they were no less angry with Great Britain. Napoleon III's intervention in Mexico was an added complication in French-American relations, but both governments acted according to what they perceived to be in their best interests. In carrying out their policies they acted with restraint and within the bounds of rationality.

There were other reasons why these difficult years left no permanent scars upon French-American relations. First must certainly be the great outpouring of French sympathy when Abraham Lincoln was assassinated. Lincoln had taken on new dimensions in French eyes during the war. His suffering, his steadiness of judgment, his steps toward emancipating the black man, and his desire to inaugurate a mild reconstruction program for the South recommended him to Frenchmen as a warm-hearted man with mellow wisdom. Consequently, the expressions of French regret upon his assassination were full and sincere. Mingled tears of two peoples sharing a common sorrow was a healing experience. Lincoln in death helped to demonstrate the shared values and perspectives of the transatlantic civilization.

Although the Union newspaper press might excoriate the policies of the French government, it informed its readers that the "enlightened" portions of the French public stood solidly with the Union. Alexis de Tocqueville, Victor Hugo, and Alphonse Guizot were names immediately recognized by literate

Americans and were part of the Union's phalanx of defenders. Edouard de Laboulaye, professor of comparative law in the Collège de France and author of a history of the United States, wrote newspaper articles favorable to the North, some so persuasive that John Bigelow had them published as pamphlets and distributed among the French oligarchy. Also friendly to the Union were Charles de Montalembert and Jean Lacordaire, liberal Catholic leaders who saw much to admire in America's church-state relationship; Augustin Cochin, editor of the Catholic journal, *Le Correspondent*; and Agénor de Gasparin, a leading Protestant layman and former deputy during days of the July Monarchy. This impressive band was convinced that a quick end to American slavery was only possible with a Union victory. They also were persuaded that the cause of republicanism, and liberty, both in America and in the Old World, was somehow intertwined with the survival of the American Union.

Although many Northerners realized that French liberal support for the Union constituted a veiled attack on the French political system, Northerners did not welcome it less enthusiastically. Any support was welcome. Americans also believed that their experiences and ideals should be a lamp to the darkened political shores of Europe. If enlightened sentiment in Europe could take advantage of America's adversity to shake Napoleon III's throne, America could congratulate itself for continuing its self-annointed role as world emancipator. And the articulation of liberal sentiment in Napoleonic France gave hope for the future that one day both nations would be republics able to share some common destiny.

CHAPTER VI

Emergence of Common Interests
1867-1913

> . . . the real estimate formed by the mass of intelligent men and
> women of each people as to the character of the other is not shaped
> by the scandalmongers of either. The understanding of each country
> by the other has steadily gained in clarity for the last fifty years,
> thanks to the candor and goodwill of the intelligent observers on
> one part and on the other. Such observers certainly are not blind to
> differences or to faults and shortcomings, but neither do they ignore
> the convincing evidence of many sound traits common to both peo-
> ple, many essential aims of a high character pursued by both, and
> forming the basis of a secure and valuable friendship between them.
>
> *New York Times*, 1912[1]

I T HAS BEEN TRADITIONAL to view American-French relations
from 1867 to the First World War as quiet and somewhat
insignificant years. There were no wars between them nor were
there even any severe quarrels.

Yet these were momentous years for America and France.
For America these decades marked its entrance into the select
circle of Great Powers. For France, these were unhappy years,
years in which she met military defeat, faced the threat of a
united and powerful Germany and struggled to devise a workable Republican government. Because they did not have serious
and directly clashing interests, America and France were seldom
concerned primarily with one another. Yet there was enough
friction, enough chances for reevaluation, and enough movement in the world of diplomacy to reorient them toward each
other in a more significant way. In the midst of their own internal disturbances and of international power realignments,

---

[1] Monday, May 20, 1912, p. 8. "Our Latest French Critic."

France and America found they had many common interests. In this era a foundation was laid for an American-French rapprochement that would survive two world wars and beyond.

France, of course, had to make the most severe adjustments, for her initial reaction to America in the period prior to 1900 was that America was the uninvited guest at the table of the Powers. And the Guest was often quite unmannerly, demanding a share of the feast without due regard to the desires of the hosts or to the established order of things. France knew the Guest was rightly there, but it was an annoyance to concentrate occasionally on American problems when Germany, who had recently joined the table, was jockeying Great Britain for the head chair. Germany was necessarily the focus of interest for France because her power was so astonishing and because her manners were so abominable. Japan, too, through an economic *tour-de-force* had edged into the charmed circle of the World Powers, making it clear that the European powers had a new competitor for the bounties of trade and influence in East Asia. France sensed that America would not immediately be a major threat to her interests but just how America would interact with the other Powers, old and new, did not become clear until well after 1900.

*   *   *   *   *

Immediately after the Civil War and through the crisis over Mexico, American-French relations were badly strained. To Napoleon III's government it appeared that a permanent barrier to good relations had been erected through Louis' wrong guesses and unwise commitments. Sampling of American opinion by French ministers, duly forwarded home, certainly indicated that American contempt for Louis was a popular passion. Louis' character, his ambitions, and his vices were mocked by many an editorial pen. And Louis received precious little credit in America for his measures to liberalize the regime; his every concession to liberal opinion stirred American hopes that France would one day throw off the yoke of Napoleonic authoritarianism and put on the mantle of enlightened Republicanism. Only then could

French sins of the past be forgotten and American and French destinies be intertwined in a complementary way. Removal of Napoleon III, then, by death or deposition, seemed to be one change necessary for the establishment of American-French relations on a reasonably cordial basis.

American desires to see Louis removed were soon fulfilled but in a way that distressed many Francophiles. Most Americans, including the minister to France, Elihu B. Washburne, were amazed when France declared war on Germany on July 19, 1870 following a dispute over who was (or rather, who was not) to occupy the throne of Spain. There had been discussion of this matter since the Spanish revolution in 1868 and the abdication of Queen Isabella. Various candidates were considered but the dispute did not become dangerous until Otto von Bismarck-Schonhausen, Chancellor of Germany, decided to push the candidacy of Prince Leopold of Hohenzollern-Sigmaringen, a distant relative of King Wilhelm of Prussia and presumably a person who would be sympathetic to German interests. Bismarck was apparently convinced that France would object to this German encirclement, would protest vehemently and perhaps even embrace the war that Bismarck needed to frighten the South German states into joining the German Union. Through astute management of a reluctant King Wilhelm and through careful editing of a dispatch that made it appear Wilhelm had insulted the French ambassador, Bismarck provoked the French government into a declaration of war.[2]

Events that followed constitute one of the most humiliating moments in French history. In rather short order, the Emperor himself was captured at the Battle of Sedan (September 1), a blow that toppled him. Two days later, a Parisian mob invaded the Palais Bourbon and compelled the Legislative Assembly to proclaim the end of empire. Revolutionary ritual was then followed and a republic proclaimed at the Hotel de Ville following the organization of a provisional government. This new government had a truly formidable task: to win a war already clearly

---

[2] On background to the war see William H. Dawson, *The German Empire, 1867–1914 and the Unity Movement*, 2 vols. (Hamden, 1966), I, pp. 288–341.

lost. Paris was soon under siege by two German armies and although fresh troops were being raised in the provinces to carry on the struggle, Paris was forced to capitulate on January 28, 1871 after a bitter four-month siege.

The National Assembly that met at Bordeaux in February elected Adolphe Thiers chief of the executive power and then waited to hear from him terms on which Germany would make peace. Bismarck's terms were hard but France was under the German boot; by a vote of 546 to 107 the French agreed to the cession of Alsace, a part of Lorraine, and to the payment of a 5,000,000,000 franc indemnity. Some twenty days after the Treaty of Frankfort was signed (May 10), Paris rose in revolt. Humiliated by the peace, angered by the marching of German troops through Paris, and alarmed that the Assembly was unfriendly to the Republic, Parisians determined to organize a government in keeping with Republican principles and one that was properly patriotic. Thiers reacted by sending in troops to crush this Paris government by Commune (municipal council); Paris put up a desperate but futile resistance, capped by Bloody Week (May 21–28, 1871) massacres that astonished a watching world. The Parisian rebellion was crushed but the hatreds engendered by this internal upheaval helped to create a realistic atmosphere, one where German terms could be met calmly and steps taken to establish a government that would command substantial support.

The American role in this time of French agony was not a large one. It first appeared that France had provoked the war by being unreasonably aggressive with Germany about the Hohenzollern candidacy; nations who seek wars, after all, must be prepared to pay the consequences of unforeseen defeats. This was certainly the view of President Ulysses S. Grant, a man whose observations of French plotting in Mexico had convinced him that France was aggressive, untrustworthy, and in need of a sound chastising. France thus paid the price, in American support, for Napoleon III's Mexican intrigue and his earlier pusillanimous conduct during the Civil War. Also, Germany's cause seemed a rather appealing one, a factor in spiking American support for France. At least it was appealing to those Americans who thought a united Germany served the cause of nation-state making and enlightened nationalism.[3] Grant and other administration officials remembered with considerable gratitude the contributions of German-American troops in the Union cause, a factor predisposing them toward sympathy with Germany.

Some shift in public opinion did occur as the thoroughness of France's defeat aroused America's traditional sympathy for the underdog. Deposition of the Emperor and French flirtations with a republic quickly convinced many Americans that they might have been premature in acclaiming German victories. The French government hoped to use this changing American opinion to France's benefit, but President Grant and Secretary of State Hamilton Fish had decided that America would stay strictly neutral in this conflict; this the American government did. Partly because Minister Elihu B. Washburne stuck by his Parisian post through its various trials, even looking after German interests for the duration of the conflict, the French government decided that America might make a useful intermediary with Germany to help bring the war to an end. When Foreign Minister Jules Faure officially asked the American government on September 8 to join other powers in mediation efforts, Secretary Fish saw some advantage for America in playing the role of peacemaker. American prestige, for one, would be notably enhanced in a mediatory role. Beyond this a conclusion of the war would re-open the channels of French-American trade, encourage European capital to seek out investments in America once again, and make possible the sale of United States government bonds within the European financial community. But the German government did not welcome efforts to end the war prematurely, a fact which prodded Grant to resolve that America must avoid mediation diplomacy unless approached by both France and Germany. This position, which the French interpreted as neutrality with a vengeance, was largely followed as well by European nations whose stake in the peace of Europe was superficially greater than America's. France thus found herself friendless in both the Old

---

[3] Allan Nevins, *Hamilton Fish: The Inner History of the Grant Administration* (New York, 1957), pp. 400–402.

World and the New World and quite unprepared to counter either Prussian arms or diplomacy.[4]

While the terms of the German *diktat* seemed harsh to France, by a strange twist they contributed to the gradual improvement of French-American relations. Although many Americans cheered for the victorious Germans, the harshness of the victor's peace terms provoked a reorientation of French diplomacy that ultimately pointed to the need for amicable transatlantic ties. How did this happen? The conclusion of the Franco-German War left France angry and bitter, determined to rectify her mutilated eastern boundary when the opportunity arose. The most stable factor in the world of European diplomacy from 1871 to 1914 became the Franco-German feud; it was one fixed point upon which statesmen could count or on which alliances could be constructed.

This hatred meant that France had to design primarily a Continental diplomacy; no dispute outside Europe could be pursued to the point where France's chances for *ravanche* would be mortally damaged; no powerful nation must be permanently alienated lest it aid Germany in the coming showdown. Friends must be wooed so that France would never again find herself diplomatically isolated as she had in 1871. Although this new superstructure of French foreign policy had no immediate impact on French-American relations, its implications were quite clear, particularly as American power continued to grow at an astonishing rate. In the Western Hemisphere, for example, France listened with growing attentiveness to American wishes. Certainly no interest of France was worth a war with this assertive colossus. As American ambitions and power expanded, expressed through construction of the new navy in the 1880s, France increasingly found it the better part of wisdom not to rag the Yankee. The Franco-German War, if not the Maximilian episode, largely buried the old French policy of trying to contain American influence.

---

[4] *Ibid.*, pp. 406, 409. In his diary for October 21, 1870, Fish recorded President Grant's "opinion that France, having without provocation entered upon the war with a scarcely concealed intention to dispossess Prussia of a portion of her territory, could not complain, and was not entitled to sympathy if the result of the war deprived her of a portion of her own territory."

*   *   *   *   *

American determination to exercise a beneficent hegemony over the Western Hemisphere was well-rooted by 1870. Of course the national conscience would not permit so bald an assertion of ambition. A resort to code words was therefore necessary. "Two spheres," "Manifest Destiny," "right of self-determination," "defending Republicanism," and "preserving the Monroe Doctrine" were some of the slogans used at various times to justify policies that served to advance American hemispheric ambitions. If European governments often found American rhetoric hypocritical and sophomoric, they nevertheless recognized that the gap between American ambitions and means was narrowing quickly. European relations with the United States within the Hemisphere would then depend on what kind of hegemony America intended to exercise. If a general attack was to be launched on European trade in Latin America and if European colonies and bases were to be forced out, then troubled days lay ahead with America.

It was obviously in the interests of European nations that American hemispheric policy develop in a constructive way, that is, with America pursuing its own ambitions yet respectful of others' rights to trade and to maintain their historic hemispheric prerogatives. This policy had certain obvious internal tensions but it was realizable since European stakes in the Western Hemisphere were generally not the kind over which wars were fought —at least not if all parties remained reasonable. Great Britain, who sensed even better than France the need to "domesticate" America's policies and ambitions, took the lead in presenting a reasonable front to American wishes for the Hemisphere. Others, including France, followed the British lead. Accommodation to American wishes thus became the overriding hemispheric policy of the powers in the latter part of the nineteenth century although many painful episodes ensued before this policy seemed equally wise to all.

Perhaps the best illustration of this new policy coordination is seen in the episodes relating to the building of a transoceanic canal. Dreams of constructing a canal extended as far back as the fifteenth century but as the technology became available, plans for a canal multiplied quickly. Eliminating seven thousand miles from an ocean voyage made sense to the dullest sea captain or merchant; and as American trade and territorial interests extended into the Pacific, the probable necessity to transfer the fleet to different theatres, and to do it quickly, made an oceanic canal attractive to the American government. It was obvious to all powers that a canal would immediately become an important link in the ocean's commercial highways and therefore of strategic importance as well. It was also obvious that whoever controlled the canal would be in a powerful position to woo hemispheric trade and to exercise political influence in the entire Caribbean area. Considerations of trade, strategy, prestige, and political influence therefore made the canal question a weighty one, particularly to a power with ambitions as large as America's.

American politicians were first sensitized to the canal issue through negotiations with Great Britain resulting in the Clayton-Bulwer Treaty of 1850. In this treaty the parties agreed to cooperate in making possible construction of an Isthmian canal and promised never to fortify or exercise an exclusive control over it. As time passed, the treaty came under increasing criticism from Americans because of the self-denying stipulations.[5]

French-American interaction over the canal began in 1878 when Lucien Napoleon-Bonaparte Wyse gained a ninety-nine year concession from the Colombian government for construction of a canal through the Panama region. On behalf of his company, the Société Civile Internationale du Canal Interocéanique du Davién, Wyse signed the Salgar-Wyse contract with Colombia, an agreement that immediately alarmed the American government. Wyse and the French government repeatedly reassured Secretary of State William Evarts that America had absolutely no basis for its anxiety. This project was purely a private one; the French government had not been consulted about the project, nor would it be. Risks and liabilities were to

---

[5] Despite several American initiatives, the Clayton-Bulwer Treaty was not superseded until November 1901, when the second Hay-Pauncefote Treaty was signed. The latter treaty gave the United States the right to build and control an interoceanic canal. See A. E. Campbell, *Great Britain and the United States, 1895–1903* (London, 1960), pp. 48–70.

be assumed entirely by the Société. In no way, officially or unofficially, would the French government lend the project its support.

Evarts and President Rutherford B. Hayes thought the French government protested too much. When Wyse consulted Evarts about sending American delegates to a great engineering congress in Paris to consider the problems related to canal building (and to drum up publicity for the project), he found Evarts notably cool. President Hayes made his government's position on general plan rather plain when he emphasized to the Congress in March 1880 that the proposed canal would be "virtually a part of the coast line of the United States" and that "the policy of this country is a canal under American control."[6] Congressmen not only nodded their heads in assent but also put both Houses on record within the year as formally protesting a canal built by foreign capital. Nevertheless, Evarts consented to send American delegates to the interoceanic canal conference but with no power to commit their government.

As expected, the conference of 136 delegates was controlled by the large French contingent. Key decisions were made, namely that a sea canal was practical and that Ferdinand de Lesseps, the aged but still spry supervising engineer for construction of the Suez Canal, should head the project. Monies were to be raised by public subscription and the financing was to be international, though undoubtedly the project would most strongly attract French investors.

De Lesseps himself came to America to negate American objections and to seek out American money. He traveled from coast to coast speaking at public banquets and even testified before the House Interoceanic Ship Canal Committee pleading for the Panama project. A Comité Américain was formed in order to rally domestic influence and money behind Panama. Secretary of the Navy Richard W. Thompson accepted its chairmanship at a salary of $25,000 per annum. Thompson's salary was miniscule compared to the total sum the American Committee expended; between 1881 and 1889 it spent about $2,400,000 to "promote" the canal and to buy goodwill.

---

[6] Richardson, *Messages of the Presidents*, VII, pp. 585–586.

Work on the canal actually began in January 1880. President Hayes' blast followed two months later, a bad omen for the Company's ambitions. Fortunately for the preservation of French-American amity, the plagues that harried the canal project led to its collapse in 1889; disease, extravagance, technical incompetence, mismanagement, and the plan itself for a sea level canal all proved part of the canal's undoing. Tremendous scandals in France accompanied collapse of the Company, disgracing high personages, abolishing private fortunes and ruining professional reputations. A multitude of investors lost over $300,000,000. The widespread effects of the Company's failure seemed even to threaten the Republic itself. To repair part of the damage the French government considered a guarantee of the Company's bonds. This potential direct intrusion by the French government into the canal business, a step it had repeatedly assured the American government would not be taken, so alarmed the United States Senate that by resolution it declared "the Government of the United States will look with serious concern and disapproval upon any connection of any European Government with the construction or control of any ship-canal across the Isthmus of Darien or across Central America, and must regard any such connection or control as injurious to the just rights and interests of the United States and as a menace to their welfare."[7] Although the resolution did not pass the House of Representatives, President Benjamin Harrison made it clear that he supported the principle it stated.

While this rather threatening statement was widely resented in France, it served the cause of Gallic-American friendship. It is difficult to imagine any more certain way to have interjected continual quarrels and crises into French-American relations than to have had the interoceanic canal fall into French hands. Even if the canal had been owned and operated by a nongovernment corporation, national monies and large French national interests would have compelled the government to take an active

---

[7] 50th Congress, 2nd Session, *Congressional Record*, XX, p. 338 (December 19, 1888). A satisfactory account of the canal story is found in Gerstle Mack, *The Land Divided: A History of the Panama Canal and Other Isthmian Canal Projects* (New York, 1944).

role in shaping corporation policy. In retrospect it is puzzling why the French government allowed the project to continue so long. Of course the French press had been corrupted by company money, a practice common in France, and key politicians had also received favors for their support. Too, American power was not yet properly appreciated in France so that the unfavorable odds on a canal gamble were not as obvious as they would have been even fifteen years later. Everything considered, the French canal project was alluring in the short run but ominous, if successful, for future French-American relations.

Other French-American contacts in the Western Hemisphere were less serious potentially but all pointed consistently toward a diminished European role. Venezuela, for example, raised the large question about how far the United States would permit European nations to press their claims against a hemispheric power. As early as 1850 Venezuela owed considerable sums to French, British, Spanish, German, Dutch, and American creditors. France was not content to be just another creditor, however, and in 1864 persuaded Venezuela to sign a convention setting aside 10% of Venezuela's customs receipts to reimburse French banks and promising France first priority in debt repayment. Other creditors naturally complained but France held Venezuela to the convention under threat of breaking diplomatic relations. In March 1881 matters took a turn for the worse. The French Chargé at Caracas withdrew in the wake of news that French warships would soon arrive to underline for Venezuela the importance France laid upon keeping contractual obligations.

Through skillful negotiation by Secretary of State James G. Blaine and because French Premier Leon Gambetta was willing to compromise, America and France reached an agreement on the Venezuelan debt issue late in 1881.[8] Successive administrations continued to be puzzled by the complexity of this issue. If the United States stood by, allowing American republics to be threatened and possibly punished by European governments,

---

[8] See U.S. *Foreign Relations, 1881*, pp. 1126–1128; 1191–1198; *1883*, pp. 364–369.

was not the Monroe Doctrine being effectively undermined? On the other hand, to warn off creditor nations who had a legitimate basis for action in international practice would hardly be serving the cause of justice nor would it motivate hemispheric governments to act in a fiscally responsible way. The experience with France over the Venezuelan debt was thus an early warning to the United States about the burdens of seeking hemispheric hegemony and a harbinger of the Roosevelt Corollary to the Monroe Doctrine. Further trouble with Venezuela in 1902 and the Dominican Republic in 1904 led directly to enunciation of the Roosevelt Corollary:

Chronic wrongdoing . . . may in America, as elsewhere, ultimately require intervention by some civilized nation, and in the Western Hemisphere the adherence of the United States to the Monroe Doctrine may force the United States, however reluctantly in flagrant cases of such wrongdoing or impotence, to the exercise of an international police power.

France's Venezuelan problems in the 1880s thus raised questions that were only answered with President Roosevelt standing the Monroe Doctrine on its head. If the French winced at the logic used to justify the Roosevelt Corollary—that in order to uphold the Monroe Doctrine and protect hemispheric neighbors from European intrusion, the United States itself would intervene— they recognized it as the virtual announcement of an American hegemony.

Another problem area of French-American relations in the hemisphere was Haiti, a country with a long history of close ties to France. Concessions made to France late in the 1870s strengthened French influence even further, enough at least to concern succeeding American administrations. Haitian trade was naturally of interest to Americans but Haiti's proximity to a possible isthmian canal considerably enhanced her importance. If America was ultimately to acquire a canal, the approaches to the canal must be either in friendly or harmless hands.

This line of thinking began to crystallize in the events following a Haitian revolt in March 1883. The revolt spread, climaxing in uncontrollable rioting in Port-au-Prince late in September. After issuing an ultimatum, France, Britain, and Spain landed troops to restore order. President Lysius Salamon, who was quite convinced that the revolt was British inspired, turned to his northern neighbor to bail him out. Salamon offered to cede Môle St. Nicholas or Tortuga, prime naval bases, to the United States in return for cash, two warships, two gunboats, a guarantee of Haitian independence, and a pledge of American good offices in Haitian disputes with foreign nations. President Chester A. Arthur and Secretary of State Frederick J. Frelinghuysen declined the offer, probably with reluctance and after the matter had been discussed by the Cabinet. Rumors that Haiti then turned to France with a similar offer visibly alarmed Frelinghuysen and revealed how carefully the administration had weighed the Haitian situation. The American minister in Paris was twice instructed to inquire at the Quai d'Orsay if the rumors were founded in fact. American fears were only quieted after the foreign minister vowed that France had no intention of making so serious a *faux pax* as challenging the Monroe Doctrine.[9] Administration concern that France not acquire a naval base in Haiti served to warn France that she might gain less advantage from a completed canal than she first supposed.

In common with other European governments, France had to be reminded many times that she must structure her hemispheric policies within the context of her relations with the United States. In the mid-1890s, for example, Grover Cleveland's administration stepped in to help restore broken Venezuelan-French relations, a situation brought about by alleged insults made by the French minister against the Venezuelan government. About this same time France became embroiled in a dispute with Brazil over 155,000 square miles of Brazil's territory, an area claimed by France but one not really interesting to her until gold was discovered in 1894–1895. Fighting broke out in May 1895 when France decided to occupy this important area, important not only because of the gold but also because it controlled the northern estuary of the Amazon River. Through the American minister in London, France was warned to go slowly, that the United States was watching the situation carefully and

[9] David M. Pletcher, *The Awkward Years: American Foreign Relations Under Garfield and Arthur* (Columbia, 1962), pp. 133–136.

would not allow any hemispheric state to "become an element in European politics."[10]

Potentially more serious was the mid-1890s crisis in Santo Domingo. America's position in Santo Domingo was well established through the Santo Domingo Improvement Company, a corporation organized by influential bankers to purchase Santo Domingo's debt. The corporation had then taken control of the nation's customs houses and proceeded to rationalize the debt. France was particularly irritated by these arrangements for they had been made largely at the expense of French interests. France chose to demonstrate its irritation following the murder of a French citizen in November 1884 and the consequent reluctance of the Santo Domingo government to pay France reparations. After some brief negotiations France delivered an ultimatum that the customs houses must guarantee a reparation payment of 400,000 francs, execute the murderer and agree to submit all matters in dispute to arbitration by the Spanish government. The ultimatum was underlined by sending a French squadron to Santo Domingo. The American government felt such strong-arm tactics were uncalled for, particularly when United States interests were directly involved. An American ship was quickly dispatched to the scene, a rather plain warning to France that such actions were no longer considered in good taste when exercised in the Western Hemisphere. On the diplomatic side, President Cleveland and Secretary of State Walter Q. Gresham offered American good offices to resolve the crisis. Fortunately the dispute was soon adjusted and the incident closed.[11]

America's rather definite responses to French hemispheric initiatives in the 1880s and 1890s presented a coherent message to France. Whether defending the Monroe Doctrine, keeping a weather eye on French naval activities in the hemisphere, or aiding American business firms in competition with European

---

[10] Thomas F. Bayard to Secretary of State Olney, October 25, 1895, cited in Walter LaFeber, *The New Empire: An Interpretation of American Expansion, 1860–1898* (Ithaca, 1963), p. 247.

[11] Summer Welles, *Naboth's Vineyard: The Dominican Republic, 1844–1924*, 2 vols. (New York, 1928), II, pp. 497–508, 556–559; *Foreign Relations, 1895*, I, pp. 397–402.

merchants, the United States obviously regarded the Western Hemisphere as her prime area of interest, a sphere that it intended to dominate. American naval power in the 1870s and 1880s could not give substance to this growing determination but rapid buildup of the American fleet made hemispheric adventures much more risky for European powers in the 1890s. American assertiveness rose in rough proportion to the increase in her navy. France was surprised but hardly shocked when the United States took an extremely belligerent attitude toward Great Britain in 1895 and 1896, telling Britain that she must settle her boundary dispute with Venezuela through arbitration or the United States itself would undertake to draw the appropriate boundary line. In the midst of the negotiations Secretary of State Richard Olney, not a belligerent man, had asserted that the "United States is practically sovereign on this continent and its fiat is law upon the subjects to which it confines its interposition. Why? . . . It is because, in addition to all other grounds, its infinite resources combined with its isolated position render it master of the situation and practically invulnerable as against any or all other powers."[12] Olney's statement was full of braggadocio, ungracious and undiplomatic; the kernel of truth, however, was a sizable one.

John Bull soon found it expedient to yield Uncle Sam his pretensions, a lesson not lost on other European powers. France, generally an apt pupil of international relations, saw her impressions of increasing American assertiveness rather sharply reinforced by this well-publicized British-American crisis. Acknowledging this development and liking it, however, were two different matters. Echoes of "the American peril" were still heard in France, an indication that French statesmen had not yet determined whether America would most likely be friend or foe in the new lineup of powers. Pending some signal France thought it reasonable that American ambitions not go unchecked any more than those other *arrivistés*, Germany and Japan, and should not be permitted to bully those nearest them.

America's aggressiveness and penchant for kicking a power

---

[12] Olney's note to Ambassador Bayard, Washington, July 20, 1895, is found in *Foreign Relations, 1895, I,* pp. 545–562.

when it was occupied or down seemed to France perfectly illustrated in the Spanish-American crisis of the 1890s. Cuba was
Spain's possession, France felt, and if rebels chose to disturb the
peace, destroy property, and generally upset the economic and
social life of the island, Spain must take all reasonable measures
to subdue the insurrection. Every great colonial power had those
problems from time to time. Patience and pressure would in time
work to subdue the rebels and to restore tranquillity to the
island. American sympathy for the rebels, it appeared to France,
made Spain's task doubly difficult and insured continuing bloodshed in Cuba. Since America was encouraging the rebels by
various means, some open and some covert, France suspected
that the United States was playing international troublemaker.
As time passed and America showered demands upon Spain to
restore peace in Cuba, France concluded that America had decided to play the part of a bully and despoiler of a nation too
weak to resist effectively. For many Frenchmen, including royal-
ists, ultramontane Catholics, and believers in the civilizing mission of empire, America's role in denuding Spain of Cuba was
a very sordid one indeed.

These judgments were not altogether fair and at least some
Frenchmen came, in time, to understand more fully how the
crisis over Cuba developed. American investment in Cuba, some
$50,000,000 when the island revolt broke out in 1895, was
threatened by the insurrectionary fire that Spain seemed unable
to quench. Yankee property, in fact, became a prime target for
insurrecto torches, their hope being that America would intervene to protect American property. In the crisis of intervention the Spanish yoke would be forever smashed. Spain was
puzzled how to proceed against the guerillas, finding, as the
United States was soon to discover in the Philippines, that eliminating resistance is not a simple matter of sending in apparently
overwhelming armed strength. Spain needed time to cope with
the uprising—time, wisdom, and new methods.

President William McKinley certainly wanted peace, of that
few historians have doubt. But he also wanted the Cuban situation resolved in such a way that the suffering be stopped and
tranquillity restored. In addition, he wanted these things to be

done within a reasonable time. He also believed that the Spanish government must take the initiative in dealing with the rebels' demands. As McKinley's policy emerged many Americans thought him the very picture of pusillanimity and obsequiousness, a contemptible weak-kneed pacifist who was afraid to exert "American principles" only ninety miles from American shores. As events developed, and particularly crucial was the unexplained destruction of the battleship *Maine* in Havana's harbor on February 15, 1898, it is difficult to resist the conclusion of historian Richard Hofstadter that the American public moved beyond a mere desire to free Cuba; the deep desire of many seemed to be a *war* to free Cuba.

From the Spanish viewpoint President McKinley was being quite unreasonable. First, the American government was making outrageous demands on the Spanish government in an internal matter—for this was how Cuba was so regarded in Spain. As Spain would not presume to lecture the American government on how best to incorporate the blacks into the national life, so courtesy, if nothing else, should have stopped American interference with Cuba. If America truly wished to restore peace in Cuba, Spanish officials emphasized, let her stop the constant gunrunning from her shores into Cuba, for this activity kept the rebels well supplied in arms. Were American investments in Cuba being damaged or destroyed? Investors must remember that they took chances in sending money abroad.

It seemed to Spain that America had it in her power to stop the insurrection simply by refusing to meddle. If McKinley ultimately found himself boxed in by a bellicose and unreasonable Congress and public, the Spanish government was in a no less difficult position. Yet not to heed American advice at all invited disaster, as her friend France repeatedly warned. But to accede to American pressure without exploring other avenues would be dishonorable to the Queen and disgraceful for Spain. Spain decided that her best course was to keep calm, to continue tinkering with the situation in hopes that the rebels would quiet down, and to call on the powers of Europe to help her persuade the United States that its policy amounted to unwarranted interference in the internal affairs of a friendly nation.

It was to France that Spain turned most consistently in this crisis. The French government, and particularly foreign minister Gabriel Hanotaux, believed Spain's cause was just. Spain under threat in the Western Hemisphere in a sense represented all European hemispheric interests that could be placed in jeopardy by the United States. Yet there were other factors to consider before approaching the Powers to coordinate their protests. If France took the lead in gaining support for a *demarche*, what would be the impact upon French-American relations? France needed to keep in mind that Spain was a decrepit power whose friendship would count for little, whereas American enmity might ultimately be very costly for France. Second, Russia was well-disposed toward the United States. Should France risk angering her newly-won ally (1893) by asking it to take part in a *demarche* against the United States for a cause that was apparently peripheral to Russian interests? French investments in Spanish bonds might also have directed the Quai d'Orsay to desire peace for Spain, as would France's desire to maintain her trade both with America and Spain. France had also to consider whether a joint *demarche* would be effective; to protest, to have that protest ignored, and then to be unprepared to take retaliatory action against the United States argued that French prestige would be better preserved simply by silence. And France could certainly not be drawn into military action on behalf of Spain since she was approaching the Fashoda incident (with a belligerent and determined Great Britain) over the mission of French Captain Marchand to the Nile River, a challenge to British imperial ambitions that provoked a grave crisis in the summer of 1898.

Also to be weighed in the scales would be the probable unfavorable reaction within France if she confronted America on behalf of Spain. France in 1898 was experiencing one of the Third Republic's most trying moments. On January 13 Émile Zola published an open letter to the President of the Republic accusing members of the general staff of practicing deception and fraud in the conviction of Captain Alfred Dreyfus (1894), a Jewish officer whose case had come to symbolize the struggle within France over the permanence of the Republic. If France dared to confront the United States on behalf of Spain, the

Dreyfusards would likely make the American cause their own with incalculable consequences to the government.[13]

French efforts on behalf of Spain were, therefore, hardly likely to be vigorous or attenuated. Nor were they. After extensive consultation among the powers, with France taking the lead, an anemic collective note was presented to the American government by France, Italy, Germany, Austria-Hungary, and Russia asking that Spanish-American negotiations be continued for the sake of peace. Although French ambassador Jules Cambon hoped that presentation of the note inaugurated an era when the nations of Europe would be willing to face down the United States, Kaiser Wilhelm II of Germany opined that "the Americans [do] not care a straw about our collective notes."[14] Both Cambon and the Kaiser were wrong, Cambon because no power was willing to risk threatening America, and the Kaiser in assessing the American attitude; the American government cared very much not to appear the New World bully. European intervention, however, was too timid and too late; moreover, the Powers' note was quite irrelevant to America's domestic situation. The *New York World* summarized the American mood early in April 1898: "Stop the nonsense! Stop the trifling, let us have peace even at the muzzle of our guns."[15]

When war came on April 25 the French government declared itself a strict neutral, a position that it honored throughout the conflict. Opinion within France and within the government itself naturally enough was not neutral. There was widespread sympathy for Spain's plight at large and a hope within the government that for Spain's sake the war would terminate quickly. Also, American naval strength, particularly after Admiral

---

[13] A well-written account of the Dreyfus affair is found in Barbara W. Tuchman, *The Proud Tower: A Portrait of the World Before the War, 1890–1914* (New York, 1963), pp. 196–263. Ernest May's *Imperial Democracy: The Emergence of America as a Great Power* (New York, 1961), is the best general analysis of European reactions to the American-Spanish crisis.

[14] German reaction to the war is analyzed in L. B. Shippee, "Germany and the Spanish-American War," *American Historical Review*, XXX (July, 1925), pp. 754–777.

[15] April 11, 1896, 6:2.

Dewey's smashing victory over the Spanish fleet at Manila Bay, stimulated new French fears about the "American peril." Now that the giant had burst its hemispheric bonds and demonstrated its power in East Asia, where would America's footsteps be heard next? French officials became convinced that statesmanship and international order itself called for a quick end to the war.

Partly because of its strict neutrality during the war, France's good offices were acceptable both to Spain and America to expedite the arrangements for peace. After Jules Cambon signed the armistice protocol on behalf of Spain on August 12, the belligerents decided that Paris was the most suitable site for drawing up the final terms of peace, a decided compliment to the French government. Foreign Minister Théophile Delcassé proved a gracious and discreet host to the Conference, which opened on October 1. Delcassé was careful not to intrude himself into the deliberations in a way likely to anger the United States. Nevertheless the French government was nervous about the fate of the Philippines; if America took the Philippines a wholly new power factor would be interjected into the political and commercial relations of East Asia, a possibility that France did not relish. Despite private French conversations with the American delegates, warning them that possession of the Philippines would automatically involve America in the politics and rivalries of Europe, the American government decided that the Philippines must become American property. France thought it prudent to say no more since the government of Great Britain supported this arrangement.[16] If the United States was to be France's neighbor in East Asia it would be well not to antagonize the Americans by futile objections. Such a policy might well have the effect of drawing America and Britain together in East Asia, a situation that France feared was developing even before the outbreak of the Spanish-American War.

Ambassador Cambon advised Delcassé that the American sugar trust was the powerful force compelling the United States

---

[16] May, *Imperial Democracy*, pp. 230–234; Royal Cortissoz, *The Life of Whitelaw Reid*, 2 vols. (New York, 1921), II, pp. 245–246; Blumenthal, *France and the United States*, pp. 208–210.

government to annex the Philippines. This trust wants "Hawaii, Cuba, Puerto Rico, and the Philippines because they want to monopolize the production of sugar in the world and destroy its fabrication in Europe." Annexation, he continued, was thus an important step in America's program to launch economic warfare against the nations of Europe.[17] Similar expressions about the economic nature of American imperialism were echoed in French newspapers and apprehensions were expressed that the whole world would soon stand in awe of American economic power. From almost every point of view France saw little advantage to herself or to the peace and well-being of Europe in the rapid rise of American power. American ambitions were apparently unlimited, its potential power colossal, and its political sense quite raw and assertive.

This rather negative view of how America would exercise its power was hardly justified by French diplomatic contacts with America outside the hemisphere. In East Asia, for example, America, France, and Great Britain had acted in general concert to establish and protect Western trading concessions in China and Korea from the 1840s through the 1870s. Even when France had turned in a new direction, toward acquiring permanent and exclusive rights in Indo-China, the United States did not object to her course. In the squabbles that developed between France and China over French rights in Indo-China (1883–1886), the United States alternately played the roles of messenger and conciliator. Feeling goodwill toward both China and France, the United States seemed to wish mainly for the disruptions and the brief French-Chinese war to end.[18] Little did most Americans realize that France had set her face on a course that was bound to bring her into conflict with American policy.

France was one of the great powers who joined in the late

---

[17] Jules Cambon to Théophile Delcassé, Washington, September 23, 1898, cited in Blumenthal, *France and the United States*, p. 210.

[18] At one point American minister to China John Russell Young proposed to Secretary of State Frelinghuysen that America try to mediate the issues between France and China. French premier, Jules Ferry, was reluctant to encourage American interference. See Pletcher, *Awkward Years*, pp. 214–218; Lloyd E. Eastman, *Throne and Mandarins: China's Search for a policy during the Sino-French Controversy* (Cambridge, 1967), pp. 144–148.

nineteenth-century scramble to establish influence in various parts of the weakened Chinese empire. This was part of that larger movement that led to the amazingly rapid partition of Africa and to the extension of European influence to Oceania. Motives for this expansion of European influence and control are still disputed, but in China the goals of the expansionists are generally not too difficult to discern. Military strategists, investors seeking promising outlets for capital, merchants wanting established markets, chauvinists seeking adventure, politicians wanting glory, nationals abroad seeking a variety of ends—all interacted to encourage the powers to establish "spheres of interest." Although France joined in this Chinese melée, indeed was one of its leaders, it is not easy to ascertain her motives. Most writers agree that economic ambition was not at the core of French policy. Prestige and the sense that France should continue to play the role of Great Power and civilizer seemed at the heart of French expansionism.

France secured her superior political position in Indo-China rather firmly in the Treaty of Tientsin (June 9, 1885). To this encroachment on Chinese suzerainty she added (in 1895–1898) political and financial concessions in the southwestern Chinese provinces of Yunnen, Kwangsi, and Kwantung that clearly marked these provinces as within France's sphere of influence. France thus embarked on a course clearly endangering the integrity of the Chinese empire and one that put her at cross-purposes as well with America's commercial objectives in East Asia. Where America wanted trade without empire, the French opted for the two in combination. By the time that America had annexed the Philippines, most of the more attractive territorial concessions had been squeezed out of China by the Powers, now including Japan. But since the United States was not interested in carving out a sphere of influence in China, why could it not simply pursue its commercial diplomacy as in earlier days? A simple but painful truth dawned that those Powers who had chosen to pursue both trade and *de facto* empire in China wished to close off their spheres to other powers, both for investment and for trading rights. This doleful circumstance prompted the McKinley administration (in September 1899) to seek promises from the concession Powers that they would allow other nations relative freedom to trade within their spheres. Though this was an embarrassing subject for most, a positive but guarded reply was given by France.

This "Open Door" policy was directly threatened a few months later when a group of incensed Chinese, called "Boxers" in the West, decided to cleanse China of Western influence. Such impertinence by the Chinese, particularly their threat to wipe out the Western diplomatic community in Peking, stimulated an international 18,000-man relief expedition in the summer of 1900. Secretary of State John Hay suspected the Powers would seize upon this uprising as an excuse to make new demands upon China and thus effectively seal off their spheres of influence from such opportunists as the United States. Hay decided to counter this intention by declaring that the United States favored preserving "Chinese territorial and administrative entity" and safeguarding "for the world [i.e. for Americans] the principle of equal and impartial trade with all parts of the Chinese Empire."[19] This declaration was now clearly at odds with French policy but France saw no need to take alarm. How could the United States argue for an open Chinese market when it closed the Philippines through application of the American tariff? If France had learned how America tried to gain a territorial concession at Samsah Bay in southern China, in November 1900, her impression of American policy would have been confirmed: it was, France believed, a policy of opportunism, regrettably moralistic in tone and marred by hypocrisy.

Thus by 1900 America and France had behind them several decades of cooperation in East Asia but were seemingly moving toward a wide divergence in policy after 1895. Even after they went their separate ways, however, conflict tended to be minimal since the United States had few commercial ambitions for Indo-China or southwestern China. Tangentially their interests did touch through competing American-Russian ambitions in Manchuria. Particularly in the era of dollar diplomacy (1909–1913) it seemed to President William Howard Taft and the State

---

[19] Circular telegram of Secretary Hay, Department of State, Washington, July 3, 1900, in *Foreign Relations, 1900*, p. 299.

Department that Russia should not be permitted to establish an exclusive concession in North Manchuria if for no other reason than it would provide Japan an excuse for like actions in Southern Manchuria where American commerce had traditionally been active. France was in a delicate position, not wishing to antagonize the United States yet aware that Russia expected her ally to give her proper diplomatic support.

American ineptness lifted this burden from French shoulders and also revealed at one stroke how little international weight America carried on Chinese questions. Late in 1909 Secretary of State Philander C. Knox proposed that an international syndicate be formed to make China so large a loan that she could buy out Russian and Japanese interests in Manchuria, and that the Manchurian railways be neutralized and internationally administered during the life of the loan. Japan and Russia were naturally incensed at this proposal and linked hands by treaty in 1910 to protect their mutual spheres.[20] French minds were put further at ease for in the process of seeking diplomatic support, the United States stimulated Great Britain to redefine her posiion on spheres of influence and the Open Door policy. In that process Great Britain decided it would be unwise to alienate her ally Japan (since 1902) by favoring neutralization or in any way attacking the spheres of influence. American policy was now declaredly without support. Spheres of influence were established and for varied reasons no great powers would support an assault upon them. The United States had originally tried to recapture the past through the first Open Door notes; it had then tried territorial concession hunting for itself without success. Through the cooperative activities of bankers, speculators, and State Department personnel it tried to gain investment concessions but had only minor gains in some areas and a firm "no" in Manchuria.

In the Russo-Japanese War of 1904–05 France saw perhaps for the first time that American power could be a constructive partner in the search for peace and a firm supporter of sensible

---

[20] See Raymond A. Esthus, "The Changing Concept of the Open Door, 1899–1910," *Mississippi Valley Historical Review*, XLVI (December 1959), pp. 435–454.

change. France was placed in a particularly delicate position by the war's outbreak. On the one hand she wished nothing too severe to be inflicted upon her Russian ally, if for no other reason than to protect the enormous French investments in Russia, estimated in 1904 at $1,500,000,000. Humiliation for Russia would also cause rejoicing in Germany with a consequent weakening of France's diplomatic position vis-a-vis Germany. Yet France was unable to support her Russian ally because of her recent (April 1904) rapprochement with Great Britain; the relationship might well deteriorate if France aided Russia in attacking Japan. France decided that her best course was to declare her neutrality, while making explanations to Russia, and hope for an early end to the war. But if the war ended disastrously for Russia she would be full of reproaches for France, and with consequences for the alliance that could be ominous.

President Theodore Roosevelt's policy of localizing the war and maintaining the East Asian balance of power by moderating Japan's peace demands upon Russia (at the Portsmouth Peace Conference, 1905) was nicely suited to French diplomatic objectives though of dubious long-term value to the United States. But France perceived at Portsmouth that American policy in East Asia had become aligned with her own. Despite their disagreement over China policy, both France and America had in general become supporters of the East Asian status quo, seeing in that condition the best guarantee of their recent territorial acquisitions. This, in effect, meant that both must frown upon Japanese ambitions and seek to restrain them, for the Philippines and Indo-China were equally vulnerable to the rising Japanese navy. Both France and America were also determined to protect those territories against outside economic competitors. Neither could therefore legitimately complain to the other about exclusionary policies though both carped considerably in a pro forma manner from time to time. By 1914 France and the United States did not enjoy cordial relations in East Asian matters but they understood the legitimacy of the other's interests, desired peace, distrusted the Japanese and hoped to make further economic gains with a minimum of disturbance.

France's experiences with the United States on African affairs before 1900 did not engender the same confidence in the reasonableness of the American government on colonial matters. American sensibilities about Liberia, for example, remained something of a mystery to France. The United States government had not officially founded it, did not subsidize it, claimed no suzerainty over it and yet undertook to warn France several times that she must not nibble away at the Liberian national domain. From 1879, when France offered its protection to Liberia, through 1892 when France and Liberia concluded a treaty adjusting their territorial and financial claims, the United States clucked in maternal fashion over Liberia. France was alternately angry and amused over this American interference but in practice came to recognize that America was exercising an informal protectorate over Liberia. France realized that the expansion of American commercial ambitions made Liberia an increasingly valuable friend to America both as a way-station to markets beyond and as a lever to help penetrate the African continent. What France failed to appreciate properly was Liberia's status as America's "conscience colony." If America had earned the world's condemnation for miserable treatment of its blacks, America would show the world its real benevolence toward the Negro by protecting helpless black Liberia.[21]

If France was occasionally annoyed over American concern for Liberia, she found American intervention in Congo and West Africa affairs incongruous and rather unseemly. When Bismarck and Jules Ferry arranged for the Berlin Conference on West African affairs (November 1884–February 1885), the United States was one of the fourteen nations that took its place around the green baize table. Why America had even been invited was a question that deserved an explanation, but one that the administration of Chester Arthur could not have answered without some embarrassment.

America was represented for several reasons. First, the administration hoped that the trade of Africa would someday be available to enterprising American merchants. America was also

---

[21] T. J. Coolidge, *The Autobiography of T. Jefferson Coolidge, 1831–1920* (Boston, 1923), pp. 166–169; Gilbert Haven, "America in Africa," *North American Review*, CXXV, Part II (November 1877), pp. 517–528. Haven argues the case for annexation of Liberia to the United States.

represented because of the skillful propaganda efforts of Henry S. Sanford, an employee of King Leopold of Belgium, who hoped to enlist American influence to protect his covert monopolizing activities in the Congo. Sanford convinced key American governmental politicians that the trade of Africa, the duty to Liberia, and America's hope to found African colonies for its own blacks obliged America to recognize Leopold's philanthropic African International Association as the government of the Congo. Sanford did his work well; in April 1884 the United States government extended recognition to the African International Association, an action that was seconded by France in the same month.

America's delegation to the Berlin Conference was an extraordinary one for two of its members, the explorer Henry M. Stanley and Henry S. Stanford, were employees of King Leopold and took their orders from him, and the third, John A. Kasson, largely followed their advice. Although Kasson managed to annoy France by seconding Stanley's proposal that the Conference support free trade "in a broad belt extending across the whole continent from the Indian Ocean to the Atlantic and including French and Portuguese colonies as well as the conventional basin," no great tensions developed between the French and American delegations.[22] What annoyed France was that America was represented at all and that its delegation was virtually the tool of King Leopold. If the United States was using the Conference to make its entrance upon the African stage, the crudity of that entrance was less excusable than America's understandable hope to open new markets for its growing wealth of surplus goods.

A brief examination of French-American economic relations after 1871 helps to explain why the surface of friction remained so large even though diplomatic questions were usually disposed of in reasonably good order. At first glance it would seem there were significant opportunities for French-American economic collaboration in the period to 1914. The United States was knocking at the doors of the world's bankers seeking investment and expansion capital; France by 1914 had sent nine billion dol-

---

[22] Pletcher, *Awkward Years*, p. 218.

lars outside her borders for investment purposes. American industry was turning to mass production of consumer goods and heavy machinery while France continued to specialize in producing high-quality luxury goods. Some reciprocity here seemed natural, indeed inevitable.

American-French trade did flourish between 1871 and 1914, as trade statistics clearly indicate, but the unrealized potential of their economic relations left both parties feeling disgruntled and all too willing to place primary blame on the other. Americans were unhappy that French bankers were so tight-fisted in releasing funds for American investments. Of France's $9,000,000,000 in foreign investments, perhaps only $200,000,000 found its way into American money markets. This appeared to some Americans the result of an orchestrated plot to retard American industry. Not at all, French bankers replied, unless "discrimination" meant avoiding overly risky investments. Cautious as a group, the bankers were dismayed when they reviewed recent American economic history. The record of crashes, recessions, repudiations, the weakness of the American banking system and the greenback system were flashing red lights, warning off all except the most risk-minded investor. French money would probably have flowed somewhat more freely into American enterprises if the federal government would have guaranteed the loans but this the government regarded as unconstitutional. French money would not have come into America in sizable quantities mainly because the French government desired to invest the franc where it would serve to reinforce national diplomatic objectives. Since cultivation of the United States was relatively low on the French scale of diplomatic priorities, the franc was directed elsewhere, primarily to Russia and parts of the French empire.

Direct trade suffered because both nations sought to protect important domestic interests against abrasive and possible destructive competition. France found the McKinley Tariff of 1890 and the Dingley Tariff of 1897 positively infuriating because, France claimed, many of the interests supposedly being protected against rigorous foreign competition were in fact using the tariff to exclude competition for the purpose of monopolizing the American market. And while enjoying an exclusive market, they charged prices that pushed their profits to unconscionable levels. This obeisance to pressure groups, so harmful to full development of American trade, was countenanced by the American government even as Americans insisted upon their right to dump low-priced farm commodities in France. American beef, wheat, and pork prices threatened ruin to the French farmer while no equivalent American industry was threatened by French imports. In fairness to its own people France felt it must retaliate until America was willing to arrive at some sensible compromise.

If French complaints were sometimes unfair, their action was no less decisive. In February 1881 American pork products were forbidden access to French markets. While the American farmer squealed in pain his government launched a campaign for repeal that was to last for ten years.[23] The supposed basis for the prohibition, the presence of trichinae in the pork, was shown quite conclusively to be without foundation. Even the French Academy of Medicine gave American pork a clean bill of health. The American government pursued the pork problem blindly, refusing to deal with larger issues that France raised by the prohibition decree. Although the pork embargo was repealed in December 1891, passage of the McKinley Tariff in October 1890 stimulated the French government to think in more creative exclusionary terms, ones that would not provoke the Americans and yet would serve to protect French agriculture and specific French industries. A year after passage of the McKinley Tariff France adopted a two-pillar tariff, one listing tariff rates chargeable to nations affording France reciprocity, the other assigning tariff rates to nations following exclusionary policies toward France. Eventually the United States was the only modern commercial nation that did not qualify for the minimum rates without exceptions. More bad blood followed conclusion of a French-American trade convention (1899), an agreement providing at least limited reciprocity. Although the American Senate refused to ratify the convention, France continued to honor the convention's terms through the summer of 1903. France complained as well that administration of the Pure Food and Drug Act of 1906 was unfair and prejudicial to French products. The State Department re-

---

[23] Bingham Duncan, "Protectionism and Pork: Whitelaw Reid as Diplomat: 1889–1891," *Agricultural History*, XXXIII (October 1959), pp. 190–195; John L. Gignilliat, "Pigs, Politics and Protection: The European Boycott of American Pork, 1879–1891," *ibid.*, XXXV (January 1961), pp. 3–12; Pletcher, *Awkward Years*, pp. 158–164.

torted that the health of American citizens compelled the government to protect its citizens against adulterated foods and shoddy packaging.

These trade barriers might have seemed less important if American and French merchants had adopted imaginative merchandising methods for new products or even stimulated personnel within the consulates to arouse domestic opinion against the tariffs. Merchants of both nations seemed reluctant to adapt themselves to living in foreign countries, to using the language of their prospective customer, to handling orders expeditiously and responsibly, or to packaging their products in ways attractive to foreign customers. Perhaps prospective profits were not large enough to intrigue the entrepreneur, or perhaps the irritated or lackadaisical attitude of the French and American merchants toward one another reflected in some way the relations of their governments. This latter speculation may be what Henry Blumenthal means by his comment that nothing "throws as much light on Franco-American diplomatic history during the last three decades of the nineteenth century as the economic relations between the two countries."[24] But even when the century ended and diplomatic relations improved, old trade hassles, continued tariff discriminations, and French reluctance to direct investment francs across the Atlantic combined to insure static economic relations between the two great powers.

*   *   *   *   *

Trade wars, French jealousy of America's increasing hemispheric hegemony, America's step toward Africa, and the apparent pursuit of rather different policies in East Asia provided evidence around 1900 that future French-American relations might not be happy ones. Yet the picture changed rapidly. What happened? America's constructive role at the Portsmouth Peace Conference and her sponsorship of arbitration treaties through the Taft and early Wilson years argued that America was peace-minded and concerned that peace not be broken because of some

---

[24] Blumenthal, *France and the United States*, p. 167.

dramatic power reordering. The United States was also acting in a "responsible" way in its own hemisphere, accepting the burdens of leadership and exerting pressure on nations who defaulted on their obligations to European creditors.

Nor was the Quai d'Orsay truly displeased by the noticeably warmer British-American relations as the twentieth century turned the corner. Nothing definite had been concluded between Britain and America, to be sure, but evolution of what Bradford Perkins has called "the great rapprochement" was soon visible to shrewd observers of the diplomatic constellations. Inept and provocative German diplomacy and the German determination to build a navy that need dip its flag to none soon directed British eyes toward France as a possible ally against certain contingencies, a thought that was formalized in the cordial visit of King Edward VII to Paris in 1903. Almost a year later, in April 1904, Britain and France signed an agreement resolving their most pressing colonial differences, an agreement marking the beginning of an *entente cordiale* that was to survive two world wars and well over fifty years.

This agreement was bound to alter the political context of French-American relations given the evolution of the alliance system, the expansion of American interests, and the diplomacy of Germany, which seemed bent on restructuring naval, colonial, and Continental affairs in ways advantageous to herself. Precisely how these elements would jell was revealed to France in the first crisis over Morocco; from that point forward France was never truly concerned that American power might be thrown into the German scales.

Perhaps the most crucial provisions of the agreement were that France was to have a free hand to develop Morocco and in return France ceded to Britain her rights and historic position in Egypt; the mortar was their promise "to afford one another their diplomatic support in order to obtain the execution of the clauses of the present Declaration." Germany was alarmed by rumors of the agreement, rumors she felt to be confirmed when France took steps in Morocco to establish her new position. Although Germany had no considerable economic or political interest in Morocco, the Kaiser was persuaded by his advisers to resist French pretensions in Morocco as contrary to the International Convention of Madrid (1880) and contrary to the wider interests of Germany. To dramatize this policy the Kaiser landed at Tangier on March 31, 1905 and dramatically announced that Germany favored independence for Morocco as well as an equal and open door there for all to trade and to invest. Panic followed in Paris where Delcassé was denounced as a dangerous adventurer, one leading an unprepared France straight toward war with Germany. Delcassé offered to compromise with Germany but the German Foreign Office was uninterested. Germany wanted an international conference on Morocco, a public showground for its new diplomatic muscle. And if affairs were handled skillfully it seemed probable that France could be humiliated and the British-French agreement smashed before their new cordiality had time to mature. France, whose alliance with Russia had lost in value since the Russo-Japanese War, would thus be left friendless and under the German gun.

Theodore Roosevelt became a key figure in the unfolding drama. Although he was on good terms with the Kaiser and had genuine admiration for Germany's stunning industrial and military progress, at bottom he believed American interests were similar to those of France. One may account for this partly on the basis of his extraordinarily close friendship with the French ambassador, Jean Jules Jusserand, but his convictions were based on a much more solid foundation than personal likes. Roosevelt thought Germany was overly ambitious, crude in its diplomatic methods, imperceptive of the dangers of its diplomacy, and led by a Kaiser who was often childish and certainly unduly influenced by his military advisers. This German bull could easily wreck the peace of Europe unless the proprietors of peace combined to restrain it. Roosevelt thus determined to aid France in this crisis while maintaining a cordial and disarming front to Germany. He communicated this determination to the Quai d'Orsay, a fact that helped to persuade France to accept convening of a conference.[25]

Kaiser Wilhelm congratulated himself when he "convinced"

---

[25] J. J. Jusserand, *What Me Befell: The Reminiscences of J. J. Jusserand* (Boston, 1933), pp. 316–320; Raymond A. Esthus, *Theodore Roosevelt and the International Rivalries* (Waltham, 1970), pp. 74–75.

Roosevelt to support the conference idea. What the Kaiser didn't know was that Roosevelt had been given a "blank check" by his ambassador to the United States, Baron Speck von Sternburg, a check which assured Roosevelt that if France and Germany were unable to resolve their differences during the conference the Kaiser "will be ready to back up the decision which you should consider to be most fair and most practical." Roosevelt communicated "Specky's" pledge to the French Foreign Office, a signal to France that the friendly Roosevelt would not permit her to be humiliated at the conference. Nor, as it turned out, was Germany humiliated although the Act of Algeciras (signed April 7, 1906) to which all the powers agreed left France in predominant control of the administration of Morocco. More important than the agreement on Morocco was the metamorphosis that took place in the British-French entente as a result of the conference. During the conference military experts of Britain and France covertly discussed plans to land 100,000 British troops in France if war should come; as André Tardieu has observed, the entente had obviously passed "from a static to a dynamic state."

France therefore had solid reason to be grateful to the United States for its support in arranging the Algeciras conference and for secretly backing her throughout its term. Algeciras also served the larger purpose of reassuring the French government that when America chose to exercise its influence it would not do so in a way disturbing to the peace of Europe. America had prospered and grown mightily during the nineteenth century when the European system had experienced an internal balance that had helped to preserve the peace. American power, it now seemed likely, would be used to perpetuate that condition. Since Germany was widely regarded as the most disturbing actor on the European stage, it seemed probable that if war came the magnificent industrial resources of the United States would not be placed at German disposal. Whether they would be available to France was another question and one that only time could answer.

*   *   *   *   *

In 1865 Edouard de Laboulaye, French historian and Union propagandist during the Civil War, concluded that the United States was the nation most closely bound to France. In their struggles to enlarge liberty and in their common aspirations for mankind, an indissoluble spiritual bond had been created. To his friend Frederic Auguste Bartholdi, a noted sculptor, Laboulaye suggested the erection of a monument to symbolize the bond. With the American centennial approaching, what better time could there be to refresh the historic transatlantic bonds established in the struggle of '76. Thus began the course of events that led to erection of the statue "Liberty Enlightening The World," a project completed only after many painful delays. Money for completion of the statue was raised mainly from the ranks of the nonaffluent in both countries, from persons who continued to believe that France and America were partners in nurturing principles that would eventually uplift all mankind and make their world a more decent place in which to live.[26]

Erection in Paris of a smaller version of "Liberty" overlooking the Seine River was meant to express symbolically the enlightened and historic partnership of France and America. Although the French gesture seemed a bit exaggerated to many Americans in the 1880s, particularly since France had only recently emerged from Napoleonic rule, by the early twentieth century there seemed to be some justice in Liberty's silent claim. France, America was commenting by 1900, had proven itself worthy of Republican government. France seemed on solid ground despite harrowing challenges to its very survival. If France had been one of the most rapacious of colonizers in the 1870s and after, one must remember that Africans and other nonindustrial peoples were being given the benefits of a sophisticated and enlightened French civilization, just as the Filipinos, Hawaiians, and Puerto Ricans were being given the benefits of American experience. Both powers, so the argument ran, also believed that progress was made through establishing ever wider international trade, that order and stability, both internally and internationally, were necessary to progress, and that the more advanced

---

[26] Robert P. Heller, "Liberty Enlightening the World," *The Franco-American Review*, I, No. 2 (Autumn 1936), pp. 135–142.

nations had the duty to preserve the peace and uplift the weak. The future for American-French relations thus held few clouds by the summer of 1914. Only the most unexpected events seemed likely to disturb significantly the slowly growing sense of French-American cordiality.

CHAPTER VII

Playing the Great Game
1914 - 1939

The United States is . . . a world power. . . . When a people have commercial interests everywhere, they are called upon to involve themselves in everything. A nation of ninety million souls, which sells wheat to the universe, coal, iron, and cotton, cannot isolate itself. . . . Its power creates for it a right. The right turns itself into a pretension. The pretension becomes a duty—to pronounce upon all those questions that hitherto have been arranged by agreement only among European powers. These powers themselves, at critical times, turn toward the United States, anxious to know its opinion. . . . The United States intervenes thus in the affairs of the universe. . . . It is seated at the table where the great game is played, and it cannot leave it.

Andre Tardieu, 1908

O cease! must hate and death return?
Cease! must men kill and die?
Cease! drain not to its dregs the wine
Of bitter prophecy!
The world is weary of the past—
O might it die or rest at last!

Shelley

We are sure the United States will ratify the [Versailles] Treaty. . . . The Americans came and they'll stay. I've told you . . . the Treaty stands; it will pay off! I don't know how they'll vote it at Washington but vote it they will. This Treaty is inscribed on the heart of the great and generous American people.

Georges Clemenceau, 1919

I know that the Americans are a dreadful people to deal with—they cannot make firm promises, but they jolly you along with fair prospects and when you are committed they let you down.

Sir Ronald Lindsay, 1932[1]

T HAT VAST CARNAGE lasting four years and three months, known to its participants as the Great War, permanently changed the substance of French-American relations. By war's end the United States had emerged as the world's greatest power in both financial and military terms. Whether America chose or not to assume a prominent role in discussion of the world's problems, all nations, including France, had constantly to be on guard concerning American attitudes and prejudices, to court Washington, and to be aware that American power was now a major arbiter in world affairs.

France, long accustomed to exercising a leading role in European and world affairs, quickly developed deep resentments about America's new status, resentments that continue to the present day. But France is presently unable, as she was in 1917–1918, to repudiate American leadership because she knows too well her potential vulnerability to a powerful and ambitious Germany. This was convincingly demonstrated by the Great War. Even with the aid of Russia, Great Britain, and her own empire, the verdict could have gone against France if America had not finally intervened in 1917. And so the context of French-American relations had to change; but France, as befitting a proud nation, did not accept the change graciously. Nonetheless, the facts of her existence, and the changed relationships of a power-conscious world, pointed after 1918 toward a new and more intimate relationship with the American colossus.

*   *   *   *   *

Americans were deeply shocked by the events of August 1914.

[1] Tardieu's analysis is in his *Notes sur les États-Unis* (Paris, 1908), quoted in May, *Imperial Democracy*, p. 242. Clemenceau's assertion was made before Parliament on September 26, 1919, and is quoted in Georges Bonnet, *Quai d'Orsay* (Isle of Man, 1965), pp. 40–41. Sir Ronald's wry comment was made in a letter to Sir J. Simon, Washington, March 3, 1932, in *Documents on British Foreign Policy, 1919–1939*, Rohan Butler et. al., Eds., 2nd Series, IX (London, 1965), p. 711.

It was bewildering that Europe should send its sons into battle because Austria-Hungary and Serbia had been at each other's throats on a question that apparently related only peripherally to larger European questions. With very little understanding of Europe's complicated rivalries or of the alliance commitments, carefully arranged and cemented by fear, Americans could only shake their heads in wonder as Europe sprang to arms. August 1914 was a time when Americans counted their blessings, and the greatest blessing of all was to be uninvolved with a Europe apparently gone mad.

Almost no one expected that the war would be a lengthy one. A six-month campaign seemed a likely guess to most lay experts. Certainly the Germans did not envision an extended war, as indicated by their Schlieffen Plan strategy. France was to be pounded quickly into submission by sending overwhelming forces against her in a great wheeling motion, launched through Belgium into northeast France, its purpose to encircle Paris, to entrap and destroy French armies in a coordinated pincers movement (the arm and hammer), and thus to forestall British intervention. Russia was to be held off for the moment and then decisively engaged once France had been defeated. It was a carefully conceived plan but, fortunately for France, German execution on the Western front was faulty to the extent that France was able in September to launch a powerful counteroffensive, the Battle of the Marne. Paris was saved and the channel ports were kept open, thus insuring that Britain would be able to forward men and supplies to the Continent. Nevertheless, huge areas of France were occupied which provided the principal battleground for the war on the Western front.

The unexpected soon happened. What everyone had envisioned as a war of mobility quickly became, on the Western front, a bloody and stalemated war. Offensive and defensive weapons and capabilities were so closely matched that major advances could be won only at terrible cost. This deathly stalemate established in the autumn of 1914 was not broken until 1918 despite desperate and heroic efforts by both sides.[2]

---

[2] Reliable military studies of the war are C. R. M. F. Cruttwell, *A History of the Great War, 1914-1918* (Oxford, 1934) and B. H. Liddell Hart, *A History of the World War, 1914-1918* (Boston, 1935).

As the nations began to face reality late in 1914 and to gird for a protracted struggle, American resources and financial potential loomed increasingly large. If American industry, farm resources, and money markets could be effectively tapped, the war could be fueled for an indefinite period and hard political decisions (particularly for the Entente powers) associated with ending the war could be postponed. Whichever side could best tap American resources would gain a marked advantage over its adversary. As fate would have it, the Entente powers were in the best position to utilize American resources, mainly because they controlled the sea lanes and were able to carry away the goods from American ports.

Much ink has been spilled by polemicists, historians, and politicians arguing whether the United States was truly neutral, what the nature of "true neutrality" was in the context of World War I, and whether President Woodrow Wilson was not so decidedly pro-Entente that his public calls for neutral attitudes and practices amounted to sham. Some of these debates have focused on non-issues. Facts largely determined American neutral practices, and the most important fact was that the Entente powers controlled the high seas and were determined to interpret maritime conventions and customs to their own advantage. The second fact was that the United States needed and welcomed European trade and was unable to challenge effectively the British and French maritime systems without resorting to embargo or war. Since most Americans favored the Entente powers, neither embargo nor a declaration of war upon them was ever very likely.

Most troubling to those who have studied these issues was the matter of the loans made to Britain and France, loans that by April 1917 exceeded $2,000,000,000. Whether or not the loans were neutral in character, and evidence at this time points in both directions, the fact is that they rescued France and Britain from dire economic straits and made possible their continuance of the war in good style. The loans also gave the United States an increasing vested interest in a victorious outcome for the Entente powers though it is not possible to demonstrate that this situation influenced the vital decision of President Wilson to enter the war.

But in September 1915 the American government permitted inauguration of the series of loans to France and Britain in response to a real situation; Entente orders to American industry would dry up unless new credit resources could be mobilized. The protests of pacifist-minded Secretary of State William Jennings Bryan notwithstanding, American economic interests demanded that the loans be negotiated. Germany was free as well to contract loans, but given Entente control of the high seas there seemed little point to hiring money in order to purchase goods that could not be transported to Germany.

Although millions of Americans identified themselves with Germany or Austria-Hungary, the majority of Americans increasingly came to believe that the cause of civilization, peace, and the preservation of Republican values somehow rested with an Entente victory. The term *"mother* England" had, if nothing else, compelling psychological overtones. And France—partially occupied by Germans who had launched a sneak attack through Belgium in defiance of an operative treaty—could only arouse America's most profound sympathies. As stories flowed into America of German cruelties, of German rape of occupied France, and of the marvelous equanimity with which France bore her sufferings, Americans joined with the poet Henry Van Dyke in chanting:

> Give us a name to fill the mind
> With stirring thoughts that lead mankind
>
> *
>
> A name like a star, a name of light.
> I give you *France!*[3]

Memories of the American Revolution, of French aid in that crisis, and of the historically ever-useful Lafayette were recalled in the literary marketplace. Past conflicts with France seemed practically forgotten by 1916 in the desire to extend a sympathizing hand to France. Such sympathies tended to gloss over any violations of American neutrality that benefitted the Entente powers.

---

[3] Henry Van Dyke, "The Name of France," *The Red Flower* (New York, 1917), p. 26.

As the war months dragged on with one campaign replaced by another, American sympathy for France mounted. In contrast, the United States experienced rather sharp conflicts with Great Britain and for good reason. It was Britain who took the lead in gradually turning the maritime screws on Germany. As early as August 20, 1914 Great Britain began the process of expanding contraband lists and moving to interfere with American shipments to Germany and to neighboring neutral countries. By November Great Britain announced that the entire North Sea area must be considered a military zone. Mines were planted in the North Sea and neutral ships could only gain route instructions by visiting an Entente port; while in port, of course, they could be searched for contraband. Beginning in March 1915, Great Britain tried quite openly to interdict all trade with Germany, ignoring the distinction between contraband and non-contraband goods. These measures caused real unhappiness in the American government, which naturally wished American merchants to have relatively free access to all markets. British-applied pressures thus forced American trade into Entente channels; American money inevitably followed. And while the American government insisted that it was genuinely neutral in its attitudes and practices, it was vulnerable to the charge by Germany and by German-Americans that in fact American weight had been placed on the Entente scales. The point here is that Britain, not France, was placing the American government in this uncomfortable position; it was Great Britain that interpreted and enforced neutrality practices in the common Entente interest; it was against Britain that American indignation had occasionally to be directed. France, meanwhile, negotiated American loans, fought and suffered, and allowed Britain to be the lightning rod for American wrath.

It is hard to say whether France was able to translate this "credit" into tangible terms. More likely, sympathy for France, who was suffering war damages that were difficult to grasp, melded into and supported the larger pro-Entente predisposition of the American people. And it became increasingly easy for Americans to join the French chorus about the barbarity of Germans as Germany, early in 1915, moved to enlarge the effectiveness of the submarine. French propaganda about German rapine in occupied northeast France and in Belgium seemed to be supported by German torpedoing of passenger ships with no provision to rescue innocent passengers. Sinking of the British Cunard liner *Lusitania* on May 7, 1915, with the loss of 1198 lives (128 of them American), constituted first-hand evidence that French and British atrocity charges were plausible if not wholly true.

Trade, loans, and sympathies were the cords connecting France and America through 1916. Each of the cords became increasingly tight as Germany enlarged her submarine campaign by fits and starts. President Wilson's attitudes in the developing maritime situation as well as his general assessment of American interests in the war and its possible outcomes were probably as crucial to American policy development as the national and historical ties to the allies. Dollars and sentiment had their place, but Wilson tried desperately to see the larger picture, to see beyond the immediate carnage to an era of peace.

Germany pleased Wilson neither in her maritime practices nor when he reflected that a victorious Germany might become the arbiter of Europe. Germany's submarine campaign he found reprehensible and inhuman even though he realized that submarines found it dangerous, if not impossible, to adhere to traditional rules of maritime warfare. He was also troubled by the thought that Germany, with her central location, enormous resources, and a warrior tradition might establish a new European hegemony. With his belief that democracy was the wave of the future, that democratic governments were generally enlightened, civilized, and peacefully inclined, Wilson could not consider the consequences of a victorious Germany with equanimity. As Wilson's vision expanded for constructing a new postwar international system, one in which democratic governments and principles could thrive and where peace would be the passion of men and governments, he felt that his dreams would be unrealizable if Germany were victorious.[4]

War did not come to America in April 1917 because President

---

[4] An excellent brief introduction to Wilson's thinking about America's role in the war and peacemaking is Arthur Link, *Wilson the Diplomatist; a look at his major foreign policies* (Baltimore, 1957).

Wilson had a dream. War came because the rulers of Germany deliberately and with full awareness of possible consequences, decided to strike for victory through virtually unrestricted use of the submarine. This decision, made at Pless Castle early in January 1917, was bound to trigger an American war declaration since it would involve disregard for American neutral rights and reneging on promises made earlier to President Wilson.[5] The possible American contribution to the Entente was carefully weighed but discounted since it was presumed that victory would precede the time that the United Sates could make a decided military impact. In the final analysis most Americans believed war was forced upon them. Neither loans to the Entente nor sympathy for France and Britain provoked the American war resolution, but the provocative acts of a calculating Germany. If this assessment appears harsh and one-sided to present-day students, it was nonetheless a judgment that was emotionally satisfying. A nation could justify considerable expense and bloodshed to subdue so dangerous and threatening an adversary. Wilson realized that arousing such primitive emotions toward Germany was poor preparation for designing a just and constructive peace, but the immediate necessity to stimulate the war spirit seemed to take precedence over longer-range goals.

*   *   *   *   *

Wilson was under no illusion that Britain and France represented the forces of reason and righteousness in the world order. Both had already suffered too much at German hands to maintain a sense of detachment as to how best to end the war and write a peace. Both were also colonial powers and were determined that the war should not undo the colonizing work of centuries. Proof of their intentions to seek national advantage from the war was made public when the revolutionary government in Russia in November 1917 began to publish a series of secret treaties concluded by the Entente powers primarily be-

---

[5] See Ernest R. May, *The World War and American Isolation, 1914–1917* (Cambridge, 1959), pp. 413–414.

tween March 1915 and March 1917.[6] Even before the treaties
were published, Wilson had seen how determined France and
Britain were to conclude the war on terms totally favorable to
themselves when he secretly tried to end the war late in 1916;
after extended maneuvering, France and Britain left Wilson no
choice but to abort his efforts. Britain and France made it plain
that his intervention would be regarded as an unfriendly act
unless the United States intervened at a time favorable to Allied
military fortunes and was prepared to help saddle Germany with
a loser's peace. Wilson's call for a "Peace Without Victory" on
January 22, 1917 put the Entente on notice that the American
perspective on the war and the future peace was fundamentally
different than that of suffering and revenge-minded France. And
although European statesmen tipped their hats to Professor
Wilson's high ideals and noble sentiments, all knew that their
constituencies would not settle for a peace where the loser
received light punishment.

It was no oversight, then, that the United States entered the
war as an associate of France and England, not as an ally.
America entered the war in anger, to defend her traditional maritime rights against Germany, a power whose only hope for
victory rested in unrestricted use of a nontraditional weapon.
In practical terms, this meant joining American efforts to those
of France and Britain. But there was never any real spiritual
union, only a joining hands of the desperate, exhausted, and
willful with those of the fresh, optimistic, and willful.

America and France could never have viewed the war and
plans for peace in the same terms, any more than residents of
Nagasaki and Omaha could have a shared perspective on World
War II. France by 1917 had endured horrible suffering and had
accumulated enormous debts, partly because she refused to tax

---

[6] Russia officially left the war in March 1918, following the November
Revolution in 1917. See George F. Kennan, *Russia Leaves the War* (Princeton, 1956). There were five secret treaties and various supplementary
agreements. They provided, in essence, for the dismemberment of enemy
empires following the war. The terms of the treaties are found in Ray S.
Baker, *Woodrow Wilson and World Settlement*, 3 vols. (Garden City,
1922), I, pp. 47–63.

herself for the war.[7] She was a world power yet shared a border with Europe's greatest power, one determined to assert her role at France's expense. France was proud of her past greatness and determined to reassert it, humiliated that she was unable to free her territory from German control, and desperately fearful that the widespread mutinies in the French army in May and June 1917, following the Aisne and third Battle of Champagne, would open the door for a German victory march to Paris. Although the United States did not realize how close France was to collapse when she entered the war early in April 1917, America was in fact the lifeline to a sinking France. But the closeness of her call and her desperate need of American resources and men little inclined France to follow American diplomatic leads or to accommodate American views of the postwar world. France did what she had to do to enlist the ever-growing flow of American aid to herself. But France had experienced German invasion twice within fifty years; she would lose 1,385,000 men in this war; monetary losses would be almost impossible to estimate, but every figure was a fearful one; her world influence was shrinking as her energies were directed almost solely to her European struggle; the war had knocked her ally Russia out of the conflict and a newly Bolshevized Russia had repudiated the enormous debts Russia owed to France; moreover, the damage to the French spirit—to French civilization—how could one gauge these immeasurable losses? The United States was free to support her own ideas, but how could Americans ever share the insights and views of a France almost mortally wounded?

These deeper feelings were submerged temporarily as Wilson, Premier Georges Clemenceau of France, and Prime Minister Lloyd George of England joined in efforts to avoid losing the war. In the second week of June 1917 Clemenceau and George, seconded by Vittorio Orlando of Italy, warned Wilson: "There

---

[7] D. W. Brogan points out that the French governments during the war "did not raise in taxes enough to pay for . . . normal peace-time expenditure." All war costs were thus borrowed. *The Development of Modern France, 1870–1939* (New York, 1966), pp. 516–517. The war wiped out 38 billion net French foreign investments. By 1919 the French owed foreigners (in terms of 1914 purchasing power) some 6.8 billion. Harold G. Moulton and Cleona Lewis, *The French Debt Problem* (New York, 1925), p. 28.

is great danger of the war being lost unless the numerical inferiority of the Allies can be remedied as rapidly as possible by the advent of American troops."[8] These were not idle words. With Russia virtually out of the war since July 1916, Germany was able to field 207 divisions on her western front by March 1917, facing only 173 divisions. Of those 173 divisions, only 4½ were American.[9] Late in March 1917 Field Marshall Erich von Ludendorff opened the German offensive that was designed to end the war before American power could become a decisive factor.

In retrospect, the American manpower contribution to the war was rather remarkable. On April 6, 1917, the date of the American war resolution, the United States Army was composed of only 200,000 officers and men. By the end of 1917 there were 180,000 American troops actually in France, although their fighting contribution was almost nil. By war's end, the American army had a strength of 4,000,000 men, more than half of whom had been shipped to France. Of that latter number about 1,300,000 had been placed in combat situations. Given the shortness of their training, the American doughboys fought commendably well and were able to help shorten the war. The navy, commanded by Admiral William S. Sims, was also able to make a substantial contribution through convoy activity, chasing German submarines, and by cooperating with the British fleet in the North Sea area.

It is certainly not true, however, that the American armed forces largely ended the war by their vigorous and heroic efforts. This distorted view became all too prevalent and easy to believe in America and contributed to an American feeling that the United States should play a role in peacemaking that seemed quite inordinate if not indecent to Frenchmen. American troops arrived on the scene when the nature of the war had changed, when stalemate and trench warfare had been replaced by movement and mobility. In this situation American troops moved

---

[8] Quoted in Samuel Eliot Morison, *The Oxford History of the American People* (New York, 1965), p. 871. Admiral Morison gives a concise overview of the American military contribution to the war, pp. 861–873.
[9] B. H. Liddell Hart, *The Real War, 1914–1918* (Boston, 1930), p. 366.

with the front, fought well, and were able to claim their share of victories. But the situation would have been quite different if Germany had chosen to continue a strategy of attrition; American glory, and the end of the war, might have been postponed indefinitely. And it is easy to forget the role of the German General Staff in bringing the war to so abrupt an end. Once it became clear (as it did in July 1918) that there would be no German breakthrough, that the Allies could take the best German punches and launch a series of counterattacks, the German high command insisted that peace must be concluded as soon as possible. American troops thus entered the war at a peculiarly fortunate moment, a moment when the changed nature of the war tended to highlight their contribution. France remembered, however, that before Americans arrived to participate in the Second Battle of the Marne, or Saint-Mihiel, or Meuse-Argonne, that there had been the First Battle of the Marne, and Ypres and Artois, the Somme, and above all Verdun, where France alone lost 350,000 men in the early part of 1916. Between August 1914 and February 1917, France calculated that she lost one Frenchman every minute!

American battle deaths were almost 50,000; an additional 230,000 were wounded. America's own direct costs for prosecuting the war had been something over $21,000,000. Yet her land remained untouched, more prosperous in fact than when the war began. All over the world her merchants had eagerly seized markets that European merchants could not service. It was doubtful that French merchants would ever regain many of their old customers. As the war drew to a close, the United States clearly emerged as the leading economic power of the world, able to make the most respectable of the Old World nations a supplicant for financial favors. As Frenchmen viewed it, the Great War had proven a profitable venture for the United States. Once again the troubles of Europe had been a boon to America.[10] Even the war loans made to the Allies had been spent

---

[10] Between 1914 and 1919 U.S. trade in Latin America alone rose from $84,000,000 to $2,332,000,000. Total American exports rose from $329,000,000 in 1914 to $4,272,000,000 in 1916. By 1916 America's surplus in balance of payments reached the fantastic figure of $2,674,000,000. Pierre Renouvin, *War and Aftermath, 1914–1929* (New York, 1968), p. 53.

largely in America, contributing to American prosperity and economic expansion.

French and British statesmen may, therefore, be pardoned for their anger when Wilson made it clear that the United States intended to end the war as soon as possible and on terms that seemed reasonable from a Wilsonian perspective. Wilson's most dramatic gesture came in an address before Congress on January 8, 1918. In his address Wilson called for a peace based upon five general principles:

1. The end of secret diplomacy.
2. Freedom of navigation on the seas in peace and in war.
3. Reduction of armaments.
4. Removal of barriers to international free trade (the "open door").
5. Impartial adjustment of colonial claims, taking into account the welfare of colonial populations.

Eight specific territorial adjustments in Europe and the Near East were called for:

6. German evacuation of Russian territory and a welcome to Russia "into the society of free nations under institutions of her own choosing."
7. German evacuation of Belgium and restoration of her sovereignty.
8. Return of Alsace-Lorraine, taken by Prussia in 1871, to France.
9. Readjustment of Italy's frontiers according to nationality.
10. Autonomy for the diverse peoples of Austria-Hungary.
11. Rearrangement of Balkan national boundaries along nationality lines with free access to the sea for Serbia (Yugoslavia).
12. Autonomous development for nationalities under Turkish rule and free passage through the Dardanelles for ships of all nations.
13. Poland to be independent and provided free access to the sea.

And the last point, to Wilson's mind the most important one:

14. "A general association of nations."[11]

Although Clemenceau's government appreciated Wilson's desire to frame a program so attractive that the Bolshevik charge of "imperialist," leveled against the Allied war aims, could be negated, and Russia even possibly attracted back into the war,[12] there was still anger that Wilson was suggesting settlements for European questions with which the United States had had little previous experience. Nor did it seem likely to French officials that a nation with so long an isolationist tradition would accept responsibility for sustaining those settlements.

French and British tempers were not assuaged when Germany and Austria appealed directly to Wilson for peace on the basis of the Fourteen Points and their supplements. Wilson, according to some historians, handled these armistice negotiations with remarkable skill. These historians, it should be noted, are not of French origin. Viewed from Paris, Wilson secured an armistice largely on the basis that a peace would be founded upon the Fourteen Points. Objections from Paris and London were met by an American threat to withdraw from the war and to negotiate separately with Germany. Also, Wilson concluded Armistice terms that left Germany for a time able to resume the war if the terms of peace proved too harsh. Foreseeing an Allied attempt to twist the Armistice terms once Germany was disarmed, Wilson thus rather cleverly parried this possible thrust. France finally accepted the terms of the Armistice with the reservation that "restoration" of invaded territories meant that "compensation will be made by Germany for all damage done to the civilian population of the Allies and their property by the aggression of Germany by land, by sea, and from the air."

---

[11] Other ideas and principles were added later. Altogether Wilson elaborated 27 points and principles that were generally associated with the fourteen points speech.

[12] Arno J. Mayer develops the theme that Nicholai Lenin soon perceived Wilson's "daring proposal . . . the most decisive challenge to his own revolutionary ideology. . . . A large-scale search for new ideological, political and social moorings was under way. In this search some would eventually turn to Wilson, others to Lenin." *Political Origins of the New Diplomacy, 1917–1918* (New Haven, 1959), p. 367.

Wilson was confident that the Armistice terms provided a satisfactory framework for concluding peace, one in which the desire for national unification and self-determination could largely be realized. In the new order tariff and armaments reductions would lighten taxation and encourage prosperity through burgeoning trade. Colonialism would be replaced by self-government. And a League of Nations would serve to dampen the eruption of new and dangerous nation-state quarrels. But as David Thomson has commented, while Wilson tried to cover all the bases and to ensure peace founded upon impartial justice, he overlooked certain facts: ". . . that national frontiers could not be tidily drawn, that nationalistic sentiment was unlikely to be pacific or reasonable, that the desire for economic self-sufficiency would resist the abandonment of tariffs and colonies as much as the desire for national security would oppose disarmament, and that to Germans or Hungarians the fact of national defeat could never be made palatable."[13] French statesmen, with their wider experience in European and world affairs, sensed the naiveté of Wilson's assumptions about how people and nations would react to even the most "reasonable" peace. Added to their distress about American presumptiveness in bringing the war to an end, therefore, was a contempt for the American President who believed that some kind of absolute justice could be achieved in a distraught and devastated Europe.

*   *   *   *   *

It is easy to view events at the Versailles Peace Conference from the perspective of 1939, to heap all responsibility for lost opportunities in the interwar period upon inept negotiators at Versailles. It is an interesting exercise and provides peculiar satisfaction to those who question the wisdom of summit diplomacy, to many who hold that a just and fair peace could have been written, or to those who believe events of the interwar years point straight back to Versailles. Particular opprobrium has been heaped on President Wilson and his French counterpart,

---

[13] Thomson, *Europe Since Napoleon*, p. 536.

Georges Clemenceau. Wilson has been accused of messianism, inordinate ambition, believing in panaceas for complex problems, and being so dedicated to "principles" that he failed to see where they were inapplicable or where their application contradicted what he hoped to achieve. Clemenceau is often scored as a nationalist whose hatred of Germany and obsession with gaining security for France blinded him to the substantial possibilities for constructive peacemaking.

These assessments have certain elements of truth in them but both are unsatisfactory because they are so one-sided and incomplete. Wilson sailed for Europe on December 4, 1918, believing it was possible that mankind could make a new start. Through redrawing national boundary lines in keeping with ethnic realities, by treating the defeated powers in a humane and constructive fashion, and, as said earlier, by abolishing armament races and reducing tariff rates and erecting an international league that would maintain a peaceful and orderly world, Wilson thought that mankind could take a positive step forward. Peace, an increase in international trade volume, lower taxes, and nations composed of relatively homogeneous populations would surely pacify the European cockpit. These steps would be taken with the assistance of the United States; in many ways the wisdom and resources of the New World would be drawn upon to guide a troubled and disoriented Europe. If Wilson saw his own role as being crucial in accomplishing these goals, his vision was not necessarily distorted. He was, after all, the leader of the world's wealthiest nation, one that through its war loans and financial potential had apparently obtained a lien on French and English diplomacy. As Wilson wrote his confidant and friend Colonel House: "England and France have not the same views with regard to peace that we have by any means. When the war is over we can force them to our way of thinking, because by that time they will, among other things, be financially in our hands. . . ."[14]

Wilson, optimistic about the future, came to Paris well-prepared to argue his program. Through his commission of ex-

---

[14] Wilson to House, July 21, 1917, in Ray Stannard Baker, *Woodrow Wilson: Life and Letters*, 8 vols. (Garden City, 1927–39), VII, p. 43, n. 3.

perts, chaired by his political adviser Colonel Edward House, and called The Inquiry, he had access to articulate and thoughtful position papers on topics likely to trouble the conference. Wilson also brought with him a supporting staff of advisers and experts who were politically weak but capable of giving sound advice. Above all, Wilson brought with him the conviction that an association of nations, if rightly constructed and endowed with ample powers, could preserve the peace and, in time, right possible injustices of the moment.

Wilson's hopes and plans, his confidence that men were basically rational and that peace could be arranged around the traditional conference table by men of good will seemed so American, so naive, to Georges Clemenceau. Premier Clemenceau—"the Tiger" of French politics—was essentially a reasonable man and a discerning veteran of French and European politics. He had assumed leadership of France during the darker days of the war (November 1917) and through sheer willpower and inspired leadership had helped to keep France harnessed to the war effort. Clemenceau knew as well as any other man the enormous physical and psychological costs of the war to France. As he gazed eastward across the Rhine he also realized that Germany remained physically untouched by the war, that Germany would not accept gracefully the position of a defeated power, that German demographic trends and natural resources could in time be parlayed into a German hegemony of Europe. His perception of Germany, a perception that had developed over a lifetime of bitter experience and observation, compelled him to distrust Germany and to fear for France's future as long as Germany was not bound by iron chains. Clemenceau suffered with equanimity jibes about his "obsession" with French security for he was inwardly confident that leniency on German questions would reap a bitter harvest not only for the sons and daughters of France but also for those of Europe and the world.

Clemenceau thus took his place at the peace table full of bitter memories, representing a nation that lay prostrate in victory. He believed that all conference questions were peripheral to the central "German question." Europe and France, he initially held, would only be secure if Germany were dismembered, the Rhineland area made an autonomous state under French control, and the Saar Valley annexed as well. Alsace and Lorraine, taken from France in 1870–1871, must be returned at once. To the east, Germany must be given neighbors powerful enough to withstand both the pressures of Germany and of Soviet Russia.[15] And Germany must be made to pay financially for the costs of the war; her total guilt for its outbreak must be matched by her total compensation for its costs! This assessment would have the advantages of helping to reconstruct France, of stripping Germany economically for the foreseeable future, and of reminding the next generation of Germans that war can be a painful exercise in national assertiveness. Even so, Clemenceau tried to see the wider implications of the peace for France and the world. He was no blind, unreasoning Germanophile. As he once commented to General Pershing, "Above France there is civilization."

Within their own frames of reference and experience, Wilson's and Clemenceau's programs for peace made sense. But how was it possible to bring these viewpoints and forebodings together in a peace program that fulfilled the expectations of France and the spirit of the Fourteen Points? British desires and aspirations, and those of the other twenty-nine official delegations attending the Conference had also to be considered as a peace program was tacked together. Over the Conference hovered the sparks of German anger and frustration at being excluded from the peace deliberations as well as the equally frightening spectre that Bolshevism would triumph in revolution-torn Russia with its tentacles reaching perhaps even into the center of historic Europe.

The Russian situation was particularly worrisome to Wilson. In the latter stages of the war Allied military leaders, particularly General Ferdinand Foch, had persuaded Wilson that German troops operating in Russia were maneuvering to capture enormous caches of Allied supplies and that American (as well as French and British) troops must be used to rescue these sup-

---

[15] Allied fears of Bolshevism spreading into central Europe is analyzed in Arno J. Mayer, *Politics and Diplomacy of Peacemaking; containment and counterrevolution at Versailles, 1918–1919* (New York, 1967). Mayer argues that fear of Bolshevist Russia was one key to President Wilson's thinking about the peace, that efforts to "tame the Russian Revolution . . . came to be central to Wilson's overall peacemaking strategy." p. 21.

plies. Unaware that he was being lied to, Wilson consented to send American troops to Murmansk and Archangel; other Americans were sent later to Vladivostok to join in a supposed rescue effort for Czech troops stranded in Siberia. Unwittingly, and against his own conviction that great revolutions will take their course despite the intervention of enemies, Wilson joined American strength to an Allied effort that was anti-Bolshevik in nature.[16]

Threats from Eastern Europe, tensions, conflicting national desires, clashing personalities, and intense domestic pressures upon the major conference participants all played some part in shaping the many vital conference decisions. When one also considers the lack of agenda, the crowded facilities, and the general confusion that engulfed the conference, it almost seems appropriate to accord the conferees some retrospective applause for their achievements.[17]

Wilson ultimately emerged from the conference largely satisfied with its work and with his own role. Paul Birdsall, a careful student of the conference, has commented that in almost every question in which Wilson interested himself, the settlement proposed was made substantially better by his suggestions and pressure.[18] From an American-liberal viewpoint, this judgment seems essentially fair. Germany was punished, but not too severely; Alsace-Lorraine was given to France; the German army was reduced to 100,000 men; the coal mines of the Saar were ceded to France for fifteen years; allied forces of occupation were to remain in the Rhineland for fifteen years as insurance that Germany would fulfill commitments she made in the peace treaty. Clemenceau was very angry that Wilson and Lloyd George would not consent to a permanent separation of the Rhineland for, as Marshal Ferdinand Foch had emphasized to

---

[16] Wilson remarked at one point that "trying to stop a revolutionary movement with armies in the field is like using a broom to hold back a great ocean." Paul J. Mantoux, *Les délibérations des Conseil des quatre, 24 mars–28 juin, 1919*, 2 vols. (Paris, 1955), I, p. 55.

[17] An excellent brief account of the conference is F. S. Marston's *The Peace Conference of 1919: Organization and Procedure* (London, 1944).

[18] See Paul Birdsall, *Versailles Twenty Years After* (New York, 1941), p. 295.

his government, French control of the Rhineland bridgeheads would make it virtually impossible for Germany ever to launch an effective surprise attack upon France. But as Wilson and Lloyd George argued, the building blocks of peace would be hay and stubble if Germany were given a permanent territorial grievance; an Alsace-Lorraine in reverse would be created if the Rhineland were permanently alienated from Germany.

In order to bring France to a more moderate position on the Rhineland question, Wilson and Lloyd George offered France a joint treaty guarantee to aid France if she were attacked by Germany.[19] Wilson and Lloyd George's offer has been criticized on varying grounds: that Wilson, for one, had no business proposing an old-style treaty without first consulting the Senate, and one that was in violation of his heralded "New Diplomacy"; and that France was foolish to accept as a partial guarantee for her security a treaty built on the sands of Anglo-American public opinion. The best explanation for the conclusion of this treaty is that it seemed like a reasonable suggestion to the principals who were working under the intense pressures of the Conference. Further, the President really saw the security treaty as a temporary one to reassure France until the League of Nations became operative. Unfortunately, Wilson did not discern that the Senate would turn its back on his work, including the triparte treaty, nor did France foresee that Great Britain would eagerly shed its treaty responsibility once it became clear that America would not participate in the guarantee. France in time came to feel betrayed by her wartime friend and associate whom, she argued, unwisely induced her to accept nominal guarantees rather than allow her to assure her security through substantial territorial annexation.

Tensions developed early in the conference on another issue related to French security: would Germany be made to pay the

---

[19] Any German violation of Articles 42 and 43, or 42 or 43, as defined in Article 44 of the Versailles Treaty was to be considered as a movement of unprovoked aggression against France; in such an event, the United States was obligated to come to French aid at once. Wilson placed the treaty before the Senate on July 29, 1919, after considerable clamor that he do so. No vote was ever taken on the treaty. See Louis A. R. Yates, *The United States and French Security, 1917–1921* (New York, 1957), pp. 118–119.

costs of the war and, if so, how would the costs be calculated and imposed? In this discussion Entente spokesmen were caught in the insidious web of their own rhetoric, for the English and French peoples had been led to believe their representatives would squeeze Germany to the last necessary pfennig. It made eminent sense to the masses that a wealthy nation, physically untouched by the war and *totally responsible* for the outbreak of war, should assume the war's total costs.

Wilson and his advisers were deeply troubled on this issue. Had he not promised Germany no punitive damages in negotiations leading to the armistice? And economic advisers whispered in Wilson's ear that assessing enormous damages against Germany and devising workable mechanisms for wealth transfers was incredibly complicated, fraught with risks to peace and a viable international economic system. Questions were proposed by politicians and economists to which there were no easy answers. Could economic health be restored to Europe if Germany were kept in the condition of international pauper? Without an economically healthy and politically stable Germany, could Europe resist the siren call of left-wing revolutionaries? And if Germany were treated as a second-class economic citizen, with perhaps unfortunate economic repercussions throughout Europe, would Europe become a lackluster purchaser of American and British surpluses?

These were serious questions, and Wilson was further disturbed by the thought that France wanted more than blood money; France, some argued, wished to place an economic millstone around the German neck. While both Wilson and Lloyd George found this idea abhorrent and thought French strategy shortsighted and bound to fail, it was hard to resist the pleas of suffering France for indemnity-like amounts. Wilson's advisers warned him that Germany's debt should be fixed, that it should be based squarely on Germany's estimated capacity to pay, and that the payment years should not exceed thirty. But France in particular wanted both the stipulated time to pay and the total assessment to be open-ended. Clemenceau commented that no matter how much he acquired for France, his people would denounce him as a traitor for not having acquired twice that sum. France won a short-term victory. Fixing the total liability and the time of repayment were assigned to a Reparation Commission provided for in the Versailles Treaty. Since the United States did not join the League, she had no representative on that important committee and did not initially act as an effective moderator in determining the first assessment schedule.[20]

It was no secret to Wilson that Germany would feel aggrieved by the financial burden placed upon her, or that in fact many injustices would be written into the treaty itself. Wilson had great faith, however, that his envisioned League of Nations would have sufficient power and collective wisdom to make political adjustments and to right obvious wrongs. Detailing Wilson's fight at the Conference for a League structure suitable to his vision is a study in heroic persistence. From Wilson's perspective, France was the major drag on his efforts to write liberal and politically cosmopolitan concepts into the League's charter. Where Wilson envisioned the community of nations cooperating within a structure that would promote peace, stability, and economic growth, France wished to see a league of victors united in its determination that 1914 would never happen again. Sensing Wilson's deep longing to see his concept of the League emerge from the Conference's deliberations, Clemenceau shrewdly forced Wilson to accept a series of concessions on territories and reparations, concessions that Wilson deeply regretted. For example, when Wilson felt compelled to ask his Conference colleagues that the Monroe Doctrine be specifically exempted from League control, Clemenceau, evidence suggests, gave French consent only after Wilson agreed to stipulations concerning military occupation of the Rhineland.

The League charter that emerged was a joint British-American product. France's delegation had little confidence in the League

---

[20] Upon recommendation of the Reparations Commission, the Supreme Council of the League stood sponsor on May 5, 1921, that Germany would pay $33 billion over an indefinite period of time. The costs of the allied occupation, or obligations in kind were not included in that figure. Receipts were assigned on a percentage basis: France, 52; Great Britain, 22; Italy, 10; Belgium, 8; Japan and other powers, 8. A well-documented account of the reparations settlement is Philip M. Burnett's *Reparation at the Paris Peace Conference from the Standpoint of the American Delegation*, 2 vols. (New York, 1940).

as constructed to maintain peace and a world safe for Frenchmen. To France, the League was a mechanism that might be able to help maintain peace if the membership were not universal, if the members shared her mortal fear of Germany and distrust of Soviet Russia, and if America's full influence was exerted through the organization to maintain the peace agreements. Any notion of a *universal* community acting in the spirit of compromise to effect a better world for all sounded like nonsense to French negotiators. It is however one of history's little ironies that doubting France joined the League and made some effort to make it work; its chief sponsor could not persuade his own nation to join. Observing the debate in America over the League, France was soon able to conclude that she had been prudent not to entrust her security entirely to American promises or to American-sponsored organizations. Her best security was a Gallic foot firmly planted on the Germanic neck. Her only regret was that France had been so moderate in its demands at Versailles.

Another irritant to French-American relations concerned the so-called war debts owed by France to the United States. This issue surfaced early at the Conference and is not resolved to this day. When all American loans and credits extended to France were combined, the bill came to about $4,000,000,000. From the American side of the ocean, the first questions posed seem both logical and fair: when did France intend to begin repayment, how long did France wish the payments to extend, and how did France wish to arrange her schedule of payments? It was first assumed by the American people and their political representatives that a grateful France would wish to pay her honest debts in full.

France saw the war debts question within quite a different framework. First, she thought some distinctions needed to be made. Reconstruction loans, for example, should be viewed in quite a different way than loans negotiated to help win the war. Monies loaned to defeat the common enemy, which were spent almost entirely in the United States, should perhaps be seen as part of wealthy America's contribution to the war effort. It was also the French viewpoint that Germany represented a real menace to American security; American greenbacks loaned to

better expend French blood seemed like a sound American investment. Was French blood not sufficient payment both for principal and interest? Reconstruction loans were on a separate footing and were accepted as contractual obligations by most French
officials. In any case, the United States must be made to realize
that the war had been a shattering experience for the French
economy, that surplus revenue must be directed primarily toward
internal reconstruction, and that French debts to America must
be seen in the larger context of reparations and intergovernmental debts.

One recent writer has traced this troubling issue through the
Republican years to 1933. What emerges from his study is a
sense of the enormous complexities of the issues and, too, that
many officials and business advisers to the Republican administrations of the 1920s were rather fully aware that an "Uncle
Shylock" approach toward the French war debts question was
economically unsound and politically unwise. Administration officials in private conceded that France's abilities to pay her war
debts were in fact related to reparations payments she extracted
from a reluctant Germany; that huge transfers of monetary sums
could be unsettling to the international economy; and that France
argued with some justice that American gains from the war fully
justified a substantial shifting of the war debts burden. The
great stumbling block to meeting France halfway was the Congress and American expectations that the taxpayer would not
have unexpected costs of the war added to his tax bill. On
December 19, 1918 the Secretary of the Treasury expressed this
conviction when he cabled the delegates: "Congress believes the
loans are good and should be collected." Both Congress and the
public thus took an active interest in the debt questions, invari-
ably from a legal rather than from a broadly political and economic perspective.[21]

Wilson's problems in approaching this issue therefore served
as a storm warning for future administrations. From the French
perspective, the hardnosed American position seemed particu-

---

[21] Melvyn P. Leffler, "The Struggle for Stability: American Policy Toward
France, 1921–1933," Unpublished Ph.D. dissertation, The Ohio State University, 1972, pp. 123–140.

larly ungracious coming from a nation that had emerged from the war as the world's creditor and banker, with its lands untouched, its industries expanding, and with dazzling prospects of invading new world markets. Both Clemenceau and Lloyd George sometimes suffered from the haunting prospect that English and French blood had been shed in order to make the world safe for American economic expansion.

* * * * *

French-American differences at the peace conference were well-defined and very sharp. In some ways France and the United States were the chief antagonists at Versailles. Fundamental political questions were approached from such different perspectives, psychologies, and experiences that in retrospect little could have been done to ameliorate the conflicts. And it is instructive to note that from the perspective of 1939, conference participants from both nations could argue that their positions had been sound. On the German question, for example, American and British conferees could emphasize that in fact it *had* been impossible to keep Germany down, that harsh attitudes and intransigent French policies written into the Treaty had simply provoked Germany, and that the recommended American and British strategy of seeking peace through prosperity and cooperation had been the epitome of wisdom. Frenchmen, however, could say that peace had been lost because their recommendation of placing the yoke on the German neck had been negated by well-meaning nations anxious to gain German markets without regard to the military consequences of a beaten but untamed Germany.

Versailles was not therefore an end, but a beginning. At Versailles the world heard the opening arguments on issues that continue to disturb contemporary statesmen. Maintaining peace in Europe, managing economies disrupted by war, fulfilling the expectations of war-ravaged peoples, propping up weakened colonial empires, distributing the spoils of war, and bringing the world's nations together into a peace-minded and creative association were all major issues at Versailles and in the interwar period. The Versailles discussions were thus mainly rehearsal for the on-going debates of the interwar years, debates that tended to underline the continuing antagonisms in French-American relations.

Clemenceau's gesture to Secretary of State Lansing when the Versailles Peace was signed, of grasping both of the secretary's hands for "that is the way France and America should greet each other today," probably seemed a little ironic to both men.[22]

* * * * *

Wilson's reluctance even to submit the French-American-British security treaty to the Senate, and the Senate's ultimate refusal to ratify the Treaty of Versailles made it appear that the wartime American presence in Europe was a mere aberration. As Clemenceau had suspected, Europe must set its own house in order, which was to say that France must maintain a constant vigilance vis-a-vis Germany. France quite clearly could not rely directly on the enormous vitality and resources of America to help reconstruct Europe and constrain Germany.

This initial French reaction, based upon America's decision neither to join the League nor to give France a treaty of guarantee, was not soundly based. American policy makers were convinced throughout the 1920s that the United States must take an active part in the search for peace and stability. France, and many other nations of the world, were confused by American refusal to join the League and by American reluctance to participate in conferences called to discuss political questions of primary concern to the nations of Europe. American public opinion, however, did not indicate that the United States ought to maintain a high profile on the international political stage. But as American policy makers argued privately, the power holding the purse strings could always have its say, and in many situations its position would be the final one.

Since it was necessary for the victorious powers to request

---

[22] Lansing Memorandum, June 28, 1919, *Foreign Relations, 1919. The Paris Peace Conference* (Washington, D.C., 1942), XI, p. 599.

American loans for purposes of reconstruction and to stabilize their currencies, pressure could be exerted upon a borrowing power that sharply challenged American policy. Germany, too, became a heavy borrower in American money markets and was thus presumably amenable to American pressure. American policy makers were therefore not overly distressed by America's constricted political role in Europe and in fact saw many advantages in influencing policy primarily through exercising the power of the purse. This evolving American approach to participation and intervention, with its emphasis on rational men arriving at common solutions through level-headed analysis of relevant data, was attuned to the "prevailing notion that appropriate solutions to international problems would emerge from the objective and scientific analysis of their economic roots."[23]

Although many Americans were under the impression that their government was not intimately involved in European affairs, the record of the 1920s argues otherwise. It is possible to document active, if discreet, American participation in almost every issue of consequence coming before the League of Nations, or considered by councils with a less international flavor. Disarmament, reparations, war debts, European security, expanding international trade, and stabilizing currencies were all matters of vital concern to the American government and issues on which it tried to exercise considerable influence. With the onslaught of the depression, American contributions toward ameliorating difficult international questions was much less constructive though the rhetoric of helpfulness often lingered on.

It is difficult to name a single major issue of the interwar period on which France and America shared common goals and ideas. Disarmament, for example, exacerbated relations from the Washington Naval Conference of 1921–1922 through the abortive World Disarmament Conference of 1932–34. Since the United States did not share France's central concern—security as it related to the containment of Germany—a sympathetic discussion of issues related to disarmament seemed virtually impossible. Where Americans talked in terms of cutting taxes through arms reductions, Frenchmen spoke of the sacrifices necessary to

---

[23] Leffler, "The Struggle for Stability," p. 14.

maintain the peace. While Americans tended to be rather cavalier about reduction of land armies and more exacting when discussing naval arms, France held that both land and naval armaments systems were vital to her survival and must be discussed together. And while Americans argued that armaments reduction itself would lessen international tensions and point the world toward peace, French governments insisted that arms reductions preceding needed political agreements would encourage aggressors to provocative acts. Americans regarded weapons systems as irritants and subversive to hopes for peace; France viewed them as her lifeline to security.

Each conference on disarmament in the interwar era highlighted differing French-American perceptions of the attendant questions. France was very reluctant, for example, to sign the Five Power Treaty on naval limitation that emerged from the Washington Conference of 1921–1922. She questioned the wisdom of establishing a ten-year holiday on construction of capital ships and the limits set on the sizes of cruisers, aircraft carriers, and capital ships. And she was outraged that as a nation with a coastline on both the Atlantic and the Mediterranean, and with naval needs relating to her overseas empire, she should be asked to accept a fixed ratio in capital ships and aircraft carrier tonnage that placed her on an equal footing with puny Italy and in a distinctly inferior position to the United States, Great Britain, and Japan.[24] France, in fact, accepted the stipulated tonnage limitations for battleships and battle cruisers but only after Secretary of State Charles Evans Hughes appealed directly to Premier Aristide Briand. Not only was France disturbed at the long-term security implications of the treaty but she felt offended that the Anglo-Saxon powers and Japan had treated her in such a preemptory fashion—and that before a watching world.

As France expected, and as events subsequently proved, the Five Power Treaty did not stop the naval race. Instead of build-

---

[24] The Five Power Treaty, signed on February 6, 1922, was to remain in force until December 31, 1936. For the United States, Great Britain, Japan, France, and Italy it set, respectively, tonnage ratios of 5 : 5 : 3 : 1.67 : 1.67 on capital ships and aircraft carriers only.

ing in the "restricted" categories, the powers raced ahead to build ships in the unrestricted categories of submarines, cruisers, and destroyers. President Calvin Coolidge was distressed by the enormous American sums appropriated for naval armaments. Therefore, in June of 1927 he asked Britain, France, Japan, and Italy to confer at Geneva with the United States, hopefully to reach an agreement "for limitation in the classes of naval vessels not covered by the Washington Treaty."[25] France, as well as Italy, refused to participate in a naval conference. Although the French government was aware of the domestic pressures on Coolidge to reduce taxes, France saw little reason to participate in another conference where she might be forced to accept naval formulas suitable to the American taxpayer but hazardous to French security. And the French government further believed that it bordered on stupidity to consider only naval armaments reduction when larger security questions called for intelligent assessment of total armaments balances.

France did decide it would be politically astute to attend the London Naval Conference, opened late in January 1930, but felt once again that the American and British views on disarmament were myopic and foolishly unrealistic. With Italy assuming an increasingly unfriendly stance toward her and with French-German relations only superficially friendly, France felt that the ratio numbers game on naval armaments created illusions of security while fundamental security questions remained unsettled. France asked the United States and Great Britain for security guarantees before she would assent to any treaty on naval reductions. President Hoover and Secretary of State Stimson knew the request could not be honored. Consequently, when the treaty was drawn, France (and Italy as well) refused to concur in Part III, the key section containing the naval ratios.[26]

The interwar merry-go-round on naval disarmament reached

---

[25] Merze Tate, *The United States and Armaments* (Cambridge, 1948), p. 141.

[26] A fine summary of the Conference is found in Robert H. Ferrell, *American Diplomacy in the Great Depression: Hoover-Stimson Foreign Policy, 1929–1933* (New Haven, 1957), pp. 87–103.

its conclusion in the mid and late 1930s against the background of a French-Italian naval race, the cynical disregard by Japan of earlier naval limitations, and the various European crises provoked by a rearming Germany. In March of 1938, America and France were joined by Great Britain in invoking the escape clause of the London Treaty of 1936.[27] For its part; the United States moved toward rapid naval rearmament, followed plans to build a two-ocean navy and a fleet that in total power would surpass the combined fleets of Japan, Italy, and Germany. For whatever it was worth, France in 1938 could argue that her position on disarmament since 1921 had been correct: armaments levels had been only discordant symptoms of political problems; American and British politicians had acted irresponsibly in trying to exorcise the symptoms rather than prescribing for causes; France had acted responsibly in refusing to disarm at the behest of America and Great Britain; yet those two nations, by their periodic insistence on disarmament, had helped to create an international atmosphere that undermined the democracies' morale and encouraged those nations wishing to overturn the postwar settlements.

Differences with the United States on disarmament matters did not deter France from efforts to associate the United States with her security system. Upon some prompting by a Columbia University law professor, James T. Shotwell, Premier Aristide Briand of France, in April 1927, sent a public message to the American people proposing a treaty that would renounce war as an instrument of national policy between France and the American people. Such a treaty, Briand privately hoped, would involve a kind of American moral commitment to France that might prompt America to assist France if she were attacked in the future. This comforting perception by Briand was precisely the point that troubled Secretary of State Frank B. Kellogg and his advisers. Much as they might wish eternal security for

---

[27] In that treaty, signed on March 25, 1936, France, Great Britain, and the United States provided for continuing naval limitations. The treaty also provided an escape clause if other nations exceeded the signatories' self-imposed limitations. Neither Japan nor Italy signed the treaty.

France, they did not intend that it be given at the possible cost of American blood.

They devised a stratagem to destroy Briand's purpose; on the suggestion of Senator William E. Borah the State Department simply suggested that the treaty be made a multilateral one. The community of nations should share so noble an idea as outlawing war; it should not be hoarded by France, America, and a few other choice friends of France. Secretary Kellogg, who forwarded this suggestion in order to take America off the hook and to bamboozle France, soon convinced himself the idea had merit and ended by bamboozling himself and the American people. Real enthusiasm for the treaty burgeoned in the United States. Briand was very annoyed at Kellogg's suggestion and thought such an idea ridiculous but as a Nobel Peace Prize winner, Briand did not see how he could withhold public applause for the apparently exalted cause of outlawing war.

Accordingly, fifteen sponsors signed the pact in Paris on August 27, 1928. All signatories promised to "renounce war as an instrument of national policy" and to solve "all disputes or conflicts of whatever nature or of whatever origin" by pacific means. France accepted the treaty but with the reservation that her right to "legitimate self-defense" remained unimpaired. American reservations were even more severe, making clear that America assumed no obligations to preserve the peace. Briand's purpose in first proposing the treaty was thus totally defeated as was the purpose of some American supporters who hoped the treaty would tie the United States into the League of Nations security system. While some commentators thought the treaty a grand international gesture, an "international kiss" as Senator Claude Swanson said, it was actually a direct indication to France that American power and resources were unavailable to France in her efforts to uphold the Treaty of Versailles.[28]

Nor would the United States give France support on questions relating to war debts and reparations. France wanted reparations

---

[28] See Robert H. Ferrell, *Peace in Their Time: The Origins of the Kellogg-Briand Pact* (New Haven, 1952), and John C. Vinson, *William E. Borah and the Outlawing of War* (Athens, 1957).

payments due her by Germany paid in full and paid on time. She expected wartime allies and associates to support the Versailles reparations settlement and thus to encourage Germany to pay France what was due her. Since France viewed the reparations arrangement as one way to retard German economic recovery and growth, she was deeply troubled to observe American money pouring into Germany on both long and short-term loans in amounts roughly equal to the reparations sums Germany owed her conquerors. The United States, to French chagrin, was obviously helping Germany to postpone the consequences of the reparations settlement. But France was most angered by British and American talk about the economic wisdom of cancelling reparations. International trade would be stimulated, economies stabilized, governments strengthened, wartime hatreds banked, and prosperity encouraged if only reparations were cancelled—or so went the revisionist arguments. France replied that cancellation of reparations would work an economic hardship on those nations who were innocent victims of German aggression, revitalize the German economy and thus the German threat to Europe, and that cancellation, or even partial cancellation, would become the fatal precedent for Germany to smash the political and economic engagements concluded at Versailles.

France was especially sensitive to the American position, for while loose talk about reparations cancellation came from America, Congress was quite explicit—even vehement—in asserting that war debts owed America were not to be cancelled. Nor would any administration in the interwar period openly recognize that French capacity to pay her war debts to Uncle Sam was related to her success in exacting reparations from Germany. This position, when combined with American tariff legislation making it most difficult for France to repay her debts in goods and services, struck the French as being completely unreasonable.[29]

From the American standpoint real efforts were made to be helpful to France. The World War Foreign Debt Commission,

---

[29] A helpful summary of war debts and reparations matters is found in L. Ethan Ellis, *Republican Foreign Policy, 1921–1933* (New Brunswick, 1968), Chapter VI.

established by Congress in February 1922, took constructive action between 1923 and 1930 to negotiate acceptable debt settlement agreements with America's debtors. In these years, the principle of "capacity to pay" was first established in the 1925 settlement with France, an important principle that was not favorably received in Congress. Interest notes were effectively lowered, the years of payment (62) were extended far beyond what Congress had earlier anticipated (25 years), and the French debt, for example, was reduced by 50 per cent.

Since the American government refused to recognize the link between reparations owed by Germany and war debts owed to the United States, it could only take an indirect part in helping to find acceptable solutions to reparations problems. Nevertheless, when Germany defaulted late in 1922 and French and Belgian troops invaded the Ruhr Valley in retaliation in January 1923, American diplomacy was very active in urging moderation on France and fertile in suggestions for some settlement.[30] Over the next seven years American citizens, acting as private agents but knowing the mind of their government, served actively on two reparations commissions that spelled out Germany's reparations obligations. Bankers Charles G. Dawes and Owen D. Young found their names attached to the reparations plans proposed in 1924 and 1929, plans which arranged for American loans to Germany, tied German payments to her rising economic growth, permitted Germany to extend her payment years to 59, and reduced German obligations by $9,000,000,000.

France could hardly be grateful to the United States for concluding terms apparently so fair, if not lenient to Germany, particularly when American loans poured into Germany and made it possible for Germany to meet her obligations with relative ease. The last bitter round of the reparations imbroglio began with the stock market crash in 1929. American investors in German bonds and other German securities began to call in their loans. The cycle of loans-reparations-war debts was thus broken since Germany found herself unable to pay her repara-

---

[30] See Royal J. Schmidt, *Versailles and the Ruhr; Seedbed of World War II* (The Hague, 1968), for a discussion of the Ruhr occupation and the role of American diplomacy in resolving the reparations questions.

tions obligations. Disaster for the international monetary and credit systems seemed imminent unless decisive action was taken. President Herbert Hoover decided in the summer of 1931 that only a temporary suspension of intergovernmental debts would give Germany time to get her economic house in order. Without consulting France, Hoover announced on June 20 that the United States would postpone all intergovernmental payments, beginning on July 1, if other governments would follow suit.

The French government was terribly angry about Hoover's announcement and with good reason. France, after all, was the major beneficiary of German payments. For Hoover to call for a moratorium without even consulting the French government seemed an act of gross discourtesy, more the act of an enemy that a friend. And the longer they examined the implications of the moratorium, the unhappier the French became. Was not the moratorium, they asked, simply the first step toward cancellation of reparations obligations? Events soon showed that it was. And was this step toward cancellation not an enormous encouragement to the Germans to break other stipulations of the Versailles settlement? As for the supposed American desire to save the "international economic order," the French took a more jaundiced view of the moratorium initiative; it seemed designed more to protect American investors who held German securities than to preserve the international monetary order.[31]

Real bitterness was thus interjected into French-American relations by the so-called Hoover moratorium. France only acceded to the Hoover plan, with reservations, following two weeks of consultation. French reluctance to concur in turn angered Hoover and administration officials. France, they complained, cared little about the welfare of the international economic system as long as she could sit on her considerable gold reserves, enjoy her relative prosperity, and exact the last pound of flesh from a near prostrate Germany.

---

[31] Ambassador Walter Evans Edge recalls the bitterness of Aristide Briand over the timing and substance of the moratorium in his *A Jerseymen's Journal: Fifty Years of American Business and Politics* (Princeton, 1948), pp. 194–195.

When the Lausanne Settlement of 1932 virtually absolved Germany of further reparations payments, France decided that she should not meet her war debts payments to the United States.[32] Americans jeered at this French decision for France had not yet been affected in a major way by the depression; her case for nonpayment was therefore not very convincing to an ill-informed American Congress and public. For her part, France thought it quite outrageous that the United States should help Germany to escape her reparations obligations to France and then chide France for discontinuing the routine of debt payments that was directly dependent upon German reparations payments to France.

Historians have often commented that no issue in European politics in the interwar years provoked as much anger and enmity as did the war debts-reparations issue. France was at the center of the storm because she felt her economic and physical security so directly tied to German reparations. America was also at the center of the controversy, in ways highly displeasing to France. In general, various administrations supported the British position of scaling down both reparations and war debts but with the hard proviso that whatever happened *re* reparations, the war debt payments to the United States were to be continued. The Hoover moratorium represented, from the French viewpoint, a continuation of American policy by drastic means. From the moratorium to the outbreak of World War II, notes of cordiality sounded in French-American relations were echoes from the past. War debts and reparations were thus issues that bore bitter fruit beyond the European scene.

*   *   *   *   *

---

[32] Ambassador Edge describes the futile struggle of the Edouard Herriot government to persuade the French National Assembly that the annual payment to the United States be made. *Jerseymen's Journal*, p. 224. President Hoover received the news with some disgust for he was aware that French citizens had on deposit over half a billion in dollar exchange on deposit in New York banks. Ferrell, *American Diplomacy in the Great Depression*, p. 237.

In a way not fully appreciated by observers living in the inter-war years, the Republican administrations had a broad international outlook. There were many highly-placed and intelligent officials in those administrations who realized that the United States must take an active and responsible part in European and world affairs. Hoover himself was acutely conscious of the complexity of trade and monetary matters and tried to act constructively in the world economic crisis. If his actions were not always appreciated by European politicians, they realized that Hoover was international-minded and trying to shape American policies in ways that acknowledged the interrelatedness of complex monetary and trade issues.

The Great Depression, of course, cast a shadow over Western governments and created fears and pressures that often resulted in paralysis or in unhelpful governmental actions. European leaders, for example, were simply appalled when Hoover consented to the high-walled Hawley-Smoot Tariff of 1930, but they realized he was under strong pressure by Congress to protect declining markets for American industry and agriculture. French officials felt, however, that even congressmen should have the intelligence to see that the Hawley-Smoot (and the earlier Fordney-McCumber Tariff of 1922) would retard foreign exports, paralyze collection of the war debts, and encourage foreign economic retaliation. Hoover's decision neither to fight the tariff measure while it was still in Congress nor to veto it when presented for his signature was widely interpreted as an indication that he was a political lightweight, a president who was unable or unwilling to defend his convictions. When followed by the Hoover moratorium on intergovernmental debts, it is understandable that the French government was pleased with the election of Franklin D. Roosevelt. Before taking office, Roosevelt gave private assurances to various individuals that he favored the maintenance of international economic stability (a prime French objective) and that he wished to work closely and in a cooperative spirit with the government of France to address the troublesome issues of war debts and monetary policy. A new era, some French officials hoped, could well be opening in French-American relations.

It is ironic, in retrospect, to compare the hopes of French officials in 1933 with the reality of French-American relations in the Roosevelt era. In few administrations were French-American relations so filled with recrimination, charges of bad faith, and feelings that the other nation was not doing its part to maintain peace or to take responsible positions on international financial questions. Essentially, neither fully understood the constraints under which each government was operating or the enormous domestic and international pressures that acted to shape the contours of national policy. French governments in the early 1930s tended to be financial internationalists and commercial nationalists whereas the United States, in contrast, was financially isolationist and commercially expansionist. Such fundamental differences were bound to make it difficult for the two governments to cooperate economically.

France was early disappointed in Roosevelt when he submarined the long-planned World Economic Conference in 1933. To stabilize currencies as the French wished, Roosevelt's advisers warned him, would impair planned American domestic financial manipulation that could lead to recovery. Apparently forced to make a choice, Roosevelt decided that international economic recovery must take a back seat to domestic recovery. Roosevelt not only destroyed the conference but he did it in such dramatic and conclusive fashion that indignant French officials tried to organize a censure vote upon the United States and ultimately left the conference bitter and disillusioned.[33] Their temper was not assuaged when, in the last weeks of the conference, the American delegation also refused even to discuss the war debts issue or to negotiate reciprocal tariff agreements so highly regarded by Secretary of State Cordell Hull.

Through this conference French officials were put on notice that the American domestic crisis was so serious that the United States would apparently take a constructive part in international affairs primarily when an action related to some American domestic need. Actually, such a conclusion would have been premature and simplistic. If one looks at the early Roosevelt years there was extensive action on the international scene. Roosevelt brought to fruition Coolidge's and Hoover's earlier initiatives

---

[33] The French viewpoint is developed in Bonnet, *Quai d'Orsay*, pp. 110–111.

to establish more cordial relations with the nations of Latin America. The administration was also acutely concerned about the deteriorating situation in East Asia. With America's rather long history of participation in the trade and politics of East Asia, and given American determination to maintain the open door for trade and investments in that part of the world, Japan's ambitions and forward movement in southeast Asia were viewed with genuine alarm. There was extensive American diplomatic consultation and action throughout the 1930s on East Asian affairs although the United States failed to provide leadership appropriate to its goals or its level of anxiety.

So the Roosevelt administration actively concerned itself with foreign relations from its early moments but that is not to say that Europe's affairs were its prime focus, for they were not. Even if Roosevelt himself had wished to place Europe in the forefront of American foreign policy, this would have been most difficult. American experiences in World War I (as perceived in the disillusioned 1930s) and the continuing controversies over war debts had convinced many Americans that noninvolvement in European politics was not only sensible but mandatory. American irritation with European "ingratitude" was clearly indicated in April 1934 when the Johnson Debt Default Act was passed prohibiting both public and private loans to governments of nations who were not current in payment of war debts. This act, of course, was a direct slap at defaulting France and it was so understood in France.[34]

America was thus in no state of mind to perceive the seriousness of European events in the 1930s. France in particular received little sympathy for her diplomatic and financial plight. Few Americans understood that France had had to accept in the 1920s and 1930s the primary responsibility for upholding the European settlements in the Versailles Treaty and that this burden, psychologically at least, was too heavy for France to carry. The United States and Russia, two powers whose participation in the war had contributed to German defeat, did not place their

---

[34] The bill, as passed, was approved by President Roosevelt. See *Franklin D. Roosevelt and Foreign Affairs*, Edgar B. Nixon, Ed., 3 vols. (Cambridge, 1969), II, pp. 26–27.

weight diplomatically in the scales against Germany. And France soon found herself confronted with a succession of British governments more anxious to please Germany and make it prosperous (and thus able to purchase British exports) than to uphold the Treaty as it related to French security. France was therefore burdened by a British ally who came increasingly to feel that the Versailles settlement had been much too harsh upon Germany and that France was playing an unworthy and destructive role in trying to maintain the settlement intact. American policy either implicitly or explicitly supported Great Britain in her wish to revise Versailles.

France reacted in various ways to this unpalatable situation. She established firm diplomatic ties with Poland and with the "Little Entente" of Rumania, Czechoslovakia, and Yugoslavia hoping thus to construct an eastern *cordon sanitaire* around Germany. She flirted periodically with Russia and Italy, hoping to keep them safely out of the German orbit. After failure of the Ruhr occupation, 1923–1925, it is true, France took a much more conciliatory line toward Germany. Without the support of her British ally, and having witnessed firsthand how difficult it was to collect reparations at gunpoint, the French decided the best approach to Germany was moderation and conciliation. Nevertheless France continued to exert herself to uphold the spirit and the law of the Versailles settlement. France, once the name that stirred the hearts of revolutionaries throughout Europe, became the bulwark of Europe's conservative forces in the interwar years.

An inordinate amount of abuse was heaped upon France for her diplomatic intransigence and for her antirevisionist stance. She was accused by friends and enemies alike of being paranoid and of aborting many possibilities for constructive international changes through her obsessive concern for security. In retrospect the criticism of France appears less enlightened than it did at the time. Even in the 1920s, however, when France was apparently able to preserve the European settlements by her own determination, the criticism had a corroding effect on her will and purpose.

Also present in French calculations, but not visible to foreign governments, was the terrible scar left upon the French military establishment by the war. Despite their public bravado on German matters and despite the maintenance of a sizable and well-regarded army, the military leaders were at one with the politicians in wishing desperately that France need never face Germany again in war. They realized how close France had come to defeat and were knowledgeable about the near-disastrous mutiny in the French army in 1917. As many analysts have pointed out, the whole psychology of victorious France was defensive, to the point where she planned her military strategy and deployed her resources in such a way that her diplomatic structure was virtually nullified. Given French military and diplomatic commitments in Eastern Europe, given her need for mobile striking forces to keep the German troops out of the Rhineland, and given the German emphasis on armored mobility and the role of air power, efforts to construct the Maginot Line fortifications now seem misplaced. Begun in 1930 along France's northeastern frontier, the Maginot fortifications spoke eloquently both of irreplaceable French manpower losses in World War I and of her probable effective support for those allies far to the east of the Rhine.

There is an extensive literature on France in the 1930s, much of it written from the perspective of French military capitulation to Germany in June 1940. The literature is highly condemnatory of the political structure and politicians of the Third Republic. Governmental instability, selfish political parties deeply factionalized along ideological and interest lines, unseemly behavior in the Parliament, scandals (such as the Stavisky scandal)[35] reaching into the highest places, politicians without courage to face the financial crises at home or to stand by French commitments abroad, and a military General Staff with more terror

---

[35] Alexander Stavisky, it was discovered in 1934, had engineered a series of swindles, the total amounting to some 200,000,000 francs. Stavisky's connections to the "best people," the desultory prosecution of the case, and Stavisky's suicide under suspicious conditions made the affair an explosive one in France. The riot in February 1934 on the Place de la Concorde, one that got out of hand and developed into a bloody street battle, was triggered partly by outrage over the government's handling of the Stavisky affair. Alexander Werth, *The Twilight of France, 1933–1940* (New York, 1942), pp. 14–21.

than iron in their souls were often noted as hallmarks of France in the 1930s. This literature also speaks of the deep rifts introduced into French society by the Depression and of the desperate efforts of the Popular Front governments, 1936–1938, to patch together domestic coalitions and policies that would resist fascism and preserve French democracy through timely social reform. Most of the viewpoints centering around the theme of French decay were well-aired in the American newspapers and received substantiation through reports by the American diplomatic staff in France or by visitors who had seen France firsthand. President Roosevelt, who received his information primarily from these three sources, himself came to believe in the decay of French society.

Historians are now assessing French life and institutions in a broader context, and those of other European nations as well. Raymond Sontag speaks of "a broken world," Laurence Lafore of "the end of glory." The day of the Euro-centered world, it is argued, had passed quite without the statesmen of Western Europe realizing it. The centers of decision had moved to America and Russia; politicians in Europe danced on invisible strings, only vaguely aware they were no longer in control. Nor did European statesmen fully recognize the terrible internal damage done to their societies by the war, by the destructive inflation that soon followed, and by the Great Depression whose impact was felt most sharply in the 1930s. It now seems fairer to argue that political developments in interwar France, for example, were not really susceptible to astute management; that the internal upheavals, inflation and devaluation, the apparent political instability, a society factionalized and at times on the verge of civil war were not primarily the fruits of faulty political structures and second-rate politicians, but were part of the burden of World War I and its aftermath. Stanley Hoffmann even speaks of France as being a "stalemated society," a phrase with negative and mechanistic overtones.[36]

These larger truths about the political and social condition of

---

[36] See Hoffmann's stimulating essay, "Paradoxes of the French Political Community," pp. 1–117 in Stanley Hoffmann, Ed., *In Search of France* (Cambridge, 1963).

France were only dimly perceived by a few contemporary observers. This level of insight was not available to the Roosevelt administration and the American people; consequently, it was impossible for them to understand the failure of nerve in the French governments as they faced the succession of challenges raised by the Third Reich and by Mussolini's Italy. It was a puzzle to Roosevelt and to the State Department, for example, that France did not challenge German reoccupation of the Rhineland on March 7, 1936. If France's physical security rested on any single arrangement of the Versailles settlement, it was the demobilization of the Rhineland; also, the Rhineland arrangement was based upon German consent freely given in the Locarno agreements of December 1925 and was, therefore, fully defensible before a watching world. As one historian has commented, Hitler transformed the entire diplomatic and military situation in Western Europe with the Rhineland occupation: "France was exposed to attack, Germany was more defensible against attack; France's allies in eastern Europe were now more cut off from French help and more at Germany's mercy; and a further evident repudiation of the peace settlement had gone unpunished."[37] French Foreign Minister Pierre-Etienne Flandin did wish the United States to issue a statement condemning on moral grounds any unilateral repudiation of the Treaty. Secretary Hull, however, stated that "we do not feel we could appropriately make any comment at this time," nor would he even allow American representatives to attend meetings of the League where the issue was discussed.[38]

President Roosevelt became increasingly sensitized to the European situation in 1935 and 1936. He was distressed by Italy's violation of Ethiopia's territory in October 1935 and called for an American "moral embargo" on shipment of oil, steel, and other commodities to Italy. Eruption of civil war in Spain in July 1936 alerted Roosevelt that the surge toward revolution was not confined to relations between nations. He was also deeply concerned when in March 1938 Nazi troops marched into Austria and Hitler later announced that Austria

---

[37] Thomson, *Europe After Napoleon*, p. 693.
[38] *Foreign Relations, 1936*, I, pp. 216–217. Hull's statement was made to Ambassador Straus, Washington, March 10, 1936, *ibid.*, p. 228.

was now a state of the German Reich, and this without a finger being lifted by France or Great Britain. An act of abandonment that provoked apprehension in the White House, however, was French and British desertion of Czechoslovakia in her hour of crisis with Hitler. France, it is true, did begin to call up reserves in September 1938 as Hitler's threats against Czechoslovakia became increasingly ominous. On September 26, Roosevelt appealed to Germany for a peaceful solution of the issue.[39] The French government decided to follow British leadership on the Czech crisis, and the British government led France quickly toward the Munich agreement of September 30, 1938. France thus took part in the dismantlement of the nation that was her diplomatic lynchpin in Eastern Europe, a nation to whom she had firm commitments and whose army and sturdy fortifications had given Hitler and his generals some reason for concern.

As the European peace deteriorated, the Roosevelt administration went as far as it felt it could to encourage British and French resistance to the increasing demands of Germany. American pats on the back, of course, were accompanied by denials of any actual or implied commitment. By the time that the Roosevelt administration began to exhibit anxiety about the European scene, the French government had long since committed itself to follow the British lead. There were certainly no concrete reasons for France to rely upon American support in diplomatic crises, as the history of the interwar decade illustrated repeatedly. And as the crisis of the 30s deepened, the American Congress made it explicit, through passage of a series of neutrality acts beginning in 1935, that it did not intend for the United States to become involved in another European war. As Roosevelt stated in his personal appeal to Hitler during the Czech crisis, the "Government of the United States has no political involvements in Europe, and will assume no obligations in the conduct of the present negotiations."[40]

In the Czech crisis French Premier Daladier and Foreign Min-

---

[39] See Cordell Hull, *The Memoirs of Cordell Hull*, 2 vols. (New York, 1948), I, pp. 591–593.

[40] Department of State, *Peace and War: United States Foreign Policy, 1931–1941* (Washington, 1943), p. 246. Development of the neutrality legislation is best followed in Robert A. Divine, *The Illusion of Neutrality* (Chicago, 1962).

ister Georges Bonnet certainly gathered direct evidence that the United States must not be counted upon, despite brave public words from the President in Chicago on October 5, 1937 that it would be wise to "quarantine" the aggressors.[41] Bonnet, blamed by many historians for leading France toward ruinous appeasement and self-castration, liked to think himself a realist. A former ambassador at Washington, Bonnet believed that France could be aided in her crisis only by the direct support of the enormously powerful United States. In July and September 1938 he secretly approached Roosevelt and begged for American arbitration of the Czech-German problem and support for France if war followed France's honoring her commitments to Czechoslovakia. Roosevelt was firm in his refusal, believing that such promises would be repudiated by an isolationist Congress and an indignant public. Bonnet then was able to assure his colleagues that there was little that a demoralized and overmatched France could do except to follow Britain's lead and to receive further German solicitations in a cooperative spirit.[42] Whether Bonnet was seeking an excuse to follow an appeasement course is a matter of debate; the fact is that France had her answer from the United States.

Hitler's gobbling up of the truncated Czech state on March 15, 1939 put new spirit into the British, if not the French, government. Now began a series of events involving German threats to Poland that convinced the Chamberlain government, at least, that Hitler's ambitions had no rational limits. In preparation for the coming crisis, Britain, France, and Germany began to bid strongly for a Russian treaty. In the meantime Britain and France signed a virtual blank check alliance with Poland on March 31, 1939, an alliance that gave Poland the power to

---

[41] Dorothy Borg has carefully analyzed Roosevelt's Quarantine Speech in *The United States and the Far Eastern Crisis of 1933–1938* (Cambridge, 1964). Her conclusion: ". . . the President was trying to find a formula which would enable nonbelligerents to exercise an influence upon a war to the extent of actually defeating an aggression while still limiting themselves to the use of methods which would not provoke reprisals that would involve them in hostilities." p. 382.

[42] J. M. Haight, "France, the United States, and the Munich Crisis," *Journal of Modern History*, XXXII (December 1960), pp. 341–348.

determine when Britain and France must enter a future war to defend Poland against attack. Five months later, on August 23, Germany and the Soviet Union concluded a nonaggression treaty, the secret portions of which provided for the partitioning of Poland and the disposition of other Eastern European states. His eastern front now secure, Hitler rushed preparations to invade Poland, an action that was taken on September 1, 1939, despite last-minute warnings from Great Britain and France. Britain and France honored their recent commitment to Poland by declaring war on Germany on September 3, 1939. The Second World War had begun.

* * * * *

There is considerable historical debate about the role played by the United States and by President Roosevelt in the series of European crises of the 1930s. Those who think that Congress and the President did what they could emphasize the paralyzing effect of the Great Depression on American society, the apparent reluctance of the American people to support intervention in Europe, the need for the United States to monitor closely the deteriorating situation in East Asia, the lack of military power-in-being that could serve to impress both friend and foe, and Roosevelt's own philosophy that a political leader dare not move so fast that he finds himself without his army of followers marching in step.

Others are more critical of Roosevelt and emphasize the enormous power of a skillful president to manipulate the public mood. Not only is Roosevelt given low marks by some for not adequately educating the public about the dangers of a revived Germany, but he is sometimes accused of being so overly cautious that the public was actually ahead of Roosevelt in wishing to take actions that might give the aggressors pause.

This debate may well be sterile if one assumes, as have various historians of Germany, that Hitler had a very low regard for American power and potential. There is a strong likelihood that nothing would have served to deflect Hitler from his purposes short of an American declaration that the United States would make war on Germany in certain circumstances. Such a declaration was clearly impossible for Roosevelt to make. Even so, Hitler was essentially a parochial politician, one whose political understanding was limited largely to the perimeters of Europe. He apparently never understood that World War I had shifted the centers of decision beyond the area encompassed by historical Europe.[43]

French governments of the late 1930s were much more perceptive about American potential in a war situation and were; therefore, most anxious to extract commitments from their associate of 1917–1918. When their hopes were not realized, and when their position vis-a-vis Germany deteriorated into a war situation, there was an understandable inclination to assign a sizable portion of the responsibility for France's desperate position to the United States. From Versailles, when the United States helped to deprive France of certain territorial security requisites, to 1937–1939 when Roosevelt and America did little except shake warning fingers at the dictators, and tried to induce the League or its most powerful members to assume the major risks in maintaining the peace, their historic American friend had undermined or simply failed to give France vital support. American-French relations in the interwar period thus sowed a harvest of resentments, ones that would deeply affect their relationship in the coming struggle with Hitler and the era of troubled peace that followed.

France, looking back in 1939 over interwar French-American relations, could attest to Sir Ronald Lindsay's cryptic if somewhat unfair comment: "I know the Americans are a dreadful people to deal with—they cannot make firm promises, but they jolly you along with fair prospects and when you are committed they let you down."[44]

---

[43] J. V. Compton has noted Hitler's remark in January 1940 that he saw no particular danger to Germany if the United States entered the war. *The Swastika and the Eagle: Hitler, the United States, and the Origins of World War II* (Boston, 1967), p. 34.

[44] See fn. 1, p. 196.

CHAPTER VIII

The De Gaulle Era

I'm fed up on all this glorification of the French, a people who have been incapable of self-government for almost two centuries.

Malcolm Bengay

O star of France . . .
Dim, smitten star
Orb not of France alone, pale symbol of my soul, its dearest hopes,
The struggle and the daring, rage divine for liberty,
Of aspirations toward the far ideal, enthusiast's dreams of brother-
    hood . . .
Again thy star, O France, fair, lustrous star,
In heavenly peace, clearer, more bright than ever,
Shall beam immortal.

Walt Whitman

Any large-scale human edifice will be arbitrary and ephemeral if the seal of France is not affixed to it.

Charles de Gaulle[1]

WORLD WAR II had much the same larger effects on France and the United States as did World War I. For the United States, the war meant an enormous expansion of its power, influence, and prosperity. By 1943 it was obvious that the United States would be active politically on the postwar international stage as she had not been in the interwar period. France emerged from the war humiliated, her power and influence dramatically reduced. Her physical destruction had been greater in some ways than in World War I, her economy was dislocated, and her bur-den of debt was enormous.[2] The fact that she had been knocked

---

[1] Bengay's comment is in the Columbus [Ohio] *Dispatch*, June 6, 1943. Charles de Gaulle's statement is found in his *War Memoirs*, 3 vols. (Paris, 1954), III, *Salvation, 1944–1946*, p. 7.

[2] René Albrecht-Carrié, *France, Europe and the Two World Wars* (New York, 1961), p. 323.

out of the war by Germany in only a few days and that she had been able to do so little to free herself left the largest scar of all, a scar upon the spirit and self-respect of France.

It is difficult for once great powers to admit that the world has moved on. Given the circumstances of her humiliation in World War II, France could not admit that her halcyon days of power and glory had passed. Alternating between rage and despair, France since 1945 has struggled to establish herself in the councils of the mighty, always insisting that French wisdom, experience, and power are necessary if European problems are to be handled wisely and if the world is not to be carved into two hegemonies by Russia and the United States. While many have scoffed at French posturing and ambitions, she has succeeded in establishing her influence within Europe to a degree never envisioned by President Franklin D. Roosevelt or Premier Josef Stalin.

In this struggle to escape humiliation France has often asserted herself at the expense of the United States. On many occasions France has refused to subserve her national interests to American policy or strategy. American visions for Europe and the Atlantic community, American perceptions and strategies in the Cold War, and American views about colonialism, arms limitations, or the United Nations were repeatedly challenged by a succession of French governments, whether of the Fourth or the Fifth Republic. This dialogue has been highly irritating to American governments but in retrospect the French challenges have often been supported by meritorious arguments and have had constructive results. The United States was thrust into a position of world leadership at a tender age through a series of catastrophic events. Her insights and wisdom in this new role have not been unerring. France's dissents and suggested alternatives have therefore played a vital role both in seasoning American policies and in helping France to establish herself as a secondary power with significant worldwide influence.

*   *   *   *   *

Although the outbreak of war deeply shocked the American people, there was a firm confidence that in Britain and France Hitler faced enemies that could take Germany's measure. The Roosevelt administration shared this view, but Roosevelt wanted to give substance to his confidence by supplying France and Great Britain with the necessities of war. While Congress rewrote the neutrality legislation in November 1939,[3] Roosevelt moved during the six-month period of the "phoney war" to forward needed supplies to America's first line of defense, France and Great Britain. Also, work was pushed ahead to produce thousands of aircraft engines for France, the arrangements for which reached well back into 1938.[4] British and French orders were expedited as quickly as possible during the *Sitzkrieg* in ways that took best advantage of the latest neutrality law.

Insofar as France was concerned, all these efforts were for naught. With the spring offensive in the West, German forces quickly occupied Denmark and successfully invaded Norway; one month later, on May 10, 1940, German forces smashed into Luxembourg, Belgium, and the Netherlands. On June 5 the Battle of France opened as German troops mounted an attack against Paris itself and east of the Maginot Line. For France the battle was little better than a rout. The Maginot Line, French armored vehicles, the Air Force, and the supposedly first-rate French army—all elements of the French defenses—were rendered incapable of effective defensive action by astute German maneuvers and by the rapid and crushing blows of the Panzer divisions.

Roosevelt did his best to support France in this hour of agony, sending messages four times to Mussolini asking that Italy not attack France. Mussolini, already committed and eager for easy spoils, invaded France on June 10. The government of Paul

---

[3] The new law repealed the arms embargo and made legal, as Roosevelt had urged, the "cash-and-carry" exports of munitions and arms to belligerents. Ninety-day loans to belligerents were also made possible under the law.

[4] John M. Haight, Jr., "Jean Monnet and the American Arsenal After the Beginning of the War," in Evelyn M. Acomb and Marvin L. Brown, Eds., *French Society and Culture since the old regime* (New York, 1966), pp. 271–272.

Reynaud was quickly faced with a military disaster. Which way should it turn, who would help? Great Britain, of course, was willing to help short of placing its own island defenses in peril if France were to fall. It was the United States, Reynaud decided, that offered France its only hope. In a series of messages addressed to President Roosevelt on behalf of a sinking France, Reynaud begged Roosevelt for aid; for the promise of an American declaration of war; for a lifeline. As he wrote on June 14: "At this grave moment in your history and ours, if you cannot give me the assurance that the United States will enter the war in the near future, then the destiny of the war will be changed. France is as a drowning man turning a last despairing look at the shore from which he expected help."[5]

From the American side, Reynaud's decision to pressure Roosevelt for help that he knew the President could not deliver was not a welcome one. The President was already deeply shaken that France had proven herself so tragically unprepared to counter the German onslaught. Reynaud's pleas simply impressed upon Roosevelt's mind the utter desperation of the French plight and that only the complete collapse of French nerve, society, and government could account for the disgraceful debacle known as the Battle of France. The idea of advancing French decadence that had been planted in Roosevelt's mind by French riots and scandals of the middle 1930s was probably nourished by the unfair public burden Reynaud thrust upon Roosevelt's shoulders in France's hour of shame.

Roosevelt, like Churchill, was deeply concerned lest a beaten and demoralized France yield its fleet to Germany. If such a contingency materialized, Great Britain would be vulnerable to invasion and probable defeat. As defeat for France became certain, the Reynaud government fell. On June 16, 1940 Marshal Henri-Philippe Pétain, the hero of World War I, became head of government. The following day Pétain sued for peace. In various direct and indirect ways the American government sent the message to the Pétain government that the powerful French fleet must remain in French hands or be disposed of in such a way that Germany and Italy could make no use of it.

---

[5] Bonnet, *Quai d'Orsay*, p. 289.

Marshal Pétain had no intention of turning over the French fleet, nor did the Germans demand it as part of the armistice agreement. Pending a victory over Britain, Hitler settled on armistice terms that were satisfactory to Germany on an interim basis. The French navy was to be disarmed and held in French ports; German troops of occupation were to occupy all northern France, including Paris, and within a broad zone along the entire western coast of France; the southern zone of France was to remain unoccupied; the French government, now removed to Vichy in south-central France, was to administer both zones subject to German needs; France was to pay the costs of German occupation; and the French prisoners of war were to remain in German hands until peace had been concluded.

France was in a unique position, conquered yet with a certain measure of self-government, partly in control of France, possessed of an "armistice army" of 100,000 men, and with the fleet and overseas territories still under the French flag. With the government headed by Pétain, most Frenchmen were apparently willing to give the Vichy regime their loyalty and support during what promised at best to be difficult days.

Both Prime Minister Winston Churchill and President Roosevelt were puzzled about the diplomatic course to be pursued toward the Vichy regime. For Britain the issue was soon decided primarily because of an understandable anxiety in London that the French fleet would somehow fall into German hands. On July 3 British ships and planes attacked French naval vessels at Mers-el-Kebir, Oran, inflicting severe casualties both on French ships and personnel. Two days later the outraged Vichy government broke diplomatic relations with Great Britain; for some influential members of the French government, a declaration of war on Great Britain seemed the most appropriate action to take. Still hopeful of somehow using French resources in the struggle with Germany, Churchill decided to capitalize on his only opportunity, that of supporting a little-known general who claimed he now spoke for the real France, the France that would never accept German suzerainty.

General Charles de Gaulle was not a national figure in France in 1940. He had achieved some recognition within military circles during the interwar years for his writing on the evolving nature of modern ground warfare and had served briefly as Paul Reynaud's Undersecretary of State for war. When it became certain that France would sue for an armistice, de Gaulle flew to London and by radio urged all Frenchmen who wished to carry on the fight against Germany and Hitler to contact him. Thus was born the Free French movement, a cause to which Great Britain gave aid and recognition in August 1940. De Gaulle was then recognized as "Leader of the Free French."

By all standards, de Gaulle's attempt to rally Frenchmen throughout the Empire was a bold, even an audacious move. It was in keeping with his character as his *Memoirs* make clear, and it was consistent with his profound love of country and his desire that France take center stage on the world scene. De Gaulle realized that unless France somehow managed to take a significant part in her redemption, French humiliation in 1940 would be compounded and she would cease to play the heroic role that de Gaulle thought so well suited the temperament and resources of France and Frenchmen. Whatever the outcome of the war, the page of shame—France's collapse in 1940—must somehow be erased. As de Gaulle wrote Roosevelt in October 1942, "Victory must reconcile France with herself and with her friends but it will not be possible if she does not participate in it."[6]

De Gaulle and the Free French movement did not really become a major factor in the American reckoning until after the United States was blown into the war by the Japanese attack on Pearl Harbor on December 7, 1941. Once in the war, however, the American government had to assess most carefully its policy toward de Gaulle. Here was a man who was fighting the same enemies, who had had some early successes in rallying parts of the French African empire, who had the steady if lukewarm support of the British government, and who promised to be a firm though difficult ally.

Why the American government turned its back on de Gaulle in the early days of the war and dealt with him only as necessary throughout the conflict is a complicated story. Those who

---

[6] Milton Viorst, *Hostile Allies: FDR and Charles de Gaulle* (New York, 1965), p. 106.

have sought to justify America's relationship with the Vichy government state there were simply overwhelming advantages in maintaining diplomatic ties with this collaborationist regime. The American diplomatic presence at Vichy, it was argued, would signal to the French people that the United States was still on the scene; hopefully, this would encourage the Pétain regime to keep its collaboration with the German government to a minimal level. Too, the Vichy government commanded the French navy and must be pressed to guard it against a German seizure. This was a crucial consideration. The extent of Roosevelt's concern was indicated when he informed Marshal Pétain that any French collaboration in a German takeover of the French fleet would result in France permanently losing the friendship of the United States. Pétain protested that France would never allow Germany to seize the fleet, and Pétain's pledge was honored. Upon Germany moving into unoccupied France on November 11, 1942, the remaining ships of the French navy, mostly stationed at Toulon, were sunk by their crews.

Other defenders of America's policy emphasized that the diplomatic listening post at Vichy could provide valuable information on German and Italian activities and military plans. Also, Vichy must be urged in every way possible not to let Germany gain control of French North or West African bases, a matter which could be pressed by an American diplomatic representative. As the war progressed, the official justifications for working with Vichy changed in emphasis but the result until the German occupation of all France in November 1942 remained the same; de Gaulle stood outside the American door looking in.[7]

De Gaulle's failure to gain sympathy and diplomatic support from the Roosevelt administration was only partly grounded in the American decision to maintain a correct relationship with Vichy. Some of the blame for what became a very trying situa-

---

[7] The standard account arguing the case for maintaining diplomatic ties with Vichy is William L. Langer, *Our Vichy Gamble* (New York, 1947). The Vichy regime itself is soundly explored in Robert O. Paxton, *Vichy France: Old Guard and New Order, 1940–1944* (New York, 1972).

tion must be laid at de Gaulle's feet. He was a most difficult man to work with, unyielding on matters where he had deep convictions and willing to go back on his word when it became inconvenient for Free French interests. In the first important contact he had with the American government, in fact, he deceived Secretary of State Cordell Hull and President Roosevelt in such a way that he gained the permanent enmity of Secretary Hull.

That contact concerned France's oldest and smallest colony, St. Pierre and Miquelon, tiny islands lying just twelve miles off the coast of Newfoundland. De Gaulle wished to "rally" the islands, by force if necessary, arguing that the radio station located on the islands could broadcast helpful information to Nazi mariners in the North Atlantic. The American government, still not at war, objected partly because of an agreement with the Vichy government that New World territories would remain in status quo, partly because it wished to avoid complications arising from a confrontation between Vichy and the Free French forces. After extended behind-the-scenes negotiations, involving Canada, Great Britain, and the United States, de Gaulle agreed not to send his colleague, Admiral Muselier, with an armed force to rally the islands.

On the very day he made his promise and just ten days after the attack on Pearl Harbor, December 17, 1941 de Gaulle sent secret orders to Muselier in Ottawa to proceed on the mission. Muselier's mission was successful and the islands were rallied. When news of the expedition reached Hull he exploded in anger. In public he said harsh things about the "so-called Free French Movement," words for which he received continuing substantial criticism but which he found hard to retract. De Gaulle's reasons for the deception have never been satisfactorily explained, but they were certainly not worth the enmity he aroused in the breasts of Hull and Roosevelt.[8] Evidence indicates that the St. Pierre-Miquelon affair was a very crucial event

---

[8] Douglas C. Anglin hypothesizes that de Gaulle possibly wished to discredit Muselier within the Free French movement, or that de Gaulle was seeking to clarify the American position vis-a-vis the Free French forces through provoking a crisis. *The St. Pierre and Miquelon affaire of 1941; a study in diplomacy in the North Atlantic Quadrangle* (Toronto, 1966), p. 80.

in forming American administration perceptions about de Gaulle and the Free French movement.

President Roosevelt saw de Gaulle and his movement in a much broader context than did Secretary Hull. To Roosevelt, de Gaulle represented both the military establishment in France that had shown itself ill-planned and incompetent in the hour of crisis, and the civilian regime that represented unstable government, scandals, and a set of opportunistic politicians who were not averse to making peace with Hitler in violation of a binding pact with Great Britain. Too, and this factor is crucial, Roosevelt entertained fanciful notions of himself as a savior of France, one who would lead France toward new political values and governmental institutions in the postwar era. If this goal was to be achieved he must have a free hand when the day of liberation arrived. De Gaulle thus represented to Roosevelt not only the discredited values and politics of the Third Republic but also a potential threat to Roosevelt's free hand in France following the war.

One must add that Roosevelt simply did not react positively to de Gaulle. He believed that de Gaulle maintained pretensions that were entirely out of keeping with his abilities, his past services to France, and the rather miniscule contribution his forces were able to make toward the common victory. Roosevelt also believed that de Gaulle's headquarters in London were a virtual sieve; the fastest way to send information to the enemy, many said in partial jest, was to send information to de Gaulle's headquarters and label it "secret." And Roosevelt was unable to comprehend why de Gaulle was so unbending and often so tactless, nor did he really try to understand. De Gaulle became a convenient whipping boy for Roosevelt's sometimes caustic wit on public occasions or at the wartime conferences. His remarks became known to de Gaulle and were not forgotten.

The war years are one long litany to American attempts to minimize the Free French movement, to see that Free French forces took little part in wartime actions, to keep de Gaulle ignorant of forthcoming military ventures, and to build up rivals to de Gaulle, ones more likely to take orders from Washington or London. Given the American determination to write off de Gaulle as a lightweight, it was not surprising that the American government made major miscalculations in assessing the rising influence of the Gaullist forces within occupied France. Nor, because of this distrust of de Gaulle, was the American government able to analyze rationally the domestic situation that would prevail in France immediately after military victory. The very thought that American GI's might fight and die in Africa and France so that Gaullism could be enthroned in Paris sent shivers of disgust through the staffs of the White House and State Department.

* * * * *

In devising strategy to bring the Axis powers to their knees, America made the decision rather early that German power must first be met and defeated. How best to do that was a matter of sharp debate. The American military first favored launching an invasion of the Continent at the earliest possible moment; Churchill, remembering the trench warfare of stalemated armies in World War I, believed that other strategies would have less risk but be as effective as a direct confrontation. Premier Stalin, whose Russian armies were bearing the brunt of the war, was predictably in favor of an early Continental invasion to relieve pressure on his armies.

A theater where some progress could be made but which entailed fewer military risks was the area of French North Africa. Foreseeing an invasion of Africa, the United States began at an early moment to woo Vichy officials in North Africa, primarily through promises of aid embodied in the Murphy-Weygand agreement. General Maxine Weygand, the supreme authority of the Vichy regime in North Africa allowed American diplomat Robert Murphy to include in the agreement that American officials could be stationed in French ports to supervise and control the shipments of American materials, a situation made to order for American intelligence activities.[9]

---

[9] Robert Murphy tells the story behind the agreement in his *Diplomat Among Warriors* (Garden City, 1964), pp. 82–86. Only 7% of the authorized quotas were delivered. p. 94.

As the date for the invasion approached there were feverish efforts to pull the teeth of potential French military resistance. Would anyone in North Africa, it was asked, have enough authority so that French troops would obey their order not to resist the Allied invasion? De Gaulle was considered but there seemed to be convincing evidence that Vichy military officers regarded de Gaulle as a deserter, one who had fled France in her hour of desperation to become a hireling of the British. General Henri Giraud, a brave French officer who had made a fine reputation in fighting (and twice escaping from) the Germans appeared more likely to command respect in the French army. Although Giraud seemed tough and insisted that he become the chief civil officer in post-invasion French North Africa, he was in fact politically incompetent and was selected partly because he seemed likely to take Allied orders with a minimum of fuss. He became the American candidate to abort resistance through an appeal to Vichy troops in North Africa.

On November 8, 1942 British and American forces landed at Oran, Algiers, and Casablanca. Giraud's authority, as events soon demonstrated, was insufficient to persuade the French army to cease resistance. There was sharp fighting and thousands of Frenchmen were killed. What was to be done? Were large numbers of French, British, and American troops to be slain that France might ultimately be freed? By design or otherwise, Admiral Jean François Darlan, the enthusiastically collaborationist commander of all French forces, was visiting his ailing son in North Africa. Acting out of desperation, Allied Commander Dwight D. Eisenhower arranged with Darlan to order French troops to cease fire against the Allies and to order French resistance to the Germans in Tunisia. In return, the Allies would recognize Darlan as the French political authority in North Africa. Darlan took this action even as the Germans were invading unoccupied France.[10]

Darlan's authority was sufficient to quell resistance. Undoubtedly many American, French, and British lives were saved by the arrangement with Darlan. De Gaulle of course was outraged

---

[10] German troops moved to occupy all of France with the invasions of French North Africa early in November, 1942.

that America continued to support a leader of the collaboration-ist regime, and Giraud sat most uncomfortably on the sidelines. In the United States a storm broke over the heads of admin-istration officials for concluding a far-reaching political arrange-ment with Darlan, one of the more willing cooperators with German rule in metropolitan France. Such fouling of the Allied cause seemed reprehensible to those who wished to see the war conducted in the spirit of its stated liberal aims.

Fortunately for everyone except Darlan, the Admiral was assassinated on Christmas Eve, 1942. Rather than seize the opportunity to bring de Gaulle and his Free French Movement forward as the civil authority in French Africa, a reluctant Eisenhower was compelled to sponsor the puppet Giraud as civil and military chief of the French forces. By late 1942, however, de Gaulle had rallied significant parts of the French Empire and could not be easily pushed aside. A compromise was in order. Accordingly Roosevelt, Churchill, de Gaulle, and Giraud met at Casablanca in June 1943 and approved formation of a French Committee of National Liberation. As de Gaulle said of the Committee, it constituted "a workable starting point."[11] That is, various elements of French leadership were brought into a work-ing partnership in such a way that General de Gaulle was soon able to assert his own dominance within the Committee. Giraud was even persuaded to sign papers in November 1943 that destroyed his position within the Committee, reduced him to a cipher, and prepared the way for de Gaulle's ascendancy.

Casablanca was to have most unfortunate consequences for French-American relations and for French-British relations as well. Roosevelt was put off by de Gaulle's stiff demeanor, his pretensions to supreme leadership of fighting Frenchmen, and his unwillingness to compromise with Giraud on cue from Churchill and the American delegation. De Gaulle took the measure of Roosevelt and found his wish to be the savior of a freed France rather incredible. As de Gaulle saw the situation, Roosevelt intended to keep the question of future French leader-ship fluid. This would provide a situation of greater flexibility for

---

[11] *War Memoirs*, II, p. 121.

the President's intended American-directed reconstruction of postwar France.

De Gaulle was also disturbed by continuing strong signals that the President was unsympathetic to the perpetuation of colonial empires following the war and that American power might be used to help free parts of the French Empire. De Gaulle regarded this position as rank meddling. The General was also profoundly disturbed that Churchill continued to support the President's position on French questions even when de Gaulle knew that Churchill's convictions lay elsewhere.

De Gaulle thus left Casablanca greatly strengthened in his own viewpoints: Roosevelt was a well-meaning dilettante whose plans to play French savior were visionary if not silly; American and British power must be welcomed in the redemption of France, but neither country must be allowed to play a role in the establishment of civil authority in metropolitan France; strenuous efforts must be made to raise and equip French troops so that Frenchmen could play a visible supporting part in the liberation of France. If this were not done France would probably be denied a role in postwar settlements, her empire might be stripped away by a jealous Britain and a crusading America, leaving France naked and humiliated, to face eventually an angry and revenge-minded Germany. His own role must be that of an unwavering spokesman for French national interests. Let others be world saviors. The plight of France was so desperate that de Gaulle must stand for her interests alone. As de Gaulle said later, conditions forced him to act as the "inflexible champion of the nation and of the state. . . ."[12]

In this atmosphere of suspicion and conflicting ambitions, American and Fighting French relations proceeded throughout the war. Once Giraud was clearly eliminated as a rival to de Gaulle, and as the evidence mounted that support for Gaullist-directed resistance movements was building within France, a more positive attitude toward de Gaulle and his forces was certainly in order. The major responsibility for the inflexible American position must be assigned to President Roosevelt.

---

[12] *War Memoirs*, I, p. 82.

The President longed with all his heart to see a healed and better-ordered world following the second holocaust in his lifetime. In his own way he was a romantic about the possibilities of human nature and rather utopian in his views and in his hopes for international cooperation following the war. To Roosevelt, the principles enshrined in the Atlantic Charter had very deep meaning and he certainly hoped the war would make possible a world where all peoples could exercise self-determination. He insisted that the wicked should be punished, and so sternly that they would not be a threat to peace for the indefinite future. Roosevelt also believed that those powers who made the major contribution to victory should remain united after the war as a power consortium to influence world developments along peaceful lines. Britain, Russia, the United States—and China by courtesy—were thought of by FDR (until 1944) as the future world policemen. The President also wished to see colonialism fade, a subject of intense anxiety to de Gaulle for he knew that Roosevelt did not wish France to recover Indochina nor to reestablish her position with Syria, Lebanon, and parts of North Africa.

Within this framework of Roosevelt's impulses and ideas, his approach to de Gaulle and his movement made sense. Self-determination for France and the French Empire would be an empty phrase if Allied power were used to establish a Gaullist regime in France, a regime which Roosevelt was convinced would have strong authoritarian overtones. Wartime France and her representatives could, in any case, be treated with relative unconcern. Her collapse in 1940 indicated a rather weak societal substructure, and her difficult experiences as an instrument of German power in the war were creating further social fissures that might lead to civil war in France following victory over Germany. Churchill's continuing plea that a strong and vital France would be necessary in future years to hold Germany in check made little impression upon Roosevelt since the President planned a punishment for Germany so harsh that he anticipated no threat from that quarter for many generations to come. If Germany did seek to create new challenges to the international order, the combined power of Britain, America, and the Soviet Union would be more than enough to put out the fire.

It is clear in retrospect how erroneous were Roosevelt's assumptions and hopes for the future. The victorious wartime alliance collapsed before the notes of triumph had been well-sounded. Germany was punished but not severely and her intrinsic strength, skills, and geographic position made her a factor to be reckoned with by 1949. France too arose from the ashes to resume a position of major importance in European councils. It is true that the postwar era witnessed the partial dissolution of the old colonial regimes, but France retained great influence within her former empire. Roosevelt's vision and perceptions were thus very cloudy indeed. Nor did he ever make concrete plans for France in his presumed role of savior. He apparently felt that for France, as well as for other territories that would in time be liberated, effective political reorganization could be planned and implemented in the train of marching armies. Within this vacuum of American postwar planning for France, de Gaulle's forces grew stronger by the day. New recruits flocked to join the forces of Fighting France. Winston Churchill and the British government, despite moments of intense anger at de Gaulle and despite negative American attitudes, continued to support de Gaulle and his military units. Through skillful maneuvering and steady work with the many resistance movements in France, the political authority of de Gaulle in France rose on a steady continuum. He clearly was the person to whom most Frenchmen looked at the man best able to establish orderly and stable government upon liberation.

Despite de Gaulle's occasional obnoxious behavior toward those who were the allies of France, he was a man of considerable vision and intellectual power. Like Churchill he believed that Germany would rise again and that a strong and stable France must be a major factor in any containment policy. De Gaulle also believed that the victorious wartime alliance would not last, that great-state rivalries would soon be resumed in traditional fashion after the war, and that it therefore behooved each nation to look to its own security and national interests first. As for France in the wake of Allied victory, de Gaulle was convinced that the alternatives were either de Gaulle or communism, a sentiment he expressed to Roosevelt early in the war.[13] Communist resistance forces were well-organized, fought steadily and heroically, and had acquired great prestige throughout France by their resistance activities. Such a closely knit force had great potential for staging a *coup* if it had marching orders from Moscow in the political vacuum following victory.

As the Allied forces under General Eisenhower prepared for the massive invasion of the Continent—Operation Overlord—the question of how France was to be governed became a pressing one. Roosevelt insisted that a vacuum in French national leadership be encouraged, that "local authorities" be allowed to assume responsibilities of a pressing nature. Eisenhower felt this position was nonsense and pressed Washington, as did the British government, to drop the petulant attitude toward de Gaulle and the French Committee and recognize the reality of de Gaulle's wide support within France. Only after de Gaulle had visited Roosevelt in Washington early in July 1944, one month after the Normandy invasion, did Roosevelt order that the French Committee of National Liberation be treated as the dominant political authority in France. Roosevelt continued to believe, until events proved otherwise, that other powerful and democratic forces would rise up in the wake of victory and dispose of the presumably authoritarian de Gaulle.

An inexcusable humiliation was placed upon the Gaullist forces by excluding them from the planning and execution of Overlord. This action was taken on the express orders of Roosevelt, presumably for security reasons. Consequently, the Allied landing at Normandy included only one Fighting French company of 180 men. General Koenig's French division disembarked at Normandy August 1, almost two full months after the initial landings. This was a particularly wounding blow, given de Gaulle's anxiety to have Frenchmen erase the humiliations of the war through extensive participation in the liberation struggle.

Although terribly angered by Roosevelt's snub, de Gaulle prepared to establish civil government under his authority as

---

[13] De Gaulle to FDR, October 1942, quoted in Viorst, *Hostile Allies*, pp. 105–106.

the Allied troops liberated successive areas of France. Ever fearful the Communist elements might decide to seize authority, de Gaulle and his associates moved quickly and dramatically behind the fighting lines to draw the strings of civil authority into the General's own hands. They were successful and in the process the General revealed political skills of a high order.

In his command of the French armies of liberation, de Gaulle demonstrated his profound belief that national forces are arms of the state and are, therefore, to be used in ways most advantageous to the state. He was determined that French troops be highly visible in the redemption of Paris, a matter on which he received Eisenhower's cooperation. More difficult questions were raised, however, over de Gaulle's desire that French troops actually invade German soil, or when he refused to withdraw French troops from a city (such as Stuttgart) or area as part of the general battle plan. Areas liberated by French troops, de Gaulle insisted, must not be allowed to fall back under German control and suffer German vengeance lest all confidence in the new civil authorities be undermined. Although de Gaulle's unbending attitude on these matters provoked outrage at SHAFE, or in London and Washington, General Eisenhower maintained a remarkably understanding attitude. De Gaulle explained his apparent uncooperativeness lucidly in his later *War Memoirs*: "It was by adopting without compromise the cause of national recovery that I could acquire authority. It was by acting as the inflexible champion of the nation and of the state that it would be possible for me to gather the consent, even the enthusiasm, of the French and to win from foreigners respect and consideration. Those who, all through the drama, were offended by this intransigence were unwilling to see that for me . . . the slightest wavering would have brought collapse."[14]

At 5 p.m. on October 23, 1944, a few days before Franklin D. Roosevelt was to stand for a fourth-term reelection bid, the United States government extended diplomatic recognition to the Provisional Government of the French Republic. The American step was taken reluctantly and with no good wishes for the Gaullist regime. Roosevelt's intransigence was not well-under-

---

[14] *War Memoirs*, I, pp. 82–83.

stood in France. To France, de Gaulle represented the French will to be free, national pride, and the first step in the national escape from humiliation. American recognition, extended so late and with such reluctance therefore soured the eventual moment of victory over the Axis. As Milton Viorst has commented, "France and the United States, united in victory, should have been the most intimate friends. But all the world knew that Roosevelt and de Gaulle were hostile allies."[15]

The case for working with the Vichy government until the invasion of North Africa, to its defenders at least, was convincing. In this policy, it should be added, the American government received considerable encouragement from the British government. Beyond November 1942 there were few viable options except to work with de Gaulle and, later, the French Committee of National Liberation. In many ways the American government came to grips with this reality. For example, Lend Lease aid was extended to Free French forces beginning in July 1942. But every such step forward taken by the American government was accompanied by grumbling and by "leaks" studded with uncomplimentary references to French leadership. Secretary Hull, who never recovered from the public chastisement he received arising out of the St. Pierre-Miquelon Affair, was one source of American unhappiness. It was President Roosevelt, however, who was primarily responsible for the hardnosed attitude toward de Gaulle. While it is true that Roosevelt simply did not like de Gaulle, there were profound differences on policy for France and the postwar world that set their relationship on edge. Given their conflicting views and ambitions, difficulties were unavoidable. But it is hard not to conclude that Roosevelt descended to uncharacteristic pettiness during the last months of his contacts with de Gaulle.

*　　*　　*　　*　　*

It was Winston Churchill and the British delegations to the later wartime conferences who sponsored the idea of a revived

---

[15] *Hostile Allies*, p. 221.

and vigorous postwar France. To Churchill it seemed predictable that Germany would in time recover, that American troops would be withdrawn from Europe as they had been following World War I, and that a stable, prosperous, and self-confident France would, therefore, be necessary if Europe were to regain its political balance and Germany to be contained.

Practically, the British position implied that representatives of France should be invited to the wartime conferences on postwar planning. Roosevelt and Stalin steadily resisted the idea, Stalin ostensibly because French capitulation in 1940 cancelled her rights to participate with the major powers on postwar decisions. Very troubling questions kept arising, however, and seemed to Churchill unlikely to be settled wisely without French input. Could Italian-French boundary questions be resolved without the concurrence of France? Was France not interested in the East European political settlements, an area where her diplomacy had been active in the interwar years and where she had assumed obligations that led her to war in 1939? Could colonial questions be intelligently resolved, or more important, could the myriad of problems and questions relating to Germany be settled without French advice and participation?

Churchill thought not, but on these matters he was actively disputed by Roosevelt and Stalin. Realizing as he did that France would—and must—revive, Churchill was repeatedly warned by de Gaulle that France would not be bound to honor agreements made at conferences from which she was excluded. France was admitted to the fighting forces of the United Nations as a full partner on January 1, 1945, yet she was excluded from the Yalta Conference held early in February.

De Gaulle regarded his exclusion from the Yalta Conference and earlier wartime conferences as a profound error, an insult to France, and a certain indication that the great victorious powers intended to manage world affairs without reference to the wishes of the lesser concerned powers. Substantive decisions were made with regard to Germany, and although it was decided to give France a zone of occupation, to place France on the Allied Control Council for Germany, and to eliminate Germany's capacity for military production—all decisions which de Gaulle thought proper—de Gaulle was still angry at France's exclusion from the Conference. So angry was he in fact that when Roosevelt asked to meet de Gaulle in Algiers following the Conference, de Gaulle not only refused but replied, none too subtly, that Roosevelt had no business landing in Algeria without first seeking the permission of the French government. The President, who saw himself as a friend of France, was deeply hurt by de Gaulle's message. Just how hurt became apparent in a speech to the Congress a few days after his return when the President complained about "a great many prima donnas in the world who want to be heard."[16]

Roosevelt missed the meaning of the exchange. The General had not intended to insult the President so much as to make the point that the great questions relating to peace must not be settled without reference to France. De Gaulle's position, which he defended throughout the war and which was subsequently adopted by French governments in the postwar era, was particularly powerful when argued vis-a-vis Germany.

As the World War drew to a close, the configurations of world power were not pleasing to traditionalists who thought of Europe as "the Continent." It was obvious to observers that the Soviet Union would no longer play the relatively passive role she had in world affairs during the interwar years, but one in keeping with her demonstrated military prowess, her enormous resources, and the hegemony she was establishing in Eastern Europe as a result of her military advances. Across the Atlantic, the American colossus had not only helped to turn the tide against Germany but had largely carried on alone the war against Japan in the Pacific. If American participation in wartime conferences was any indication, the United States intended to take a direct part in world political affairs as it had not in the interwar era. With America in possession of a terrible new atomic weapon, its wishes would be crossed at some risk to the transgressor. Great Britain had faded in triumph, much as had France in World War I, but the emergence of the Superpowers made Britain's new position explicit. Germany was a rubble heap, but with her potential intact. China, although treated by courtesy as a great power, was in a state of continuing revolu-

---

[16] Quoted in Viorst, *Hostile Allies*, p. 233.

tion that made her role in world affairs doubtful. France was left badly scarred by the war, but she was ambitious and determined to devise ways to maximize her influence. The two world wars had drastically weakened the ties of the old colonial empires although it was not always obvious to the mother countries.

* * * * *

Precisely how the world was to be put back together was unclear in 1945. There were two major new factors on the world scene, the first being the United Nations and the apparent American determination that the UN would be the focus of a new international system. Although nations that had been interwar participants in the old League of Nations discounted much of the overblown American rhetoric concerning the potential role of the UN, there was a new factor which held promise for UN success; the greatest world powers would not only be members of the organization, but their real weight in world affairs would be recognized by positions and privileges accorded them within the United Nations Organization.

The second major new condition in world affairs was the expansion of American and Russian influence to the point where their interests were literally global in nature. This was a by-product of the war and was not unforeseen as early as 1941.[17] Even more disturbing than this profound assignment of power within the international system was the apparent animus developing between these two colossi. Partners in victory, they nevertheless circled each other warily during the war even though President Roosevelt tried his best to introduce notes of cordiality into the relationship. To perceptive students of international relations it seemed highly likely that these two giants would soon find their relationship full of tensions and that the rivalries

---

[17] Alexis de Tocqueville, in fact, had predicted this state of affairs in the mid-1830s. America and Russia, he commented, seem "marked out by the will of Heaven to sway the destinies of half the globe." *Democracy in America* (New York, 1838), p. 414.

inherent in the nation-state system would be fully expressed in the American-Russian relationship. A disturbing potential of this new rivalry and this reordering of world power was that the lesser powers of the world would find their national interests and their viewpoints subordinated to the interests of the two superpowers.

This was indeed the direction of events as the Cold War developed. And the tensions inherent in this new rivalry found expression through nearly every conceivable avenue other than armed conflict. In order to mobilize for "victory," both nations emphasized differences in their ideology and value systems. A highly emotional content was thus added to the contest and nations in all parts of the world were called upon to stand up and be counted in the struggle for civilization and history. In this drama, in this titanic struggle of wills, it was apparently the duty of lesser powers to commit their resources to implementation of their bloc leader's perceptions and program. Within the United Nations, as participants in various international conferences, on matters related to the emerging "Third World," on armaments and defense policy and on matters of trade and monetary policy, both the Soviet Union and the United States increasingly came to expect that their viewpoints should take precedence over those of their allies and that their allies should recognize the logic of the situation and cooperate willingly.[18]

France was reluctant to accept the role of American Sambo even in the immediate postwar years when her economic dependence on America weakened her power to resist. It was essentially this ongoing reluctance that has lain at the core of American-French tensions since the end of World War II. There were many reasons for her decision to maximize French influence on world councils. France could not—did not—believe that the configuration of power had so changed that her interwar role as keystone of the Versailles peace should now be permanently changed to

---

[18] Charles O. Lerche, *The Cold War and After* (Englewood Cliffs, 1965), offers an astute analysis of the assumptions and strategies of America and Russia during the Cold War era. Also useful is Louis J. Halle, *The Cold War as History* (New York, 1967).

that of international cipher. Her central position of the European continent, her industrial resources, her tradition of Continental leadership, her revolutionary traditions in a changing world, her colonial empire, her world-wide cultural influence and her long experience in the vicissitudes of world politics all argued that France should continue to play her role of world power.

With their keen sense of the past the French were also convinced that France must ultimately play a central role in maintaining whatever settlement was made with regard to Germany. To stand abjectly by while the great powers plotted their strategy concerning Germany seemed potentially suicidal to French politicians of every stripe. Consequently, there was widespread support within French political circles for France to claim a seat with the great powers, if for no other reason than to protect French interests on evolving Germany policy.

Too, the French had an internal political situation that gave them a perspective on the developing Cold War highly displeasing to their would-be American mentors. Living in a nation with a powerful Communist Party, it was difficult for many Frenchmen to sympathize with the American position that containing "international communism" should be the first priority of all "civilized" nations. Also, in their cynical way the French were amused at the nations and leaders who were often included on the American "free world" list and thus eligible for American military, monetary, and diplomatic support. Dictators of the right, if willing to commit their territory or resources to American purposes, were happily included on the list. Apparently the American government did not object to rightest totalitarian governments, only to those with leftist orientation and therefore likely to be associated with the Soviet Union. America's emphasis on ideology as a factor dividing the world was in the final analysis not very convincing to French governments of varying political hue. Ideology, many Frenchmen argued throughout much of the Cold War, was simply a blind to disguise what was at bottom a great-state power conflict, and nations were foolish who placed stock in protestations of ideological principles. Furthermore, American-Russian antagonism distressed France if for no other reason than that it was those two powers who had rescued France from Germany in the previous world wars; Russia, for fifty years, had been viewed in France as her natural ally against an ambitious Germany.

While Americans and Russians were nourishing their demonological fancies, French politicians were concerned about the hazardous nature of a bipolar world. They believed it was dangerous to world peace first because it was a new fact of international life and therefore created uncertainty and instability. With the new atomic weapons of mass destruction in the hands of both protagonists after 1949, an international system revolving around their mutual hatred and intense competition was highly dangerous to peace and ought to be changed. It was in the interests of everyone, France came to argue, that the power centers of the world multiply. A return to an older system where there were several real power centers would not ensure peace and stability but it would most likely be less dangerous than the bipolar international system that emerged after World War II.

It was not in the interests of peace, therefore, and certainly not in the interests of France that she follow willy-nilly the lead of her American ally. One must remember, Frenchmen cautioned each other, that American power was relatively new, that Americans were inexperienced in the exercise of world power, and that Americans had proven themselves an unreliable source of stability in the interwar years. Furthermore, their messianic complex and impetuousness made it doubtful that they would be willing to weigh carefully the interests of their friends and allies before adopting policies that were appealing to the American electorate or in keeping with American security needs. These sentiments were expressed not only by de Gaulle, who resigned as President of the Provisional Government in January 1946, not to return to power until 1958, but by the subsequent governments in the Fourth Republic.

*   *   *   *   *

America's wildly varying policies on Germany between 1944 and 1950 encouraged little French confidence that America was sensitive to the security needs of France or aware of the profound implications for the world of a revived and rearmed Germany. De Gaulle, Roosevelt, and their successors had rather different concepts of how Germany was to be divided and administered but all agreed that a prosperous and united Germany would be a menace to the world. Whether Germany was to be turned into a vast pasture, as envisioned in the American Morgenthau Plan of 1944, or weakened through strategic annexation of certain territories, exacting reparations, and decentralization of the powers of government, as envisioned by de Gaulle, was really a matter of strategy.[19] But as de Gaulle said early in September 1945, "Germany was amputated in the east but not in the west. The current of German vitality is thus turned westwards. One day German aggressiveness might well face westwards too. There must therefore be in the west a settlement counterbalancing that in the east."[20]

Partly at Churchill's insistence, Roosevelt finally came to support the idea that France should be given a zone of occupation in a Germany that was to be temporarily divided four ways. France was not reluctant to exploit her zone of occupation, nor would France cooperate with the decisions of the Allies made at the Potsdam Conference in July and August of 1945 that Germany should be treated as a single economic unit. For four years French governments fought the American-British plan to form a Trizone of their three areas of occupation, sabotaged as effectively as they could American plans to shift responsibility for German affairs to German hands, and opposed bitterly writing a German constitution that provided for a centralized German Federal Republic. French insistence on German territorial adjustments, on the need to internationalize the resources of the Ruhr, and on written military guarantees for France before the devolution of power in time became highly annoying to the American government.

The Cold War developed rather quickly after 1945 and it

---

[19] De Gaulle told President Truman in August 1945 that France favored the separation of the Rhineland from any future German state or states, economic fusion of the Saar with France, internationalization of the Ruhr and destruction of centralized power in Germany.

[20] *The Times* (London), September 10, 1945, quoted in F. Roy Willis, *France, Germany, and the New Europe, 1945–1963* (Stanford, 1965), p. 15.

became ever more tempting for the American government to view the German question within the Cold War construct. If a military showdown with the Soviet Union was a real possibility, policy makers in the Truman administration gradually convinced themselves that positive steps must be taken to enlist German resources in this struggle.

There were other factors evident in the American drive to normalize the status of Germany. For one, the Truman administration perceived that the staggering economies of Western Europe and Great Britain would not take a decisive turn toward recovery unless German talents and resources were drawn upon. As the American government moved toward establishment of massive economic assistance for European nations in 1948, known to history as the Marshall Plan, it made considerable sense to help Germany to its feet as part of the larger strategy of recovery. Too, the American government was fearful that a prolonged and harsh occupation of Germany would sow seeds of bitterness that might adversely affect development of democratic institutions in Germany. Finally, the American and British governments had little stomach for the role of occupier. They were accordingly indignant at French and Russian stripping of their zones and were thus inclined to normalize the German situation partly to bring this practice to an end. Too, they believed that French appropriation of German resources meant that the American taxpayer would ultimately pay the bill for a prostrated Germany.

De Gaulle and his successors[21] were convinced that Americans were taking much too short and too optimistic a view of German questions. A deep bitterness developed against the United States as the French saw how helpless they were to combat American assumptions and actions on Germany, either through normal diplomatic channels or through conferences of the powers. Early American hints that it might even be necessary to rearm Ger-

---

[21] De Gaulle resigned in January 1946 for several reasons: he was unable to influence sufficiently American policy on Germany; there was profound economic discontent in France; the Cold War was developing rapidly, an event that would affect France domestically and make France's role as arbiter between East and West an unlikely one. See Alexander Werth, *De Gaulle; a political biography* (New York, 1966), pp. 194–196.

many enraged French politicians of all parties and successive French governments were urged by the Chamber of Deputies never to accede to such a request.

Outbreak of the Korean War on June 25, 1950 was to have a profound effect on French-American relations. Based upon rather tenuous evidence, the American government decided that the North Koreans had been sent into South Korea at the express wish of the Soviet Union. This attack was presumably the herald of further Soviet probings to follow shortly. In all likelihood the Soviet Union had adopted a design for world conquest; in time it became a popular political game to discuss the coming "year of maximum danger." Placed in the context of the dangerous confrontation in Berlin created by Russian cutoff of Allied access routes in 1948, Soviet explosion of a nuclear weapon in 1949, the "loss" of China to Communist forces in 1949, and the hysteria that developed around the Alger Hiss security case, the fear of Russian forward movement had some basis in perceived reality.

The French governments of René Pleven and Henri Queville shared the American fear of Soviet invasion of North Europe but entertained grave doubts about the American prescription: creation of a European Defense Community in which a rearmed Germany would play a major role. France had been happy with creation of the North Atlantic Treaty Organization in August 1949, but the United States now insisted that a Soviet invasion could not be repulsed without including Germany in the defense community. Unfortunately for the French governments involved, they had no reasonable alternatives to suggest. France was unwilling or economically unable to field an army that was minimal even for her own defense needs; she admitted that Western Europe was utterly vulnerable to a Soviet ground attack. Even if France did wish to assume full responsibility for the protection of Western Europe, there was simply not enough French manpower to do the job. Only in Germany was there sufficient manpower to help provide Western Europe with the ability to defend itself against a possible Soviet onslaught.

What was France to do, given the factors of a defense need and of intense American pressure to rearm Germany? The French themselves first suggested creating an integrated European army, linked to the political institutions of a united Europe. This plan, called the Pleven Plan after its proposer, Premier René Pleven, was discussed for many months without positive results.[22] Finally, in May 1952, after lengthy and painful negotiation, the French government initialed its agreement to the creation of a European Defense Community. Under the agreement Germany was to contribute twelve divisions within a European army but was not to join the North Atlantic Treaty Organization.[23] Approval of EDC was linked to the end of the German occupation.

Before the agreement could be implemented it first had to be approved by the concerned governments, in the case of France by the National Assembly. From the American perspective French ratification was certain. What other choice did the French have given the American determination to have Germany rearmed in the face of a possible Soviet invasion.

The Eisenhower administration was therefore taken aback by the vociferous, raging debate that was triggered in France by the EDC proposals. It was probably the most profound debate in France since the Dreyfus Affair, for its consequences were perceived as linked to the survival of the French state. Disagreement about EDC came from all points on the political spectrum. Gaullists were adamant in their opposition because it implied integration of the French army within a European army and, therefore, some diminishment in French sovereignty. Communists, who took their cue from Moscow, and others believed that German rearmament would be a tragic error under any circumstances. A "European" faction opposed EDC because they were convinced it would retard or abort movements afoot to integrate Europe politically and economically. French involvement in the Indochinese War also played a part in shaping French attitudes toward EDC. The deeper France sank into the Indochinese quagmire (with powerful American encouragement and economic

---

[22] Edgar S. Furniss, Jr., *France, Troubled Ally; De Gaulle's Heritage and Prospects* (New York, 1960), p. 65. Furniss argues that the Pleven Plan "was shrewdly calculated to prevent the emergence of any German army."
[23] The six signers were the United States, Great Britain, France, Belgium, Holland, and Luxembourg.

assistance) the easier it became to argue that France would certainly not emerge as the dominant nation within EDC; that role would obviously be played by an American-backed, prosperous, and unencumbered Germany. Too, many were angry that the United States reacted negatively to French suggestions that serious diplomacy be carried out with the Soviet Union. If America and Russia would bargain in good faith, some argued, the issue of German rearmament need not be faced.

After many months of arguments, postponement, and the final dramatic debate in the National Assembly in late August 1954, the EDC proposal was soundly defeated. The scare tactic of "EDC or Wehrmacht" was not enough to convince the opposition. Pandemonium broke loose upon announcement of the indicative Assembly vote. France, many felt, had been spared the spectacle of a rearmed Germany and the submergence of the French national army into an integrated and faceless armed force.

Actually, as events soon proved, French rejection of EDC merely stimulated the United States and Great Britain to choose a different path toward German rearmament. The government of Pierre Mendes-France, although it had not supported EDC, chose to participate fully in the discussions concerning German rearmament. Through an amended Brussels Treaty, German occupation was to be ended and Germany and Italy were to be brought into NATO. By December 1954 the French National Assembly accepted the Paris agreements providing for an amended Brussels Treaty and did so decisively. As Alfred Grosser wryly commented, "the National Assembly accepted the [German] Federal Republic's membership in the Atlantic Pact as an alternative solution to EDC. Four years before, the French government had suggested the idea of a European army as an alternative solution to the Federal Republic's membership in the Atlantic Pact."[24]

The irony of that situation did not escape the Mendes-France government nor members of the National Assembly. Nor did many forget that the agony of this decision had been forced upon France by successive American governments hinting at

---

[24] Alfred Grosser, *La IVième République et sa politique extérieure* (Paris, 1961), p. 326.

imminent Soviet invasions of Western Europe that never materialized. A point of interest was the French decision to opt for a defense solution that emphasized the continuation of distinctly national armies. The decision was not made by a Gaullist government, a fact that was arresting to Americans who chose to perceive de Gaulle's nationalistic bent as an aberration in French postwar politics.

America's forcing some resolution of the German rearmament issue provoked profound speculation in France about how the new and rearmed West German government could be defanged insofar as France was concerned. Should new political approaches be made to the Soviet Union, a natural and historical ally, when confronting the German problems?[25] This course would have several disadvantages. Most obviously it would antagonize the United States. Perhaps more important in the long run, it would antagonize the Germans and make any true reconciliation most unlikely. French statesmen were inclined to think that the safest path for France was to seek a genuine reconciliation with Germany. It was ultimately de Gaulle, coming to power in June 1958, who gave fullest expression to this desire.

France's program of reconciliation with Germany was certain to take on anti-American overtones and to cause considerable indignation in Washington. Basically de Gaulle offered the West German government led by Konrad Adenauer a political partnership that both hoped would be able to wield considerable clout in European and world affairs. France, as befitting de Gaulle's conception, would be the senior partner. The close American-German relationship, de Gaulle presumed, would atrophy as Bonn looked to Paris rather than to Washington for leadership. Konrad Adenauer took the first steps toward contracting into this new German-French relationship in January 1963 but to de Gaulle's anger and disappointment both the German Parliament and Adenauer's successor, Ludwig Erhard, had quite dif-

---

[25] De Gaulle concluded a treaty of friendship with the Soviet Union on December 21, 1944 partly because he wished to firm up the ties of the two nations who had fought as allies in two world wars against Germany. A detailed discussion of his trip to Moscow in 1944 is found in *War Memoirs*, III, pp. 66–96.

ferent ideas about the value of Germany's Atlantic associations and the recently written treaty with France.

It was also de Gaulle's misfortune that his concepts about how to move toward a settlement of the German question and to bring together the nations of Europe into an effective political and military bloc were contested by President Kennedy. The young, self-confident American President believed in strengthening the economic and political bonds uniting a revived Europe but he was determined that American interests and influence would be protected in an envisioned Atlantic community. As early as July 1962 Kennedy publicly proposed in Philadelphia a vast Atlantic zone of free trade, a development that would have opened France to competition from American agricultural exports. In keeping with this goal Kennedy was anxious that America's special ally, Great Britain, be taken into the European Common Market so that American viewpoints would be fully heard in European councils. It was precisely this kind of development that de Gaulle was determined to avoid; this influenced his decision to veto Britain's application for entry into the Common Market in January 1963. If Europe and France were to have their proper say in world affairs, de Gaulle argued, they must protect their vital economic interests and speak with a distinct voice on political affairs. The new Europe must be neither the tool of America nor the Soviet Union. Nevertheless it was quite clear that de Gaulle's "Europe of the Fatherlands" would be dominated and led by France.

To impartial observers it appeared that French and American differences in the 1960s involved a rival clash of hegemonic ambitions. This was undoubtedly so. Unfortunately for France she was not in a position to outbid the United States in competition for influence and position with the West European states. But France was in a position to disrupt American ambitions as her veto of British application for Common Market membership made clear. Through challenges to the dollar as the world's reserve currency, through withdrawal of French troops from the NATO military command beginning in 1959, through verbal condemnations of American military action in Indochina, and through repeated diplomatic challenges to United States Cold War policies (such as France establishing diplomatic relations with Red China in January 1964), France made it known that her views on world problems and the place of a revived Europe in the postwar world were quite different than were those of her American ally.

*   *   *   *   *

To many Americans in the late 1950s and throughout the 1960s, Charles de Gaulle appeared to be a temperamental obstructionist, irascible, unreasonable, pursuing dreams of French glory that were last appropriate in the age of Louis XIV. But de Gaulle raised some hard questions that indicated his government's policy positions were not without substance. One major question concerned the defense of Europe in a possible showdown with the Soviet Union. Reports of enormous Soviet standing armies in East Europe, together with rather modest conventional defense forces in West Europe apparently made it mandatory that atomic weapons would be used in the event of a Soviet invasion. Actually, American possession of atomic and hydrogen bombs, with adequate means of delivery, made it seem improbable that the Soviet Union would cross the German frontier line, knowing certainly that terrible destruction would rain upon Russian cities and defense systems.

Soviet explosion of an atomic bomb in 1949 and a hydrogen bomb in 1953 exercised a profound change in strategic thought concerning the defense of Western Europe. Through organization of the North Atlantic Treaty Organization, sending American troops to Europe to serve in potential front line areas, and naming General Eisenhower to command NATO, the Truman administration tried to make it clear that American commitment to the defense of Europe was firm and unequivocal. American "trip wire" troops in Germany's front line areas were a guarantee, European governments were assured, that any confrontation with the Soviet Union would bring to Europe the full resources of the American nation.

It was the French, and the Gaullists in particular, who stimulated increasing doubt about the credibility of the American "atomic umbrella." The incredible destructiveness of atomic weapons made it easy to foresee the day when the United States would never use its atomic arsenal unless there was a direct threat to American survival. Was Soviet invasion of Western Europe a threat of this magnitude to American interests? Despite a protracted chorus from Washington that this was so, and always would be so, logic and some knowledge of the horrible destructiveness of atomic and hydrogen weapons systems argued otherwise. It followed that placing western European security in American hands was likely a risky proposition.

De Gaulle and his coterie also made the point that there would inevitably be political or military matters perceived by individual European nations to be vital to their national interests but which might seem peripheral to the United States. De Gaulle had in mind colonial questions, or the protection of key supply lines such as was involved in the Suez Crisis in 1956. What recourse then had France, or the other nations of Western Europe, if America chose not to rattle its atomic arsenal in defense of interests Europeans perceived to be vital. To ask the question was to suggest that the members of NATO had already yielded a significant function of their sovereignty, the ultimate responsibility to defend the state against external crises. Many Frenchmen were also deeply disturbed by the concept of nuclear "graduated response," a concept made popular by Secretary of Defense Robert S. McNamara. Opponents of graduated response argued that only a certainty that the full American arsenal would be hurled at the Soviet Union if aggression occurred would prevent that aggression. Graduated response also implied that the superpowers would "trade" pieces of territory as the war escalated. Gaullists and others argued that Europe could be incinerated piece by piece if the United States and the USSR began a game of nuclear chicken; neither, it was presumed, would begin the game in such a way that its own territory would become an immediate target.

The only answer to these problems that partially satisfied de Gaulle was French development of an atomic arsenal. Even with limited atomic weapons and limited means to deliver them, France would be able to make a potential attacker weigh carefully the cost of aggression. Furthermore, it was stated, atomic weapons would give France a means to make likely American involvement in a nuclear showdown with the Soviet Union. Bombs dropped by France to protect her own or Western European interests would serve as a "trigger" on the American atomic reserve. National arsenals could thus serve as a partial assurance that American defense commitments were in fact to be honored.

A last reason for the development of a French arsenal, one that carried great weight with France, was that no nation could demand a seat at the table of the great powers without atomic weapons. In the last analysis, de Gaulle believed, respect and position among the nations stood in rough proportion to the damage one state could inflict upon the other. France's international position, the defense of her present and future vital interests, and the maintenance of a fully sovereign state thus appeared to rest in the development of atomic weapons.[26] Initiation of an atomic technology did *not* begin in France with the advent of the Fifth Republic in 1958. Development of this technology was begun in 1945 and assiduously cultivated by a succession of French premiers.[27] It was General de Gaulle, however, who happened to be in office when French technology made production of atomic bombs feasible and it was de Gaulle who pressed the case for building a French atomic striking force that he called the *force de frappe*.

From the beginning of French nuclear testing, the American government took a strongly negative position on development of this new arsenal. The American government perceived it in the interest of peace that the world's atomic weapons be kept to a minimum. Proliferation of atomic arsenals, with weapons ultimately falling into the hands of irresponsible governments, provoked real nightmares among American scientists, politicians, and military personnel. For France to acquire atomic weapons was seen as likely to encourage other second-line na-

---

[26] It need hardly be said that General de Gaulle was unsympathetic to these arguments when they were stated on behalf of West Germany.

[27] Grosser, *La IVième République*, pp. 124–126. An excellent study is Lawrence Scheinman, *Atomic Energy Policy in France Under the Fourth Republic* (Princeton, 1965).

tions to set out on this hazardous path. Each nation that acquired atomic weapons, it was argued, made the world that much more dangerous and certainly would inject new risks into future world crises. American reluctance to share atomic know-how with France was due in part to the view of President Kennedy and his advisers that dealing with de Gaulle would not be any less difficult if France were given nuclear technology assistance. This viewpoint was probably well taken if somewhat beside the point.

De Gaulle's arguments for the acquisition of atomic weapons made the American government particularly uneasy as it contemplated the future of Germany. All the arguments used by the General to justify French acquisition of atomic weapons would in time be fully applicable to the West German government. How then could West Germany (or a united Germany) ultimately be denied atomic weapons if France had them? De Gaulle appreciated the power of the objection but believed the problem would not arise in an acute fashion if the cordial French-German partnership evolved that he envisioned. Any possibility, however, that Germany might eventually acquire atomic weapons was not only a nightmare for France but for the Soviet Union as well. De Gaulle thus hoped that Soviet hostility to German acquisition of atomic weapons would reinforce France's own determination that this event never occur.

French access to American atomic technology became for de Gaulle one acid test of French-American relations. The fact that the United States made much of its atomic know-how and certain weapons systems available to Great Britain, while largely denying assistance to France, was an indication to de Gaulle that the United States did not accept France as a full partner in defense and would not therefore defend vital French national interests. De Gaulle was determined that France would be a member of the inner circle of great powers making decisions for Europe and the world. He even made approaches to President Eisenhower in September 1958 and June 1960 asking that France be so included, and in other forums indicated that France should be given access to American atomic expertise on the same terms as Great Britain. His requests were not granted. Such developments gave de Gaulle further ammunition for his views that France must move away from America, develop her own atomic arsenal, and deny the American trojan horse, Great Britain, access to the Common Market if France were to play her proper role in world affairs.

The United States made some effort to placate the French on the issue of atomic weapons. In 1959, for example, a secret French-American treaty provided that America supply uranium enriched fuel for France, an agreement that the United States unilaterally cancelled, apparently due to French intransigence on European defense questions. Another effort was made in 1961 when President Kennedy proposed that surface vessels carrying atomic weapons be manned by mixed crews from participating NATO countries. This was really a cosmetic maneuver, for the United States would not yield on the issue that only the American president would have the authority to push the button. Two years later, in 1963, the United States sold refueling planes for the French Mirage bombers thus making the *force de frappe* technically more credible.[28]

Also in 1963 a serious if incomplete attempt was made to satisfy French desires. France was offered Polaris missiles on terms identical to those made to Great Britain; that is, the missiles would be assigned to NATO but in time of a national emergency they could be deployed for national purposes. The General quickly rejected the proposal in one of his famous press conferences (January 14, 1963). He was obviously offended that the offer came as a result of the Nassau Conference between Britain and America, a conference where the chief agenda item had been to revise the nuclear defenses of the Atlantic Alliance. France had not even been invited to the Conference, a grievous insult. Furthermore, France did not have the submarines to deliver the missiles nor did the United States offer France the needed marine technology. The General was also offended that the American offer was made to France publicly; furthermore, he was suspicious that the "Anglo-Saxons" were maneuvering to bring his *force de frappe* under American control. France, de Gaulle thundered, would "adhere to the decision we have made: to con-

---

[28] Wilfrid L. Kohl, *French Nuclear Diplomacy* (Princeton, 1971), p. 180.

struct and, if necessary, to employ our atomic force ourselves."[29]

Storage of American atomic weapons on French soil once she acquired her own arsenal was considered unwise in France. A powerful American arsenal stored in France, it was argued, would draw Soviet atomic lightning upon France if the United States and Russia engaged in open conflict. This horrible destruction might take place without France having a say in pushing the American-controlled button; it might even happen on an issue totally unrelated to French vital interests; Soviet weaponry might fall, in fact, merely as part of a scenario in a carefully escalated conflict in which the Superpowers' allies were the first to be sacrificed.

Such prospects were not pleasant for any member of NATO to contemplate. For France, the decision was made not to permit American atomic weapons on French soil. De Gaulle decided as well in 1958, or even earlier when in political retirement, that integration of French supporting forces in NATO no longer best served French national interests. In 1959 elements of the French fleet were withdrawn from NATO command. In March 1966 de Gaulle completed the process by announcing that France was withdrawing all French military units under NATO command, indicating that NATO headquarters must be moved from French soil by April 1967 and unilaterally denouncing five agreements with the United States concerning bases, communications networks, and an important NATO fuel pipeline.

These French moves angered American officials. France, many argued, was pursuing a very cynical and selfish course, for France knew that in a confrontation with the Soviet Union that threatened Western Europe, America would use her resources to protect France. This defense was mandatory because of France's central geographical position. France was thus following a course that minimized her costs and dangers while continuing to enjoy the privileges of American nuclear protection.

American-French nuclear quarrels revolved, it is quite clear, around a number of central issues: the extent to which France and Western Europe should be involved in Cold War politics;

---

[29] *Major Addresses, Statements and Press Conferences of General Charles de Gaulle, May 19, 1958–January 31, 1964* (New York, 1964), p. 219.

the scope of France's role in the Great Powers' club; the political influence that the United States was to exercise on Continental affairs; the strategy France was to follow in protecting herself against a possible German resurgence; the extent to which a nation was sovereign when its life-and-death decisions were to be made in the capital of a foreign nation; and the Gaullist vision of a "European Europe," independent both of American and Soviet control.

There was another fundamental difference that troubled not only French-American relations but the relations of France with her European neighbors as well. This difference related to the future of Western Europe and how best to insure that another destructive war would not break out. For many Europeans and Americans it seemed that Europe's best future lay in the integration of her national economies and in the growth of common political institutions that would develop a supranational perspective. Establishment of the European Coal and Steel Community in April 1951; establishment of the European Economic Community, or Common Market, in March 1957; and integration of European defense through NATO and EDC were viewed by good "Europeans" as steps toward the development of an organic Europe. Although the United States grew increasingly uneasy as it reflected upon the potential economic and political power of a "United States of Europe," American governments continued to believe that Europe's best hopes for prosperity and peace lay in the integration of its national economies and in resource sharing.

France accepted this viewpoint but with serious reservations. Some of the most profound reservations were articulated by the Gaullists. At the heart of the Gaullist argument had been the belief in the persistence of the nation-state and that through this vehicle the peoples of Europe (and certainly the people of France) could be most creative and forward-looking in fulfillment of their varying national tasks. And while all governments should welcome integrative steps within Europe, whether political or economic, integration should not be permitted to proceed to the point that the great decisions relating to a nation's best interests are made outside her own political structure. Thus foreign money, for example, should not be permitted to buy controlling interest in the major economic enterprises within one's national boundaries. If other European governments were willing to abdicate their sovereignty through concessions to integration, France was not. It was also de Gaulle's firm belief that a Europe united through supranational institutions would be much more amenable to American pressures and influence than would a "Europe of the States."

American-expressed unhappiness at de Gaulle's occasional obstructionist course on political and economic integration of European institutions was not taken very seriously in Paris. America's continuing assertion of economic hegemony in Latin America and its apparent desire to exercise economic and military hegemony over Western Europe hardly placed the United States in a position to argue for moderation of the French thesis. Nevertheless, Americans intensely criticized the Gaullist regime for glorifying the anachronism of nationalism and for hazarding future French security vis-a-vis Germany by placing roadblocks in the development of supranational institutions.

France in the postwar era had been given little reason to suppose that her vital interests outside Europe would be protected in a multinational framework or as part of the American Empire. The United States, both during and since the war, either opposed reestablishment of French control in areas such as Indochina, Syria, and Lebanon, or took ambivalent positions in the 1950s when France was under enormous pressure to alter her relationship with her African Empire, particularly her relationship with Algeria. France believed deeply in the benefits of her "civilizing mission" to colonial peoples, and she believed as well that an ally such as the United States should support her in her time of troubles. But the United States remained skeptical of the French *mission civilisatrice* and in any case was so involved in the Cold War competition for the underdeveloped nations' commitment that it was unwilling to encourage French retention of her colonial empire unless the issue was placed in the Cold War context. Even then the American support seemed problematical, as the Vietnam situation highlighted.

During the Second World War, American sympathies were notably aligned with those Indochinese who wished for independence. President Truman likewise made it clear that he favored some form of self-government for the Vietnamese. France did bend apparently, to the extent of granting Vietnam a limited autonomy. But disagreements arose over implementing the new policy and in mid-December 1946 the Viet Minh, led by Ho Chi Minh, attacked the French in Hanoi. This attack opened seven and one-half years of bitter warfare.

American policy at first was even-handed, neither supporting the French nor the insurgents. In June 1949 the French established Bao Dai as head of the new State of Vietnam, partly to mobilize native support against the Viet Minh. France was not faring well in this contest but the American government did not become unduly concerned until the Chinese Communists reached the Indochinese frontier at the beginning of 1950. With added supplies from Red China, the Viet Minh began to expand their operations.

Red Chinese assistance now brought the Indochina struggle into the Cold War context, a development that made it easy for the American government to begin supporting the French effort. Diplomatic recognition was extended to Bao Dai's regime in May 1950 and in June, with the outbreak of war in Korea, Vietnam was seen as a frontier outpost of the Cold War struggle.

Now it became American policy to urge the French forward and the French were encouraged with subsidies that by 1954 paid for eighty percent of all French military expenditures in Indochina. Nevertheless, the French position deteriorated. Even as preparations were underway for a peace conference at Geneva, France found itself with a major crisis in the spring of 1954 when a French and loyalist Vietnamese force was trapped in a remote northern fortress, Dien Bien Phu. In desperation the French government made it clear to President Eisenhower that only direct American intervention could save the situation. Although personally sympathetic to the French plight, President Eisenhower and Secretary of State Dulles found Great Britain opposed to intervention and Congressional leaders reluctant to begin a land war in Asia. Dien Bien Phu fell early in May 1954 and the French prepared at Geneva to abandon their position in Indochina.[30]

---

[30] Herbert Tint, *French Foreign Policy since the Second World War* (London, 1972), p. 23. Don R. and Arthur Larson, *Vietnam and Beyond* (Durham, 1965).

America's subsequent and gradual assumption of France's military role in Vietnam added a bizarre twist to the story. While America pointed to its obligations to Vietnam under the Southeast Asia Collective Defense Treaty of February 1955, France perceived only American folly and opportunism. Once France was ejected from Vietnam, it was noted, American resistance to initiating a land war faded rapidly. The United States was apparently launched on a colonial venture of its own but under the banner of a "crusade against communism." Remembering American resistance to reestablishment of French authority in Indochina in 1945, many Frenchmen concluded that the reason was now clear: America had hegemonic ambitions of its own for Indochina. As the United States gradually sank into the Vietnam quagmire, French sympathy for the American position was notably scarce.

America's uncertain support for France was likewise highlighted in 1956 when France and Great Britain struck back at Egypt and President Gamal Abdel Nasser for nationalizing the Universal Suez Canal Company, a company largely owned by French and British citizens. Both nations were disturbed that an international waterway vital to their economies was nationalized and placed under the control of Nasser, a man the French National Assembly labeled "a permanent menace to peace."[31] While President Eisenhower and Secretary of State Dulles proposed solutions unacceptable to everyone involved, France and Great Britain secretly determined to invade the Canal Zone area, topple the Nasser regime, and reestablish the authority of the Canal Company. In late October and early November, in concert with Israel, Egypt was bombed and her territory invaded by those three nations.

Eisenhower and Dulles were terribly angry that France and Britain would initiate a move so hazardous to peace without even consulting the United States. In a step with enormous implication for French-American relations, the United States and the Soviet Union joined their influence within the United Nations to condemn the actions of America's closest allies. On November

---

[31] Richard P. Stebbins, *The United States in World Affairs, 1956* (New York, 1957), p. 259.

2, 1956 the General Assembly passed a resolution introduced by Secretary of State Dulles calling for a cease-fire and the withdrawal of foreign troops from Egypt. Russia, in the meantime, had threatened to send "volunteers" to Egypt and to use guided missiles against France, Britain, and Israel. The Superpowers, for very different reasons, thus combined to crush one venture of the old colonial powers and Israel.

And what was significance of this episode? As Vice-President Nixon saw it, for "the first time in history we had shown independence of Anglo-French policies toward Asia and Africa which seemed to us to reflect the colonial tradition. That declaration of independence has had an electrifying effect throughout the world."[32] Nixon was essentially right. Furthermore, French and British influence was temporarily reduced to a nullity in the Middle East. American prestige within the old colonial areas accelerated appreciably. But the North Atlantic Treaty Organization was nearly ruined. France and Britain were profoundly disturbed, partly because they had been so pointedly humiliated by their American friend who had pledged to defend their vital interests, even at the implied cost of the American homeland.

The lesson to France was quite clear; American power was not to be relied upon to defend the vital national interests of their NATO allies, particularly if those interests fell outside Europe. The American "protector," it was widely noted in France, had not even the grace to take a neutral position over Suez within the United Nations. Perceptions of the world were so different in Washington and Paris, as Suez graphically demonstrated, that to place all the French eggs in the American basket struck French strategists as deplorable folly. The rather different perceptions recalled a wartime conversation between Churchill and de Gaulle and their conclusion that "when all is said and done, Great Britain is an island; France, the cape of a continent; America, another world."[33]

Too, successive French governments lived in perpetual fear that the United States and the Soviet Union would have a meet-

---

[32] November 2, 1956, quoted in Stebbins, *ibid.,* p. 327. See also Murphy, *Diplomat Among Warriors,* pp. 382–393.
[33] De Gaulle, *War Memoirs,* I, p. 104.

ing of the minds on the Berlin and German questions and would conclude a settlement without regard to French policy or interests. Berlin and the question of German unification became a particularly divisive issue in French-American relations during the Kennedy administration. The crisis was originally precipitated by the Soviet Union's Nikita Khrushchev in early November 1958 when he announced that the USSR had decided "to renounce the remnants of the occupation regime in Berlin." He subsequently demanded that Britain, France, and the United States withdraw their occupation forces from West Berlin, declare it a "free city," and negotiate directly with the East German government concerning access rights to Berlin. If the Allies failed to reach agreement with the East German government within six months, Khrushchev warned, the Soviet Union would turn over Western access routes to Berlin to supervision by the German Democratic Republic.

Khrushchev in effect raised the larger question concerning a possible German settlement: was Germany to be divided permanently, as implied in Khrushchev's demand that the NATO Allies recognize the legality of the East German government; or if Germany was to be unified, by what steps would unification be achieved and how would Germany be governed; would the Allies have any controls over a new and unified Germany; and how would the unification of Germany affect other security arrangements in Europe? In short, Khrushchev had raised fundamental questions on the most important unsettled issues arising from World War II and ones that had been immeasurably sensitized by the Cold War.

Within Allied councils and in the negotiations with the Soviet Union that followed, de Gaulle and Konrad Adenauer were continually distressed at American and British apparent willingness to make fundamental concessions on Berlin and on recognition of the East German government without driving a hard bargain on German unification issues or on continuing Allied rights in Berlin. De Gaulle was particularly anxious because President Kennedy was reportedly willing to make concessions on East Berlin in order to freeze the status quo on West Berlin. As de Gaulle saw it, the Allies must take a hard line on West Berlin, insist that Allied rights were founded in duly negotiated agreements and, if necessary, threaten atomic war to preserve Allied rights. He also adamantly objected to extending diplomatic or *de facto* recognition to the East German Democratic Republic; to do so would signify that the West had given up on German unification. This admission would inevitably turn Germany eastward for it would be obvious that German unification could be achieved only through arrangements made with the Soviet Union.

The fact that President Kennedy and Secretary of State Dean Rusk insisted upon a high-level conference to negotiate these issues convinced de Gaulle that the United States had little grasp of Europe's security problem and how the security issues could be most intelligently handled.[34] And when the United States went ahead to open discussions unilaterally on the issues, first on Berlin and then disarmament, against the vigorous opposition of de Gaulle, further support was given to de Gaulle's position that America was not to be trusted on Europe's most vital concern: security.

Unease over Germany strengthened de Gaulle's conviction that it was dangerous for world peace to have only two major power centers. It was therefore the role of enlightened statesmanship to erode the position of both Superpowers to argue for alternative solutions to major problems before the assembly of nations, to provide alternative leadership to those nations and peoples who wished no part in the Cold War, and to insist that the lesser nations had vital interests that should be given a fair hearing before the major powers imposed solutions. France was the logical nation to play the role of spoiler to the Superpowers. It was within this general framework of policy that when de Gaulle twice visited Latin America, and toured Quebec, Canada (in 1967), he invoked their French or Latin heritage and encouraged them to look to France for leadership and culture. Cultural proselytizing, especially through sending thousands of French language teachers overseas, became another means to enhance French prestige and influence. Too, French diplomacy and weapons sales were stepped up to the Middle East, encourage-

---

[34] An enlightening discussion of the Berlin issue is found in Robert Kleiman, *Atlantic Crisis, American Diplomacy Confronts a Resurgent Europe* (New York, 1964), pp. 38–43.

ment was given to East European nations to resist Russian hegemony, the Bretton Woods agreements of 1944 which established the American dollar as the prime medium of international exchange were undermined, and technical aid programs with obvious political implications were developed—these policies and activities were all in keeping with the Gaullist philosophy that the world would be a safer place with power dispersed and that France should be an important center of world influence.[35]

De Gaulle stated his position succinctly in 1965:

The fact that we have resumed independence of judgment and action regarding all problems seems at times to displease a state which might believe that because of its power it is invested with a supreme and universal responsibility. . . . The reappearance of a nation whose hands are free, which we have again become, obviously modifies world politics which, since Yalta, seemed to be confined to two partners only. But since this division of the world between two hegemonies, and therefore two camps, clearly does not benefit the liberty, equality and fraternity of peoples, a different order, a different equilibrium, are necessary for peace.[36]

To the United States, the French *non* became increasingly exasperating. Convinced of the rightness of its motives and the wisdom of its actions, the United States was unable to appreciate the philosophy and viewpoints behind de Gaulle's actions. It was popular to say that de Gaulle was following a course of revenge for his ill treatment by Roosevelt during World War II, or that he was the intellectual and emotional captive of eighteenth-century concepts concerning the glory of the nation-state. These kinds of analyses were satisfying to Americans, apparently explained French resistance to an enlightened American hegemony, and made it unnecessary to consider carefully the fundamental questions so often raised by the General and by other non-Gaullist French governments.

* * * * *

---

[35] Tint, *French Foreign Policy*, pp. 163–179.

[36] *Le Monde*, April 29–May 5, 1965, No. 863, cited in W. W. Kulski, *De Gaulle and the World; the foreign policy of the Fifth Republic* (New York, 1966), p. 155.

In retrospect, many of the French contentions in the era of de Gaulle have proven correct. The Cold War, it increasingly appears, was at bottom a traditional nation-state conflict with ideological window dressing; the Superpowers did try to divide the world into two blocs to their own advantage, but the persistence of nationalism worked in open and hidden ways to defeat their hegemonic ambitions; the nation-state continues to thrive as the primary political unit in the international system; a variety of power centers have emerged from the rubble of World War II, with several more likely to show their muscle in the next two decades; Europe has increasingly awakened to its possibilities for profits and international leadership as its common economic institutions have gained experience and authority; old style colonialism became largely extinct but the freed colonies continue to look to the mother country for skills and building resources; the United Nations, once described by de Gaulle as a *machin* (what's-its-name) has demonstrated little ability to cope with major crises; the American military presence has gradually diminished in Western Europe, and the nations of Europe must increasingly work out their relationships while American attention focuses elsewhere.

This is hardly to argue that French—and particular Gaullist—contentions have all been soundly based. Much of the Gaullist argument for a *force de frappe* is highly questionable, as has been the French contention about the diplomatic value of possessing an atomic arsenal. French willingness to use its atomic arsenal in defense of its neighbors is ultimately as questionable as is American determination to use its arsenal to defend Western Europe, French protests to the contrary. Americans may also wonder at Gaullist reasoning for eroding the two-power hegemony when French purpose was to create a four- or five-power hegemony. Apparently the world will be a safer place only when the great power club is large enough to accommodate France!

* * * * *

In the era since World War II American-French relations have evolved in what for them has been a revolutionary setting.

The United States in 1945 was acclaimed as one of France's liberators. From 1948 to 1950 America poured over $2,500,000,-000 into France in order to revive her economy and to prevent social chaos and a communist takeover.[37] Although Frenchmen were as grateful to their liberator and financier as people can be in such humiliating circumstances, their ambition was to put behind them those days of defeat, poverty, and mortification. Reassertion of French leadership in Europe and beyond was made necessarily at the expense of Superpower ambitions. In a most fundamental sense, her policy goals became subversive of American influence and policies. But her resurgence in world affairs has been, in part, a testimony to the American largesse of dollars distributed through the European Recovery Plan (Marshall Plan) and to prolonged American support for a revived and healthy Europe. If the achievement has occasionally been bittersweet for the United States, that is often the nature of international relations and of life itself.

Despite the continuing tensions in French-American relations, the alliance of these two nations goes beyond any formal ties through military or economic treaties. Their fundamental, though badly articulated, commitment to common values and to the preservation of Western civilization is the real cement of the alliance. Both nations are broadly aware of the talents and resources that each contributes to the common civilization. If Americans sometimes feel that French views of America are jaundiced and unkind, for example, that American capital and American diplomacy are threats to the sovereignty of nations and to international peace, Americans must also remember how General de Gaulle gave the Kennedy administration unconditional support in the terrifying Cuban missile crisis of 1962.[38]

---

[37] Harry B. Price has commented, however, that "France did not achieve economic viability or financial equilibrium during the Marshall Plan period." *The Marshall Plan and Its Meaning* (Ithaca, 1955), p. 282. An authoritative work on the forms of aid channeled to France is William A. Brown, Jr., and Redvers Opie, *American Foreign Assistance* (Washington, 1953).

[38] Elie Abel, *The Missile Crisis* (Philadelphia and New York, 1966), p. 112. See also Sylvia K. Crosbie, *A Tacit Alliance: France and Israel from Suez to the Six-Day War* (Princeton, 1974).

This episode underscored for many Americans that a difficult ally should not be equated with an unreliable ally.

Nevertheless, the postwar era has introduced at least two factors that will permanently alter the French-American relationship. One is development of the Common Market, a factor that has already had a major impact on Atlantic trading patterns. And despite French resistance to evolution of supranational European political institutions, it is difficult to see how they can be stunted permanently if the framework of the Common Market is maintained. This development too will certainly reshape America's economic and political relationships not only with France but also with other Common Market members.

Likewise, the development of atomic weapons has profoundly changed the value of military alliances. Adherence to an alliance that in crisis will probably bring immolation rather than liberation inevitably alters alliance perceptions and commitments. As the Cold War has waned, fear receded, and as France regained her self-confidence, she has gradually defined her position toward the United States essentially as one of an uncommitted ally. While annoying to the United States, it appears unlikely that this relationship will be sharply redefined unless war clouds begin to form or unless technology works in some unforeseen way to alter drastically the present balance of terror.

Suggestions for Additional Reading

The primary and secondary materials that proved most helpful to me are reflected in the footnotes. There is a vast literature that bears on French-American relations, but few works of a survey nature. Henry Blumenthal, *France and the United States: Their Diplomatic Relations, 1789–1914* (Chapel Hill, 1970) is a sterling survey and also provides a good brief guide to the scholarly resources and literature for this period. Other general works that are stimulating are Crane Brinton, *The Americans and the French* (Cambridge, 1968); Donald C. McKay, *The United States and France* (Cambridge, 1951); Howard M. Jones, *America and French Culture* (Chapel Hill, 1927); Edward Fecteau, *French Contributions to America* (Methuen, 1945); and Elizabeth B. White, *American Opinion of France from Lafayette to Poincaré* (New York, 1927). Anne C. Loveland explores that eminently usable symbol, Lafayette, in *Emblem of Liberty: Image of Lafayette in the American Mind* (Baton Rouge, 1971). Beckles Willson has written an anecdotal and entertaining book on *America's Ambassadors to France, 1771–1927* (New York, 1928).

Still stimulating on French exploration and settlement in America are Francis Parkman's *Pioneers of France in the New World* (Boston, 1891); *A Half Century of Conflict*, 2 vols. (Boston, 1892); and *The Old Régime in Canada* (Boston, 1874). George M. Wrong, *The Rise and Fall of New France* (New York, 1928) is still useful as are newer works, such as Yves F. Zoltvany, comp., *The French Tradition in America* (Columbia, 1969); John F. McDermott, Ed., *Frenchmen and French Ways in the Mississippi Valley* (Urbana, 1969); and John A. Caruso, *The Mississippi Valley Frontier: The Age of French Exploration and Settlement* (Indianapolis, 1966). Samuel E. Morison has given us a delightful biography of *Samuel de Champlain: Father of New France* (Boston, 1972). Other special studies of substantial value are Emmett F. O'Neil, "English Fear of French Encirclement in North America, 1680–1763," unpublished Ph.D. dissertation, University of Michigan, 1941; Jacob M. Price, *France and the Chesapeake: A History of the French Tobacco Monopoly, 1674–1791*, 2 vols. (Ann Arbor, 1973); Natalia M. Belting, *Kaskaskia under the French Regime* (Urbana, 1948); Allen Forbes and Paul Cadman, *France and New England* (Boston, 1925); and Durand Echeverria, *Mirage in the West: A History of the French Image of American Society to 1815* (Princeton, 1957).

Samuel Flagg Bemis, Richard W. Van Alstyne, Richard B. Morris, and William C. Stinchcombe have written the finest monographs on the diplomacy of the Revolutionary War years and are cited in the text. Old but still useful are Congressman James B. Perkins' *France in the American Revolution* (Boston, 1911); E. S. Corwin, *French Policy and the American Alliance of 1778* (Princeton, 1916); and P. C. Phillips, *The West in the Diplomacy of the American Revolution* (Urbana, 1913). Parts of Lawrence S. Kaplan's excellent survey, *Colonies Into Nation: American Diplomacy, 1763–1801* (New York, 1972) can be read with profit as can Kaplan's *Jefferson and France; an essay on politics and political ideas* (New Haven, 1967). French background to the Revolution is explored in John J. Meng, *The comte de Vergennes; European phases of his American diplomacy, 1774–1780* (Washington, D.C., 1930); Elizabeth S. Kite, *Beaumarchais and the War for American Independence*, 2 vols. (Boston, 1918); and Dallas D. Irvine, "The New-Foundland Fishery; a French Objective in the War of American Independence," *The Canadian Historical Review*, XIII, No. 3 (September 1932), pp. 268-284. Different aspects of Franklin's thought and influence are detailed in Gerald Stourzh, *Benjamin Franklin and American Foreign Policy* (Chicago, 1954); Claude Anne Lopez, *Mon Cher Papa: Franklin and the Ladies of Paris* (New Haven, 1966); and Alfred O. Aldridge, *Franklin and his French Contemporaries* (New York, 1957). Some idea of French reactions to Americans and their institutions is found in Genevieve G.

Hubbard, "French Travelers in America, 1775–1840; A Study of Their Observations," unpublished Ph.D. dissertation, American University, 1936, and Gilbert M. Fess, *The American Revolution in Creative French Literature, 1775–1937* (Columbia, 1941).

Diplomatic literature on the period from 1789 to 1815 is notably rich. Lawrence S. Kaplan's earlier mentioned monograph, *Colonies Into Nation*, is especially perceptive on the Federalist era. Alexander DeConde has written two standard works on the Federalist years, *Entangling Alliance: Politics and Diplomacy under George Washington* (Durham, 1958) and *The Quasi War: The Politics and Diplomacy of the Undeclared War With France 1797–1801* (New York, 1966). Albert Hall Bowman's *The Struggle for Neutrality: Franco-American Diplomacy During the Federalist Era* (Knoxville, 1974) is also an impressive monograph and will become a standard work on the Federalist period. Other books or essays on the Federalist period that are useful are Forrest McDonald, *The Presidency of George Washington* (Lawrence, 1974); Jerald A. Combs, *The Jay Treaty: Political Battleground of the Founding Fathers* (Berkeley, 1970); Peter P. Hill, *William Vans Murray, Federalist Diplomat: The Shaping of Peace With France, 1797–1801* (Syracuse, 1971); Robert R. Palmer, "The French Idea of American Independence on the Eve of the French Revolution," unpublished Ph.D. dissertation, Cornell University, 1934; Charles D. Hazen, *Contemporary American Opinion of the French Revolution* (Baltimore, 1897); and Bernard Faÿ, *The Revolutionary Spirit in France and America* (New York, 1927).

In approaching the Jeffersonian era, one must still begin by reading Henry Adams' *History of the United States of America during the Administrations of Jefferson and Madison*, 9 vols. (New York, 1889–1909). A fine single volume survey is Marshall Smelser, *The Democratic Republic, 1801–1815* (New York, 1968). These works can be supplemented by specialized studies, such as Louis M. Sears, *Jefferson and the Embargo* (Durham, 1927); Reginald Horsman, *The Causes of the War of 1812* (New York, 1962); Bradford Perkins' two thorough studies, *The First Rapprochement: England and the United States, 1795–1805*

(Philadelphia, 1955) and *Prologue to War: England and the United States, 1805–1812* (Berkeley, 1963); and the many fine biographical studies of Jefferson, Madison, and Albert Gallatin. An excellent synthesis of the war is in Harry L. Coles, *The War of 1812* (Chicago, 1965). American press reactions to Napoleon and Napoleonic France have been studied in Charles W. Meinert, "The American Periodical Press and Napoleonic France, 1800–1815," unpublished Ph.D. dissertation, Syracuse University, 1960.

Scholarship on French-American relations between 1815 and 1861 is relatively sparse, underlining the less intense contacts between the nations in these years. Useful studies touching on political issues are C. K. Webster, "British Mediation between France and the United States in 1834–6," *English Historical Review*, XLII, No. CLXV (January 1927), pp. 58–78; R. A. McLemore, "The Influence of French Diplomatic Policy on the Annexation of Texas," *Southwestern Historical Quarterly*, XLIII (1940), pp. 342–347; Jesse S. Reeves, *American Diplomacy under Tyler and Polk* (Baltimore, 1907); Stanley J. Pincetl, Jr., "Relations de la France et des États-Unis pendant la Seconde République, 1848–1851," unpublished Ph.D. dissertation, Université de Paris, 1950; John F. Cady, *Foreign Intervention in the Rio de la Plata, 1835–50* (Philadelphia, 1929); Frederick Merk, *The Oregon Question: Essays in Anglo-American Diplomacy and Politics* (Cambridge, 1967); and the several specialized studies on the Monroe Doctrine by Dexter Perkins. Also of value are works relating to diplomatic personnel of the era. See, for example, *Mémoires et souvenirs du Baron Hyde de Neuville*, Viscountess de Bardonnet, Ed., 3 vols. (Paris, 1888–1892); J. Fred Rippy, *Joel R. Poinsett, Versatile American* (Durham, 1935); J. H. Powell, *Richard Rush, Republican Diplomat, 1780–1859* (Philadelphia, 1942); and Ann E. Liston, "W. C. Rives: Diplomat and Politician, 1829–53," unpublished Ph.D. dissertation, The Ohio State University, 1972. There are numerous "opinion" studies on this period, the most useful being Henry W. Casper, *American Attitudes Toward the Rise of Napoleon III* (Washington, D.C., 1947); and Lynn M. Case, *French Opinion on War and Diplomacy during the Second Empire*

(Philadelphia, 1954). Alexis de Tocqueville's *Democracy in America* is, of course, the premier study of American society by a Frenchman and is still enjoyable reading some 140 years after being first published.

Lynn M. Case and Warren E. Spencer have done such a superb job on their *The United States and France: Civil War Diplomacy* (Philadelphia, 1969) that many older studies need no longer be consulted. Other recently published monographs that have real value are Daniel B. Carroll, *Henry Mercier and the American Civil War* (Princeton, 1971); Glyndon G. Van Deusen, *William Henry Seward* (New York, 1967); Maurice Melton, *The Confederate Ironclads* (New York, 1968); Serge Gavronsky, *The French Liberal Opposition and the American Civil War* (New York, 1968); and David P. Crook, *The North, the South and the Powers* (New York, 1974).

Carl H. Bock's definitive *Prelude to Tragedy* is nicely complemented by reading Charles Blanchot's *Mémoires; l'Intervention française au Mexique*, 3 vols. (Paris, 1911); Nancy Barker, *Distaff Diplomacy: The Empress Eugénie and the foreign policy of the Second Empire* (Austin, 1967); and Pierre Renouvin, *La politique extérieure du Second Empire* (Paris, 1940).

The goals and setting of French diplomacy after 1871 is clearly explained in M. Jacques Chastenet, *Histoire de la Troisième République*, 7 vols. (Paris, 1952–1963). Also useful is H. J. Priestley, *France Overseas; a Study of Modern Imperialism* (New York, 1938); and G. P. Gooch, *Franco-German Relations, 1871–1941* (New York, 1967). Some of the more important issues in French-American relations are explored in Richard M. Packard, "The French Pork Prohibition in American Diplomacy, 1881–1891," unpublished Ph.D. dissertation, Harvard University, 1954, and Samuel T. Chambers, "Franco-American Relations, 1897–1914," unpublished Ph.D. dissertation, Georgetown University, 1951. America's increasingly friendly stance toward France is demonstrated in Seward W. Livermore, "The American Navy as a Factor in World Politics, 1903–1913," *American Historical Review*, LXIII, No. 4 (July 1958), pp. 863–879. Henry Blumenthal's *France and the United States* is especially insightful for the period between 1870 and 1914. Elihu B. Washburne's *Recollections of a Minister to France, 1869–1877*, 2 vols. (New York, 1887) are entertaining and still worth reading. Some background on the Statue of Liberty is found in Hertha E. Pauli and E. B. Ashton, *I Lift My Lamp: The Way of a Symbol* (New York, 1948).

Probably the best short overview of American diplomacy relating to World War I is Daniel M. Smith's *The Great Departure: The United States and World War I, 1914–1920* (New York, 1965). Special studies of help in understanding French-American relations are Lawrence E. Gelfand, *The Inquiry: American Preparations for Peace, 1917–1919* (New Haven, 1963); Howard M. Merriman, "The French and Woodrow Wilson, 1912–1918: A Study in Public Opinion," unpublished Ph.D. dissertation, Harvard University, 1937; Edward H. Buehrig, *Woodrow Wilson and the Balance of Power* (Bloomington, 1955); Carl P. Parrini, *Heir to Empire: United States Economic Diplomacy, 1916–1923* (Pittsburgh, 1969); Gordon N. Levin, *Woodrow Wilson and World Politics* (New York, 1968); Henry R. Rudin, *Armistice, 1918* (New Haven, 1944); Dorothy S. White, "Franco-American Relations in 1917–1918: War Aims and Peace Prospects," unpublished Ph.D. dissertation, University of Pennsylvania, 1954; David F. Trask, *The United States in the Supreme War Council: American War Aims and Inter-Allied Strategy, 1917–1918* (Middletown, 1961); Thomas A. Bailey, *Woodrow Wilson and the Lost Peace* (New York, 1963); and Betty M. Unterberger, *America's Siberian Expedition, 1918–1920* (Durham, 1956). There are dozens of memoirs on the war and peacemaking that are worth perusing. Three of the most pertinent are Secretary of State Robert Lansing's *The Peace Negotiations: A Personal Narrative* (Boston, 1921); Ferdinand Foch, *The Memoirs of Marshal Foch*, 3 vols. (New York, 1931); and Georges Clemenceau, *Grandeur and Misery of Victory* (New York, 1930).

For the 1920s, the works by L. Ethan Ellis, Melvyn P. Leffler, and Robert H. Ferrell cited in the text constitute the best guides to French-American relations and to the general directions of

American diplomacy. Special studies of value for the interwar period are Margaret E. Redman, "Franco-American Diplomatic Relations, 1919–1926," unpublished Ph.D. dissertation, Stanford University, 1945; Thomas H. Buckley, *The United States and the Washington Conference: 1921–1922* (Knoxville, 1970); John E. Stoner, *S. O. Levinson and the Pact of Paris* (Chicago, 1943); Denna F. Fleming, *The United States and World Organization, 1920–1933* (New York, 1938); Herbert Feis, *1933, Characters in Crisis* (New York, 1966); Raymond G. O'Connor, *Perilous Equilibrium; The United States and the London Naval Conference of 1930* (Columbia, 1963); Richard P. Traina, *American Diplomacy and the Spanish Civil War* (Bloomington, 1968); Donald F. Drummond, *The Passing of American Neutrality, 1937–1941* (Ann Arbor, 1955); and John McVickar Haight, *American Aid to France, 1938–1940* (New York, 1970).

French diplomacy in the interwar years can only be understood within the context of European developments and France's internal political situation. Helpful studies are E. H. Carr, *The Twenty Years' Crisis, 1919–1939* (London, 1939); Arnold Wolfers, *Britain and France Between Two Wars: Conflicting Strategies of Peace Since Versailles* (New York, 1940); Denis W. Brogan, *France Under the Republic; the Development of Modern France, 1870–1939* (New York, 1940); John W. Wheeler-Bennett, *The Pipe Dream of Peace: The Story of the Collapse of Disarmament* (New York, 1935); Elizabeth R. Cameron, *Prologue to Appeasement; a Study in French Foreign Policy, 1933–1936* (Washington, D.C., 1942); Joel Colton, *Leon Blum: Humanist in Politics* (New York, 1966); Hubert Cole, *Laval: a Biography* (New York, 1963); Alexander Werth, *France and Munich* (London, 1939); and Gaetano Salvemini, *Prelude to World War II* (Garden City, 1954).

There has been a strong historical interest in the Vichy regime and with American-Vichy relations. See, for example, Paul Farmer, *Vichy, Political Dilemma* (New York, 1955); "Our Vichy Fumble," by Louis Gottschalk, intended as an answer to William L. Langer and published in *The Journal of Modern History*, XX, No. 1 (March 1948), pp. 47–56; and Adrienne Hytier,

Two Years of French Foreign Policy: Vichy, 1940–1942 (Geneva, 1958). Ambassador William L. Leahy's *I Was There* (New York, 1950) and appropriate passages from the *Memoirs of Cordell Hull*, 2 vols. (New York, 1948) help to give special insight into the diplomatic questions raised by Vichy.

De Gaulle is best understood by reading his multi-volume memoirs. Winston Churchill says much about de Gaulle in wartime London in his *The Second World War*, 6 vols. (Boston, 1948–1953). A stimulating brief biography of de Gaulle is Jean Lacouture's *De Gaulle* (New York, 1965). Also useful are Arthur L. Funk, *Charles de Gaulle: The Crucial Years, 1943–44* (Norman, 1959) and Robert Aron, *De Gaulle Triumphant: the Liberation of France* (London, 1964). Monographs on de Gaulle roll off the presses at an accelerating rate, many of them of high quality.

Wartime diplomacy has also produced a vast literature. The best brief guide to American diplomacy is Gaddis Smith, *American Diplomacy During the Second World War, 1941–1945* (New York, 1965). Herbert Feis has written a detailed and highly useful account of decision-making by the Big Three in his *Churchill, Roosevelt, Stalin: The War They Waged and the Peace They Sought* (Princeton, 1957). See also his *The Potsdam Conference* (Princeton, 1960). Issues important for French-American relations are also recounted in George Kirk, *The Middle East in the War* (London, 1952); F. C. Jones and others, *The Far East, 1942–1946* (London, 1955); and Willard D. Range, *Franklin D. Roosevelt's World Order* (Athens, 1959).

In order to grasp the world context of French-American relations since 1945, it is helpful to peruse a diplomatic survey textbook, such as Alexander DeConde's *A History of American Foreign Policy* (New York, 1971). Special studies of great value are A. W. DePorte, *De Gaulle's Foreign Policy, 1944–46* (Cambridge, 1968); Alexander Werth, *France, 1940–1955* (New York, 1956); and Simon Serfaty, *France, De Gaulle, and Europe: The Policy of the 4th and 5th Republics Toward the Continent* (Baltimore, 1968). France's postwar economic plight and American assistance is recounted in Theodore White, *Fire in the Ashes* (New York, 1953); Joseph Jones, *The Fifteen Weeks* (New York, 1955); and Ernst H. van der Beugel, *From Marshall Aid to Atlantic Partnership; European Integration as a Concern of American Foreign Policy* (New York, 1966).

Other books useful for understanding French-American relations in the postwar period are Edward Newhouse, *De Gaulle and the Anglo-Saxons* (London, 1970); Roy C. Macridis, *De Gaulle: Implacable Ally* (New York, 1966); John L. Gaddis, *The United States and the Origins of the Cold War, 1941–1947* (New York, 1972); Jack M. Schick, *The Berlin Crisis, 1958–1962* (Philadelphia, 1971); William Diebold, Jr., *The Schuman Plan* (New York, 1959); Seyom Brown, *The Faces of Power: Constancy and Change in United States Foreign Policy from Truman to Johnson* (New York, 1968); and Roger Hilsman, *To Move a Nation: The Politics of Foreign Policy in the Administration of John F. Kennedy* (Garden City, 1967). Claude Julien, foreign editor of *Le Monde*, has written a searching criticism of twentieth-century American diplomacy in *America's Empire* (New York, 1973). On the whole, the goals and direction of French foreign policy since World War II have been explained more cogently by historians than has American foreign policy.

Index

Act of Algeciras, 1906, 191
Adams, John, disapproves of
Franklin, 30; undermined by
Vergennes, 46-47; peace negotiations, 49; on French Revolution, 55; election of 1796,
71; peace mission to France,
72; comments on France, 73;
protests French policy, 75;
signs Naturalization Act, 76;
moderates views of France,
77-78; mentioned, 12
Adams, John Quincy, on American claims, 101; defends Andrew Jackson, 105; Monroe
Doctrine, 107; on merchant
marine, 118; interest in Cuba,
123
Adams, Samuel, 43
Adams, Thomas, 77
Adenauer, Konrad, and reconciliation with France, 270; Berlin
crisis, 283
Adet, Pierre, attack on Jay Treaty, 70-71
Africa, and Berlin Conference on
West African Affairs, 184-185;
World War II, 250-251; mentioned, 254
Africa International Association,
185
Aisne, battle of, 204
Aix-la-chapelle, 105, 106

Alabama, 143
Algeciras Conference, 191
Algeria, 127, 251, 279
Alien and Sedition Acts, 76
Alsace and Alsace-Lorraine, 162,
213
Amiens, Peace of, 1801, 83
Aranjuez, Convention of, 1779,
37, 38
Archangel, 213
Argentina, French interest in,
107, 112; and Monroe Doc-
trine, 109-110
Arman, M., 144-145
Armstrong, John, minister to
France, 90
Arthur, Chester A., and Haiti,
171; and Berlin West Africa
Conference, 184
Artois, battle of, 206
Assembly of Notables (Mexico),
149
Atlantic Charter, 254
Atomic weapons, 260, 288
Austria, and War of Succession,
10; beaten by Napoleon, 72;
invades Naples, 106; and Itali-
an unification, 126; war with
Prussia, 153-154; Spanish-
American crisis, 177; men-
tioned, 114, 197

Bancroft, Edward, 32